# EMOTION, SOCIAL THEORY, AND SOCIAL STRUCTURE

*Emotion, Social Theory, and Social Structure* takes sociology in a new direction. It examines key aspects of social structure by using a fresh understanding of emotions categories. Through this exciting synthesis emerge original perspectives on rationality, class structure, social action, conformity, basic rights, and social change. As well as giving an innovative view of social processes, J. M. Barbalet's study reveals unappreciated aspects of emotions by considering fear, resentment, vengefulness, shame, and confidence in the context of social structure. While much has been written on the social consequences of excessive or pathological emotions, this book demonstrates the centrality of emotions to routine operations of social interaction. Dr. Barbalet also re-evaluates the nature of social theory, for once the importance of emotions to social processes becomes clear, the intellectual constitution of sociology, and therefore its history, must be rethought.

J. M. BARBALET is Reader in Sociology at the Australian National University. He is the author of *Marx's Construction of Social Theory* (1983), and *Citizenship: Rights, Struggle and Class Inequality* (1988), as well as numerous articles for scholarly journals on various aspects of political sociology and sociological theory.

# Emotion, Social Theory, and Social Structure

*A Macrosociological Approach*

J. M. Barbalet

CAMBRIDGE
UNIVERSITY PRESS

302
B22e

PUBLISHED BY THE PRESS SYNDICATE OF THE UNIVERSITY OF CAMBRIDGE
The Pitt Building, Trumpington Street, Cambridge CB2 1RP, United Kingdom

CAMBRIDGE UNIVERSITY PRESS
The Edinburgh Building, Cambridge CB2 2RU, United Kingdom
40 West 20th Street, New York, NY 10011-4211, USA
10 Stamford Road, Oakleigh, Melbourne 3166, Australia

First published 1998

Printed in the United Kingdom at the University Press, Cambridge

Typeset in Plantin 10/12 [SE]

*A catalogue record for this book is available from the British Library*

*Library of Congress Cataloguing in Publication data*

Barbalet, J. M., 1946–
    Emotion, social theory, and social structure: a
    macrosociological approach / J. M. Barbalet.
        p.   cm.
    Includes bibliographical references and index.
    ISBN 0 521 62190 9 (hardback)
    1. Emotions – Sociological aspects.   2. Social structure.
    3. Social interaction.   I. Title.
    HM291.B269   1998   302–dc21   97–25639   CIP

ISBN 0 521 62190 9 hardback

*e*
*r*

For my eldest son, Tom

# Contents

# Acknowledgments

Debts incurred in producing a work such as this are always greatly in excess of what can be properly acknowledged. But two names which must be mentioned in this context are Tom Scheff and Dave Kemper. Through the example of their publications, and their personal encouragement, it became possible to see that the sociological understanding of emotions is not only attainable, but offers insights and approaches which otherwise could not be achieved. My methods and style are not theirs, however, and neither of them is responsible for what follows.

Earlier versions of three chapters were previously published, and I would like to acknowledge that a paper which became chapter 3 first appeared in *Sociological Theory*, and that papers which became chapters 4 and 7 first appeared in the *Journal for the Theory of Social Behaviour*.

Through my membership of the Emotions Section of the American Sociological Association and the International Society for Research on Emotions I have enjoyed many discussions about emotion. By a circuitous route, such encounters and subsequent reflection have contributed more than I can indicate to what is written in the following, and I wish to acknowledge my gratitude to those organizations and their members.

In a less organized way I have enjoyed much stimulating conversation about emotions with Joe de Rivera, of Clark University, Bertell Ollman, of New York University, Doug Porpora, of Drexel University, and Suzanne Dee, of the Australian National University. I wish to thank each of them for their friendship and encouragement.

Catherine Max, of CUP, is especially thanked for her guidance, and for selecting three anonymous reviewers who led me into clarity on a number of points. These three also have my sincere thanks.

With Margot Lyon, of the Australian National University, I have much discussed and experienced emotions. My thanks to her cover more than the span of the pages that follow.

Finally, my greatest thanks are owed to my children, Tom, Felix, and David. Life and work are simple words, but the meanings of what they refer to are ultimately unfathomable. My sense of those things, however, comes in large measure from my children, and my feelings for them.

# Note on citations

In the text and the References section, reference to sources indicate the year of first publication and that of the edition used, so that Smith ([1776] 1979) refers to Adam Smith's *Wealth of Nations*, first published in 1776, and indicates that the 1979 Oxford University Press edition was used. This is to preserve something of the historical context of authors who have contributed to the discussion.

# Introduction

Two things are attempted in this book. First, key aspects of social structure are examined through the development and application of emotions categories. Thus rationality, class structure, social action, social conformity, basic rights, and social change are considered through discussion of a particular emotion or set of emotions which both characteristically pertains to each of them and elucidates the processes to which each is subject. Second, the development and application of emotions categories to the analysis of social-structural components are used in the refinement and elaboration of sociological theory.

The dual interests of understanding social structure and enriching sociological theory have always been central in sociology. Less frequently have endeavors to achieve these aims been attempted through a focus on emotion. Emotion is not readily thought of as a category which either belongs in or has anything important to offer sociology. Nevertheless, the following chapters will show that emotions terms can be developed in and applied to the analysis of social structure. They will also show that theorizing which offers a central place to emotions categories risks nothing of its sociological character.

But any conclusions which are drawn from these chapters must be made in light of their intentions, and therefore of the limits on what they attempt to achieve. While it is not an author's place to prime the critics, although all authors do that unintentionally and inadvertently, I do want to indicate some of the things not attempted in this book.

One obvious omission, which some readers may regret, is a full statement of a general theory of emotion. This absence is fully intended. There are some robust theories of emotion, and parts of my discussion are obviously informed by certain of them. Of the sociological theories of emotion in general, Kemper's (1978) stands out as the most influential on my own work. In two chapters, chapters 5 and 7, his social interactional theory of emotions is addressed explicitly with a view to extending it. But these extensions are with regard to particular emotions, not the overall

1

framework of the theory. And this is the point. A theory of emotion in general has not been attempted here because this book is concerned instead with certain particular emotions.

Emotion in general is simply a category, while particular emotions have the reality of actual experience. What is needed in sociology is not another general theory of emotion but a deeper understanding of particular emotions, and especially those central to social processes. The emotions which are treated in the chapters to follow include fear, resentment, vengefulness, shame, and confidence. All of these have previously attracted the attention of researchers; but by considering them in the context of social structure it is possible to discover new things about them. Fear, for example, has always been held to be a paralyzing emotion which holds back change. But a study of elite fear leads to a reconsideration of fear itself, as we shall see in chapter 7.

The particular emotions explored in the following chapters will each be considered in terms of singular aspects of social structure. The coverage cannot be complete, and aspects of social structure not discussed here, and other emotions, deserve to be researched. If this book achieves anything of value it will be to further encourage the building of what used to be called middle-range theories of social-structural components in terms of efficacious emotions.

Some problems require a different approach, however. One such is the problem of rationality, in which no single dominant emotion or emotion type is implicated, but the conventional conceptualization of emotion itself, and also of rationality, must be brought into question. Rationality is not a component of social structure so much as a quality of social agency. It is shown in chapter 2 that the bases or social foundations of rationality include a range of particular emotions. It is also shown that the concepts of rationality and also emotion cannot be taken at face-value.

A method employed here for unraveling the connections of rationality and emotion is a critical analysis of the sociological theory of Max Weber. When emotions are understood to be central in social structure and social processes, the capacity of sociological theory to convey that fact becomes a matter of real concern. Much of the discussion of the chapters that follow will be devoted to the evaluation and construction of sociological theory. But, again, this is not comprehensively executed and much has been left undone.

Weber is given his due in the following discussion, but what of the other classical theorists, especially Durkheim and Marx? The importance of Durkheim to a sociology of emotion has not gone unnoticed (see Barbalet 1994; Collins 1975; Fisher and Chon 1989). Marx has drawn very little attention in this regard, however, although his work does warrant consideration (see Barbalet 1996b). But for the purposes of understanding those aspects of social structure and the correlative emotions discussed later, it would be entirely artificial to simply survey classical sociological theory in this book. Nevertheless, theorists who have typically been ignored by sociologists are drawn upon when their contribution is of critical importance to the discussion.

Two theorists in particular, almost never allowed to contribute to sociological theory, prove to be crucial at key points of discussion: Adam Smith and William James. Their work is discussed here as it touches on the themes of the various chapters. During research, it emerged that, once the importance of emotions to social processes becomes clear, the intellectual constitution of sociology, and therefore the history of sociology and those who have contributed to it, have to be rethought. In this process the current standing of both Smith and James will inevitably undergo a transformation, from neglect to a recognition of their considerable importance. But this is work for the future, and, briefly, the Epilogue that follows.

It is necessary to add another caveat regarding what is to follow. The social science discussion of the role of emotion in large social units and processes has typically focussed on pathological manifestations of emotions which have destructive consequences. Perhaps the best known of these is Gustave Le Bon's classic of the late nineteenth century, *The Crowd* (1895). The deleterious consequences for social order and historical change of excessive and pathological emotions is an important topic. Indeed, some of the best recent sociological writing on emotion is in this vein. I am thinking especially of Thomas Scheff and Suzanne Retzinger's *Emotions and Violence: Shame and Rage in Destructive Conflict* (1991), and Thomas Scheff's *Bloody Revenge: Emotions, Nationalism, and War* (1994). The purpose of this book, however, is not to pursue such a line of thought.

Many of the emotions to be discussed in the following, especially resentment, vengefulness, shame, and fear, have typically been treated in terms of their pathological forms. This book, however, is focussed on the explanation of what might be called normal or functioning social processes. The challenge is to demonstrate the centrality of emotion to the routine operations of non-deviant structures of social interaction. In doing so, it is sufficient to stick to normal not extreme expressions of emotion. The discussion here, then, is confined to the emotions necessary for structures of social order and harmonious social change. This is not to deny that conflict or even fundamental challenge are not regular occurrences in social systems. Rather, it is to say that emotion is central to and not deviant in the everyday operations of social processes.

One more thing must be said before the chapters which make up this book are described. A good deal could be made in these brief remarks of the book's macrosociological focus. But much of what is covered here pertains also to the social psychological or micro realm, and it would be disingenuous to not acknowledge the fact. Our concern in discussing microsociological matters, however, is to indicate a clear appreciation of what an emotions perspective can offer an understanding of the linkages between the micro and macro domains. This is an under-explored set of problems to which an emotions approach is well placed to contribute.

The chapters which follow explain particular social processes through the application of conceptualizations of certain emotions. The exception to this are chapters 1 and 2. Chapter 1 situates the discussion of emotion in the recent history of sociology, and explains that emotions categories hold a place in the foundations of sociology. It also explains how emotion came to be displaced from sociology. In considering the new sociological interest in emotion, this chapter discusses the relationship of emotion with culture and with social structure.

In chapter 2 the discussion is directed to the relationship between rationality and emotion in general. This chapter demonstrates the limitations of the taken-for-granted assumptions about the contribution of emotion to irrationality, especially in the work of Max Weber. Against this conventional and still widely accepted partial understanding of emotion, the discussion explores instead the contribution to rationality made by emotion.

Chapter 3 focusses on an emotion which is key to fundamental aspects of social structure, namely class resentment. It is frequently commented that the theory of social class is at an impasse, which some writers believe will be overcome through the application of rational choice theory to the analysis of class situations. This chapter shows that a focus on class resentment encourages the identification of aspects of social structure and culture which are crucial in understanding propensities to class formation and action. This chapter demonstrates how emotion may be conceptualized as inhering simultaneously in individual experience and in the social structures and relationships in which individuals are embedded.

Moving from class structure to social action, chapter 4 is concerned with the emotional basis of action and agency. Confidence, in particular, is shown to be an emotion which, in overcoming the uncertainty of engaging an unknowable future, is a necessary basis for social action. By referring to the future in this way, we therefore introduce temporality into considerations of action when its emotional dimensions are highlighted. The macrosociological significance of the perspective developed in this chapter is demonstrated by a consideration of business confidence.

The contribution of shame to social conformity is treated in chapter 5. This has recently become well-covered ground through a mushrooming of popular interest in shame (Karen 1992). This chapter examines the argument that shame is central to conforming behavior as it was presented by Adam Smith in the eighteenth century, by Charles Darwin in the nineteenth, and in the various forms of twentieth-century claims for and doubts about the importance of shame as a social emotion. Through a critique of leading sociological accounts of shame, a new typology of shame and the ambiguous relationship of shame with social conformity is presented.

Human or basic rights are increasingly drawing attention from sociological writers. Chapter 6 presents a theory of basic rights in which the emotions of resentment and vengefulness are shown to be principal factors. The chapter argues that claims to rights are directed and energized primarily by resentment and vengefulness. It is also argued that rights are claimed not when physical needs are not met, but when social standing is violated. Resentment and vengefulness are distinguished in terms of the types of social violation each is a reaction against. By approaching basic rights through emotions it is also possible to account for historical variability in the efficacy of the vocabulary of rights in political practices.

The final chapter, chapter 7, is concerned with the problem of social and organizational change, and especially the importance of fear in influencing social processes. The relevance of fear in these matters has been insufficiently explored, and the conceptualization of fear in previous discussions of it has been incomplete and partial. It is shown, for instance, that in addition to the flight–fight or subjugation and rebellion fear behaviors, a third typical fear response is containment. This last response can be described as an attempt to limit or redirect the source of fear. While fear can be characterized as a consequence of insufficient power, it is important to recognize that this may be experienced relatively as well as absolutely. Elites, therefore, may experience a loss of power relative to what they had previously experienced, with resulting fear. Thus fear is not exclusively an emotion of subordinate groups. Elite fear, in particular, leads to attempts to contain what is perceived as a threatening force. In this way elite fear is a significant but neglected source of change.

At the end of the book is an Epilogue, in which some earlier themes are revisited. First, the present vernacular standing of emotions is discussed. The problem of sociological critique through an emotions perspective is next taken up. Internal to this part of the discussion is a critique of the notion of emotional labor in which an alternative presentation of emotional processes is provided. Third, the importance of temporality and its connection with emotions and action are treated. Finally, the impact on sociological traditions of an emotions approach is outlined. A unifying theme of this epilogic discussion is the concept of "the self."

Discerning readers will have noted an apparent inconsistency between the theoretical orientation of some of the chapters. It is therefore necessary to qualify the use of terminology more clearly to indicate the focus of the different chapters. In particular, the concept of class is employed in chapter 3, whereas in chapter 7 the term elite is used. These terms are widely understood to belong to antithetical conceptualizations of social organization. The use of these quite different terms in different chapters is intentional. The focus of chapter 7 is broader than that of social class and also includes political strata. The consideration of this chapter is not class structure, as it is in chapter 3, but the structure of power, and the implications of this for the experience of fear.

Additionally, in chapter 3 the discussion of resentment attaches to class differences in social structure, whereas in chapter 6 the account of resentment is developed in terms of the division of labor, without any reference to class. Again, these two terms, class and division of labor, have been associated with alternative characterizations of social structure. The term class is typically situated in arguments concerning conflict, exploitation, and social cleavage, whereas the term division of labor finds its place in discussions of reciprocity, social exchange and order, and stratification. But as Bertell Ollman, for instance, has recently shown (1993, pp. 53–67), these distinct terms can be understood as referring to different levels of generality and not necessarily to opposed theoretical formations.

The discussion of basic rights and the attendant emotions of resentment and vengefulness is certainly applicable to class societies. But it is also relevant to analyses of those societies in which class is underdeveloped or complicated by overriding social forces, but in which the division of labor underpins social organization. This is a more general account than that which functions in terms of class relations: and this is precisely the character of the account in chapter 6.

In each of the chapters to follow emotions categories are developed through sociological, and frequently macrosociological, analysis. Also, social processes are explained and theoretical accounts of these developed through an application of emotions terms. The idea that emotions can only be dealt with psychologically, for instance, is therefore demonstrated to be simply untrue. Indeed, the following chapters indicate the significance of emotions to social processes and the ways in which emotions concepts can be applied to the development of sociological explanation and theory building.

In summary, then, this book explores particular emotions in order to extend our understanding of social structure, and to enhance the competence of our social theory. Its real purpose is not to settle matters and answer questions definitively. Rather, it is a book whose success will be realized if it serves to prepare and not conclude investigation.

# 1   Emotion in social life and social theory

This chapter addresses the question of the place of emotion in sociology, and therefore in social processes. The matter is dealt with in this manner, rather than beginning with emotion in society, because while the role of emotion in social life can be taken to be more or less constant, the category of emotion has had a varied career in social analysis. This anomaly requires explanation.

The chapter begins with a discussion of sociology in general, and where emotion might fit into it. It is shown that in its historical origins, in the eighteenth-century Scottish Enlightenment, and in later European and American sociological writing, there was ample space for emotion. But through a number of changes in social organization and intellectual trends, the category of emotion lost its footing in social explanation. And yet, even during the period of overarching cognitivism in social thought, certain sociologists continued to draw upon emotions categories in their accounts of social processes.

Within a more recent generation, some sociologists have returned to a more explicit exploration of emotion in their research. How this redirection arose is also discussed in the chapter, along with a number of the questions it raises. These include the constructionist approach to emotion, the relationship between emotion and culture, and emotion and social structure. Finally, the chapter emphasizes that, while emotion in general is an abstract category, experience is always of particular emotions. More important still: while emotional feelings tend to merge into each other, the particularity of an emotion is to be located in its social sources and consequences.

## Emotion and sociology: the odd couple

What is sociology's business with emotion? One answer is that sociology attempts to explain social phenomena; and emotion is a social phenomenon. That emotion has a social nature is not immediately obvious, however. An individual's experience of emotion more readily reveals the personal and intimate side of emotion than its collective or social dimension. Nevertheless, it has been shown by anthropologists, historians, and sociologists, that the patterns of emotional experiences are different in different societies. In this sense emotion can be regarded as an outcome or effect of social processes. As a social product, emotion is in principle amenable to sociological examination and explanation. There is in fact a large and growing literature which shows, from a number of different perspectives, that emotion is a social thing (Kemper 1991; McCarthy 1989).

There is another answer to the question, "What is sociology's business with emotion?" Sociology might be concerned with emotion because emotion is somehow necessary to explain the very fundamentals of social behavior. This idea, that emotion is a social cause, is more likely to be resisted by sociologists than the idea that it is a social effect. As this is the more difficult to accept of the two answers concerning sociology's business with emotion, it is the one that we shall focus on here. The only good reason to offer a sociological explanation of emotion is if emotion is itself significant in the constitution of social relationships, institutions, and processes.

Resistance to the idea of a causal capacity of emotion in social life and social processes follows fairly directly from the present state of sociology itself. This claim is by no means exaggerated, as a brief summary of the structure of sociology will demonstrate. It is necessary, therefore, to diverge into a discussion of sociology and its variant forms, which exclude consideration of emotion. In examining the quality of their deficit we will better appreciate the important role emotion might play in reconstituted sociological explanations.

Sociology, unlike academic history, for instance, is committed to the possibility of general explanation. But, unlike academic economics, say, sociology does not operate within a single unifying paradigm. While agreeing on the necessity to go beyond description, sociologists are likely to disagree about the particular form of explanation which can take them there. There is not one sociology; rather, there are many sociologies. Drawing upon conceptualizations of varying breadth, we may count the number of general types of sociological theory as five (Martindale 1961), say, or four (Collins 1994), or three (Giddens 1971), or two (Dawe 1970). For our present purposes, the simplest approach is the best. Dawe (1970) distinguishes between a sociology of social system and a sociology of social action.

Accounts of social behavior which operate in terms of a sociology of social system assume that factors which are external to social actors determine what they do. Such accounts do not propose that external forces simply compel actors to act. Rather, they offer two possibilities.

Social-system accounts hold that structural factors create particular and limited ranges of opportunities, so that possibilities for action are materially constrained. Or, relatedly, social-system accounts hold that structural factors imbue agents with particular interests, so that there are objective imperatives of action. Both of these types of account refer to conditions important for social analysis, but neither of them can be construed as offering complete statements concerning the source of social action, as we shall see. For these reasons, such approaches offer little encouragement to an emotions perspective, although we shall have more to say about that also, shortly.

The social-system approach regards social actors as necessarily constrained. In the face of limited options, actors must choose from among them. Even in the absence of a choice of options the actor can choose not to act. The choices referred to here are matters of sociological concern. How the choices, and indeed the interests, of actors are translated into actions, also requires sociological explanation. These considerations take us to the realm of the sociology of social action. Accounts of social action typically assume that actors are self-conscious or reflective decision-makers. But such a perspective seems to be more optimistic than realistic.

The actions of most people most of the time do not arise from self-conscious decisions. The assumption that social actors know the relevant facts of their situation, or even their own preferences within it, and also how to best match the opportunities they face and the preferences they have, is overstretched. Indeed, to the extent that social action involves cooperation with others, actors can never know, at the time they take it, whether their decision to cooperate is correct. The success or otherwise of any cooperative act, which would indicate whether the decision to cooperate was correct, is necessarily posterior to the decision itself.

In addition to the cognitive basis of action, sociology has frequently taken habit, or what is usually called custom or tradition, to be an adequate source of a significant proportion of social behavior. Habit as such is not much discussed in sociology today, but Emile Durkheim, Max Weber, Thorstein Veblen, George Herbert Mead, and others treated it explicitly as a basis of action. Its importance is still implicitly acknowledged in role theory and other accounts which emphasize routinizing aspects of social learning. The importance of habit cannot be denied. But habits change, and the differential inclination to habituation of distinct types of social action has itself to be explained.

Those accounts of social processes which operate in terms of either reflective decision-making or habit tend to exclude emotion from consideration as a basis of social action. It should be noted, however, that there are theories of emotion which function through strongly cognitive categories, involving interpretive processes, which facilitate emotional experiences. But these are typically accounts of emotion which regard it not as a source of agency but as a reflection or construction of cultural values and cues. In these accounts, therefore, emotion is at best an intermediary between social rules and social behavior. In its conventional constitution, sociology offers little space for emotion as a basis of action.

The limitations alluded to above of a sociology of action founded on cognitive principles are widely acknowledged. It is ironic that the category excluded by such principles, namely emotion as a basis of social action, offers a viable alternative approach which avoids the unrealistic assumptions and untenable heuristic pretensions of a sociology of the self-conscious decision-making actor. This is not to say that rational action is not possible or does not occur. But, as we shall see in the following chapter, emotion facilitates rational action when it does occur, and can be used to explain those actions which take place in the absence of conditions of knowledgeable decision-making.

Habitual behavior, to the extent that it occurs, can also be shown to have an emotional basis. And even a sociology of social system can be improved by the introduction of emotion, as we shall see in the discussion of class resentment in chapter 3, because it can indicate which particular social structures are primary in the process of class formation.

Having set out to suggest that it is not immediately easy to find a space for socially efficacious emotion in sociology, it does not follow that there is no place for such emotion. Indeed, the chapters which follow have the purpose of convincing readers that emotion deserves a central role in sociological research and theorizing. The commonplace notion that emotion is not amenable to sociological application because it is an essentially psychological phenomenon, for instance, will in the chapters to follow be shown to be a misconception. It can also be observed that while many sociologists today are hostile to the application of emotions categories to sociological explanation, writers who must be regarded as the founders of modern sociology were clear exponents of what might be called an emotions approach.

## Emotion in the origins of sociology

The eighteenth-century Scottish origins of sociology have been frequently noted (Bierstedt 1979; Bryson 1945; Lehmann 1930; Meek 1976; Swingewood 1991). Adam Smith, for instance, in *The Wealth of Nations* ([1776] 1979), is credited with anticipating comparative historical sociology and a macrosociology of institutions. Adam Ferguson, in *An Essay on the History of Civil Society* ([1767] 1966), is even more secure as a precursor of modern sociology in his explicit understanding of the social as distinct from the economic consequences of the division of labor and for his account of historic development. What is seldom noted, however, but which is essential for an understanding of each of these thinkers, and for an appreciation of the intellectual formation of the Scottish Enlightenment of which they are a part, is the importance they attach to emotion in making sense of social relationships and as a foundation for their larger social theories.

There is a view that in *The Wealth of Nations* Smith developed a line antithetical to that of his earlier book, *The Theory of Moral Sentiments* ([1759] 1982). It is held that whereas one pursues the thread of economic self-interest, the other expands on sympathy as a basis of moral behavior. This reading of the relationship between Smith's books misinterprets each of them (Macfie and Raphael 1976, pp. 20–5). What must be emphasized here is that the much narrower focus of *The Wealth of Nations*, a detailed working out of the consequences for economic actions and institutions of "self-love," derives from Smith's earlier theory. *Moral Sentiments* accounts for moral judgment and social interaction in terms of particular emotions, and argues that the capacity for a sympathetic echo of these emotions in other actors is a further determinant of social conduct.

The underpinning emotions framework of Ferguson's *Essay on the History of Civil Society* ([1767] 1966) is unavoidable to its readers. The book consists of six parts. The first and by far the longest is "Of the General Characteristics of Human Nature." This forms the methodological and theoretical basis of what follows, and is largely concerned with the emotional dispositions associated with social and political relations and organization.

The explanatory value of emotions categories can also be located in the major sociologists of the nineteenth and early twentieth centuries. Alexis de Tocqueville, Gustave Le Bon, Emile Durkheim, Vilfredo Pareto, Ferdinand Tönnies, and Georg Simmel are some of the more notable European sociologists who, in a number of different ways, regarded emotions categories as important explanatory variables. During this same period American sociology, in the works of such figures as Albion Small, William Graham Summner, and Lester Frank Ward, as well as Edward Ross and Charles Horton Cooley, found explanatory roles for emotions categories. All of this is mentioned here simply to indicate that during an earlier time it would not have been necessary, as it is now, to show that a sociologically robust understanding of emotion makes good sense.

The absence of Max Weber from the lists of the preceding paragraph is not accidental. A number of commentators with projects similar to my own have recruited Weber to their purpose, arguing that Weber was one sociologist who recognized the explanatory importance of emotion.

Weber did have an ideal type conception of "affectual action," certainly; but as Talcott Parsons ([1937] 1968, pp. 647–9), for instance, has noted, this category is primarily residual, and was not positively used in Weber's empirical work. Parsons may exaggerate the absence of emotion in Weber's explanations: it is notionally central to (although wholly undeveloped in) his account of charismatic authority. There are, in fact, many references to emotion in Weber's work. He insists on the necessity of passion in the calling of science. The discussion of the role and practice of the priesthood in *Ancient Judaism* (Weber [1917] 1967) includes much on the generation of emotion and its manipulation. Emotion is also important in Weber's discussion of the Protestant ethic and the spirit of capitalism. A consideration of this latter discussion will be developed in the following chapter. It will be shown that Weber's account of emotion is not only in itself seriously flawed, but is associated with the expulsion of emotion from sociology. It is this theme which will be taken up here.

## The expulsion of emotion from sociology

The rise of Weber's stock in recent sociology has been the result of a trend which took to heart Weber's idea that the increasing rationalization of the world means the decreasing significance of emotion in human affairs and conduct. In the following chapter it will be shown that this formulation, while misunderstanding the relationship between rationality and emotion, was accepted for a number of reasons and, in being accepted, led to the formation of sociologies without emotion. This raises the question of how to account for the fact that, in its formative period, sociology typically proffered explanations of social processes in terms of emotion, but then ceased to do so and does so infrequently today.

The conventional opposition between emotion and reason provides only a part of the answer. From this conventional perspective emotion is held to deform reason. Emotion is seen as the product of an agitated individual or group psychology. Reason, on the other hand, comes to be regarded as an expanding web which is both produced by and supports social organization. If this is a fair statement of the seasoned prejudice, then it is not difficult to appreciate the atrophying of emotion in sociology, and elsewhere. The validity of such a perspective will be discussed in the following chapter. Here, we briefly consider how it gained currency.

### Romanticism

The application of general categories of intellectual and cultural development to analyses of specific occurrences can be more misleading than helpful. This is because general categories summarize and exaggerate, whereas detailed analyses require discerning and differentiated conceptions. Nevertheless, an account of the rise and decline of emotion in sociology cannot fail to refer to the impact of Romanticism. The Romantic Movement had a profound influence on European thought and politics during the eighteenth and nineteenth centuries. It emerged as a reaction to that aspect of the Enlightenment and French classicism which emphasized the pervasive power of human reason and the prospects of the capacity of reason for human emancipation.

Romanticism denied the possibility of objectively arbitrating between differences of value, rejected the assumption that society could be ordered by rational principles, and instead acclaimed emotion as the basis of value, affiliation, and conduct. The influence of Romanticism can be appreciated from the fact that it was associated with the pervasive nationalist movements of the nineteenth century, and touched all areas of intellectual and creative life. The Byronic model of Romanticism was to engage what Weber would later call "value rationality," in which a passionately held ideal was to be pursued without regard to its costs. Indeed, the Romantic convention was to elevate emotion over reason.

A significant historic root of the Romantic Movement was German Pietism. Weber captures the relevant aspect of Pietism when he distinguishes it from Calvinism in terms of the former's laying "greater emphasis on the emotional side of religion." His characteristic summary of its consequences, as "a weakening of the inhibitions which protected the rational personality of the Calvinist from his passions" (Weber [1905a] 1991, pp. 130, 131), accepted the flavor of conventional conceptions of reason and emotion as alternatives in which the possession of one destroys the other.

As Romanticism was a reaction to the excessive rationalism of the Enlightenment, so in turn did the unbalanced appeal to emotion in Romanticism sponsor a counter-reaction. The point is not that sociology was a product of Romanticism, but that in the reaction against Romanticism those elements of sociology which emphasized emotion were discredited. It is necessary to say that an insistence on the significance of emotion in social processes is not necessarily an acceptance of a Romantic disposition. The opposition between reason and emotion, and the political conservatism which became associated with later Romanticism, are unequivocally rejected in the present work, for instance. What is being claimed, though, is that the Modernism of the twentieth century did not question Romanticism's inadequate conceptualization of emotion, but only its adherence to emotion at all.

## Changing fortunes of mass society

It is an enduring feature of political life that those who exercise power experience their enthusiasms as reasonable, but the enthusiasms of those who challenge them as unreasonable and emotional. Etymologically, "enthusiasm" is a state of supernatural possession or inspiration, and in that sense, as a state of being moved by an external concern, it is inherently non-rational. The nineteenth-century theorists of mass society, for instance, were at least partly stimulated in their accounts of contemporary society by a concern for, if not a fear of, the enthusiasm of the popular masses for anarchist, socialist, and syndicalist ideas and engagements. Social analysts do not necessarily express themselves through a political vocabulary. But the salience of an emotions terminology in the sociology of the nineteenth and early twentieth centuries resonates well with the emotions which the researchers themselves experienced during an historic period of unruly crowds, urban masses, and economic, political, and social transformations.

By the end of the First World War, however, and certainly by the 1920s, in western Europe and America, the general image of a wholly threatening seething social landscape appeared less tenable. The war itself had permitted political states to regulate economies and populations in a way which reinforced the constitutionalism that had been developing throughout Europe during the nineteenth century. At the same time, the industrial heart-land could by now be regarded as largely pacified. In the post-war period of reconstruction, militant workers and marginalized radical elements of labor movements were calmed by full employment (Gallie 1983; Middlemas 1979). With the consolidation of industrial order the working classes ceased to be regarded as a threat to "civilization" in the way that they had previously been.

In addition, economic organizations were by this time increasingly large and impersonal (Bendix 1974, pp. 211–26). An associated development was not only a rise in the number of blue-collar workers but at the same time their relative decline as a proportion of the workforce as a whole. This was through a rise in the numbers of white-collar clerical, administrative, and sales workers which accompanied growth in the size and importance of organizations. These factors together enhanced the sense of a less passionate and an increasingly rational social order.

Out of these and associated developments, a new model of social action gained currency, which seemed more commensurate with the emergent social and civic experience, and which gained prominence in sociological thinking. It is from about this time that emotion ceases to find ready acceptance as an explanatory variable in sociology. In fact, the term and concept cease to hold any real interest for sociologists at all. These changes which we have accounted for in political economies were supported by intellectual developments in allied disciplines.

In psychology, in particular, the period between the end of the First World War and the beginning of the Second, say from 1920 to 1940, was one in which Behaviorism gained ascendancy and dominated the field. As a consequence, introspective methods were discredited and the statistical manipulation of measurements of observed behavior advanced. Where one had favored the concept of emotion in understanding mental life, the other favored conditioning and learning theory in the explanation of behavior. Where the first of these developments denied emotion, the other simply displaced it from the concern of psychology, and from those disciplines which accepted the authority of psychological accounts of behavior.

### Cognitivist emphasis: 1930s–1970s

A characteristic of sociology, at least since the 1930s, has thus been an almost exclusive emphasis on the cognitive bases of social action. This orientation is shared by a number of approaches, including functionalism, symbolic interactionism, ethnomethodology, rational choice theory, and also conflict theory in both its neo-Weberian and its neo-Marxian forms. The role of Talcott Parsons's translation of Max Weber's *The Protestant Ethic and the Spirit of Capitalism* in the rationalization of sociology cannot be overlooked. Parsons's translation of Weber was made available to English-reading and especially American sociologists from 1930.

The Americanization of Weber's sociology was made possible by the removal of its political and historical dimensions, and through the emphasis instead on its formal and methodological characteristics (Cohen, Hazelrigg, and Pope 1975; Mommsen 1989, pp. 181–2; Turner and Factor 1984). In this way it served the purpose of promoting a cognitive rational sociology to the exclusion of other approaches. "Affective neutrality" (Parsons 1951), as an aspect of modern social development, insists that emotion is irrelevant to the secondary institutions and relations of modern society, indeed, is undermining of them. Under the aegis of this conceptualization, emotion was regarded as not only irrational but pre-modern: such views became sociological conventions.

Like all conventions, there is a degree of distortion in the summary representation of the conception of affective neutrality. It is instructive to consider Parsons's account of it in detail because it is a paradigm case of a sophisticated discounting of the significance of emotion for understanding social processes. The condition of affective neutrality is located at one extreme of a continuum along which affectivity occupies the opposite pole. Thus Parsons does not wish to deny that emotion occupies a place in modern society. But the full context of Parsons's account and the details of his discussion of this pattern variable indicates that for him the processes of advanced societies tend to confine emotional expression to limited arenas of experience, and generally to contain if not suppress emotion.

Parsons treats affectivity–neutrality as a "polarity" which "formulates the patterning out of action" of "some gratifications," namely those "which might interfere with the . . . instrumental pursuit of a certain class of goals" (1951, pp. 60–1; see also Parsons and Shils 1951, p. 80). This characterization, by fiat, understands emotion to be disorganizing of societal processes and goal-directed systems of action. We shall discuss this approach to emotion in more detail in the following chapter. But Parsons is not asserting that emotion is absent from modern society. While instrumental action is realized through the denial of emotion, emotion may flourish in family relations and friendship. Emotion is expelled from the secondary institutions and expressed in the primary institutions of society.

There is an additional part of Parsons's argument, more original than the first. The problem of social order is one of the balance between deviance and control: emotional reactions are generated in certain social processes, which other social processes must contain. For Parsons, social control is not the elimination of deviant factors from motivational systems of social actors, but the limitation of their consequences (1951, p. 298). This is because the "strains [which may] eventuate in deviant motivation" are endemic in social systems, and strain and deviance are therefore unavoidable and ineliminable, though containable, aspects of social systems (1951, p. 298).

Strain is ever likely because of the impossibility of pattern consistency (Parsons and Shils 1951, pp. 172–3, 175), that is, the impossibility of alignment between the normative system of expectations and the social system of interactions. Strain, Parsons says, provokes the reactions of anxiety, fantasy, hostility or aggression, and defensiveness (1951, p. 299). As the consequences of strain are therefore predominantly emotions disruptive of order or withdrawal from it, control must be directed to "all these elements of the motivational structure" (1951, p. 299). This is to say that a significant component of social control will be the suppression of the emotional consequences of strain.

This latter activity, Parsons says, is part of "the normal processes of interaction in an institutionally integrated social system" (1951, p. 301).

Included in these processes is a "limited permissiveness for . . . types of emotional expression which would be tabooed in ordinary everyday life," but, in being given limited expression in certain contexts, these become "continuous with the main institutionalized social structure" (1951, p. 306). In this account Parsons has in mind such things as youth culture and grief at funeral ceremonies. He returns to these cases in a later discussion, in which he repeats that the function of funeral ceremonies is to permit "'grief' reactions beyond the normal level of emotional demonstrativeness," while at the same time to deny "reciprocity for unduly extreme sentiments of grief" (Parsons, Bales, and Shils 1953, p. 76). The consistency in this structure of control, Parsons immediately adds, is "to put a premium on 'getting back' onto track the resumption of 'normal' social functioning."

Affective neutrality, thus, does not deny affectivity. But as Parsons understands it, affectivity is irrelevant to systems of instrumental action. Also, emotions are conceptualized as consequences of strain, which are disruptive of normal social functioning. The purpose of social control, then, includes the direct containment of affectivity, and its managed expression through which it might dissipate. Parsons does allow for emotion in society, but only as a flea on the dog.

To return to our theme: from the 1930s to the late 1970s, emotion had no secure place in sociology. Yet the real significance of emotion in social processes is such that even during this period the concept, even if not always the word, found its way into sociological explanation. A selection of cases will make the point. A central category of George Homans's study, *The Human Group* (1951), for instance, is "sentiment." In examining what social science had established about human behavior, Homans was able to escape contemporary sociological conventions by distilling the work of an earlier generation and by drawing upon anthropology, which, in studying rustic populations, was not embarrassed to find emotion.

The observation of C. Wright Mills, in *White Collar* ([1951] 1956), that emotion is a commodity in late-capitalist society, and that service workers must manage their emotions, predates the literature on emotion management by three decades. But the absence of the currency of the term emotion, and the unavailability of the concept of emotional efficacy in social relations, robbed the observation of the intellectual support such insights require if they are to be developed into an argument about social processes.

Mills says that when "white collar-people get jobs, they sell not only their time and energy, but their personalities as well." He immediately goes on to say that: "They sell by the week or month their smiles and their kindly gestures, and they must practice the prompt repression of resentment and aggression. For these intimate traits are of commercial relevance and required for the more efficient and profitable distribution of goods and services" ([1951] 1956, p. xvii). Rather than proceed to treat these transactions for what they are, namely emotional exchanges in commercial processes, Mills immediately slips into a discussion of the changing nature of rationality. He reports that the locus of rationality has shifted from individual persons to bureaucratic social institutions. The implication is that commodified emotions and emotion management are *ipso facto* within the domain of irrationality. The hegemonic intellectual categories of the day therefore take Mills away from an exploration of the nature of emotion in organization and instead to a misdirected discussion about the highly abstract category of rationality.

Other writers also used emotions categories during what might be called the non-emotions period of sociology. Neil Smelser (1959), for instance, was able to develop a theoretical account of social change through an unacknowledged abandonment of the functionalist theory he claimed to be developing and by drawing instead upon an argument concerning the consequences for social relations of what he calls "negative emotional reactions." As the character of this part of Smelser's argument was unacknowledged by its author, so it was unnoticed by his readers. In a similar way, Alvin Gouldner (1955, p. 498) outlined a discerning insight on the emotional basis of the ascendence of theories. His argument was to be more fully developed fifteen years later (Gouldner 1970), but still too early for his readers at least to realize that an important statement concerning the significance of emotion in theoretical development was being presented.

More forthright than any of the work referred to so far is Erving Goffman's article on "Embarrassment and Social Organization" (1956). Goffman shows that "embarrassment is not an irrational impulse breaking through socially prescribed behavior but part of this orderly behavior itself" (1956, p. 271). Indeed, at a time when sociology was most committed to exploring the calculative possibilities of organization (Blau 1955; Gouldner 1954; Merton [1940] 1968; Parsons 1956; Selznick 1948) Goffman was able to show that a sustaining mechanism of organization is not only formal rationality or the interest articulation of bureaucrats, but the emotional process of embarrassment. Goffman's is a most explicit characterization of the significance of an emotion in social processes. This major affront to the dominant focus of the sociology of the day was mounted from the psychiatric wards of Bethesda, where Goffman conducted research in the early 1950s.

Some writers, then, did acknowledge the significance of emotion as an explanatory variable in sociology, if not always consistently. But they were only able to do so in a manner which indicates the deviant nature of such particular intellectual activities. The taboo on emotion was therefore never complete because the consequences of emotion in social processes are always effective and compelling, and therefore likely to draw some notice irrespective of prevailing ideologies.

This process is reminiscent of Arthur Bentley's ([1908] 1949, pp. 3–109) discussion of more than a hundred pages in his now classic study *The Process of Government*, in which he attempted to discredit the idea of "Feelings and Faculties as Causes." He succeeded in showing that common-sense is not social science and that even good ideas can be badly presented. Much later in the book, however, Bentley acknowledged that his attack in the earlier chapter contained "certain exaggerations" or "shades of overemphasis": while feelings have no "independent existence," as he had earlier stated, he now wanted to say that "they do indicate a very important part of the social activity" ([1908] 1949, p. 443). The strongest denial of the relevance of emotion in social processes eventually yields to fundamental qualification.

### The new rise of emotion

The deviations from the dominant orthodoxy referred to above were not essentially challenges to it. But the orthodox refusal to accept the significance of emotion in social processes did find opposition from the late 1970s, when a number of sociological works expressly dealing with emotion in social processes began to appear. The creative burst, from the late 1970s to the mid-1980s, of papers and books on emotion in social processes was of a sufficient critical mass to generate serious discussion and debate and to encourage others to join in. If any single source can be pinpointed as initiating a renewal of sociological interest in emotion it is probably Randall Collins's general textbook, *Conflict Sociology* (1975).

From this time there followed a number of publications which explicitly treated emotion as a proper object of sociological concern and developed sociological theories in which emotions categories featured as key factors. Articles by Arlie Hochschild (1975, 1979), David Heise (1977), Susan Shott (1979), Steven Gordon (1981), and Randall Collins (1981) must be mentioned in this regard. The publication of three major books during this period further demonstrated not only the importance of emotion to sociology, but also how it could be theorized from quite different perspectives: Theodore Kemper's *A Social Interactional Theory of Emotions* (1978), Arlie Hochschild's *The Managed Heart* (1983), and Norman Denzin's *On Understanding Emotion* (1984). With these publications the intellectual prospects of sociology changed course again.

As in all intellectual sea-changes, emergent trends are never confined to a single discipline. So it was with the renewed interest in emotion. Historical starting-dates can only be indicative, even speculative, openings for discussion, never definitive demarcations. The refocus of psychology on to emotion might be dated as early as 1964, if Silvan Tomkins's aggressive "Introduction to Affect Symposium, APA 1964" (Tomkins and Izard 1966, p. vii) can be taken as a guide. Certainly, from the 1970s there was enormous growth in psychological research on emotion (Leventhal and Tomarken 1986). In anthropology also, the early 1970s saw the beginning of new interest in emotion (Briggs 1970; Levy 1973), which continued to gain momentum (Lutz and White 1986). Philosophy was another discipline in which the renewed interest in emotion can be dated from the 1970s (Neu 1977; Solomon 1976), although the process was set in motion rather earlier (Bedford 1957; Kenny 1964; Ryle 1949).

The degree to which there was cross-fertilization in the renewed interest in emotion between the distinct academic disciplines is not clear, but the evidence suggests that it was not strong. The sociological return to emotion, in particular, although aware of research in other disciplines, developed genuinely sociological themes and drew on sociological sources (Scheff 1983; Thoits 1989). These intellectual developments were consolidated by organizational ones. In 1984, the International Society for Research on Emotions (ISRE) was founded. From the beginning this was a cross-national, cross-disciplinary organization. Nevertheless, the bulk of its membership is drawn from North American psychologists, although non-Americans, as well as philosophers, anthropologists, and sociologists, are included in its ranks. The Sociology of Emotions section of the American Sociological Association was founded in 1986. In 1990, a Sociology of Emotions Interest Group was formed within the British Sociological Association. A Sociology of Emotions panel has been part of the Annual Conference of the Australian Sociological Association since 1992.

While the changes in sociology relate to modifications in intellectual agendas they cannot be explained in terms of purely intellectual dynamics. The problems broached in academic disciplines are dealt with in terms of the traditions and innovations within the disciplines themselves. But the problems they deal with are intellectualized translations of concerns which are properly to be located in a wider arena. The changes which reintroduced emotions categories into the study of social processes can ultimately be traced back to historic transformations in which the vulnerabilities of social power, and therefore also of the inadequacy of conventional understandings of reason, became apparent. Under these

conditions new socio-political loyalties are formed and new understandings of identity emerge. The salience of emotion becomes ever
apparent to participants of such changes.

Emotion is not a simple category, although those skeptical of its
explanatory value see it as no more complex than an interrupter of
ordered behavior, the latter being a position as discredited (Leeper 1948)
as it is persistent. Among other considerations, it must be acknowledged
that emotion has a dual aspect, which was summarized by the seventeenth-century philosopher Baruch Spinoza. He argued that passions, as
the carriers of external forces (as he saw them), control those who experience them. But in forming an idea of their passions, he continued,
persons may free themselves from their grip. This is to say that people are
spontaneously moved by their emotions, but at the same time they may
attempt to control or manage them.

This dual aspect of emotion is at the root of quite different approaches
to it. The notion that social agents are spontaneously moved by and
subject to emotion is central to the position that emotions are universal,
objectively ascertainable, and biologically rooted. The idea that social
agents may control or manage their emotions is core to the view that emotions are cultural artifacts relative to particular societies, significantly subjective, and phenomenologically grounded. In sociology these different
aspects of emotion are differentially emphasized by different approaches.
The idea that emotion is responsible for social outcomes has been
emphasized by writers such as Thomas Scheff and Theodore Kemper.
The other possibility, which seems to dominate certain sociological
accounts of emotion at the present time, is that emotion is principally a
consequence of cultural and cognitive, as opposed to social-structural
and relational, processes. This is the approach which concentrates on the
"social construction" of emotion.

### Constructionism and culture

New Social Movements, from the 1970s, challenged prevailing political
arrangements and undermined received conventions of social status.
These Movements, which include the Women's, the Environmental, and
the Black Movements, also contributed to the new awareness of the significance of emotion in social and cultural processes. A major concern of
the New Social Movements has been that of identity. The politics of identity, in getting away from the idea that the political standing of persons is
bequeathed to them by factors they are subordinate to and cannot influence, emphasized instead the conventional and customary as opposed to
the natural elements of being. That is, they emphasized the cultural and

social construction of the "person" and their "identity." Emotion, too, can be seen in this light. But if this is its only illumination the image is distorted, and the value of the concept for sociological research and analysis is lost: in the constructionist view emotion remains a consequence of other forces and its capacity for influencing social processes is neglected if not implicitly denied.

The constructionist approach typically holds that emotions are principally strategic evaluational claims associated with local meaning systems, based on cultural cues and precepts. There is a certain voluntarism in the approach, which emphasizes actors' manipulation of emotion rather than the effect of emotion on their actions and the processes in which they are implicated. It is true that emotional expression does have strategic significance in social exchanges. It is also true that the objects of emotions and aspects of experience of them are subject to variation through changes in socialization and prevailing values and norms. But the idea that there are "feeling rules" in a given culture, and that the socially significant emotions are likely to be subjected to modification through a social actor's "emotion work" (Hochschild 1979), while part of a new orthodoxy, deserve to be treated skeptically.

To be effective, "feeling rules" must have a discernible cultural existence. But what we know of the cultural norms relating to emotion and feelings is that they are too broad or general and too contradictory to function as rules or guides for individual emotional occurrences (Heller 1979, pp. 128–9, 156; Russell 1991). Indeed, as Pierre Bourdieu (1990) has shown, norms are never guides for action but outcomes of practices, and are therefore constantly subject to revision, differentiation, and instability. To say, as constructionists do, that such norms are not directive rules but only the parameters within which emotion work takes place is simply to beg the question.

Persons may attempt to manage their emotions, certainly. But to treat this as an independent process is misleading. A person's emotions with regard to an event may change, and they may feel that such a change resulted from their own efforts. In fact, emotional experience is continuous and emotional changes occur as a result of a number of processes, many of which result from the structural dynamics of emotions rather than the directing force of culture. These structural dynamics of emotions include emotional reactions to emotional experiences, such as being ashamed of being angry, being guilty about being jealous, and being happy about being in love. The emotional patterns which occur with an individual's experience are transformed and change as a result of relational and circumstantial changes, which provoke further emotions. These latter may include emotions which not only modify existing emotions but displace them, as when love turns to hate. It is also possible that through relational changes there may arise an emotion of emotionlessness. One form of this is depression, another is what Georg Simmel, in his discussion of "The Metropolis and Mental Life" ([1903] 1971), has called the blasé feeling. We shall have more to say about this in the following chapter.

There are other problems with the constructionist approach to emotions. Socially constructed emotions are given cultural labels or names; but the absence of a word for an emotion does not mean that an emotion is not experienced and behaviorally influential (de Rivera 1977, p. 128; Ortony, Clore, and Collins [1988] 1990, p. 8; Russell 1991, p. 445). Indeed, Thomas Scheff (1988) has shown that socially efficacious emotions are likely to be experienced below the threshold of awareness, rendering emotion work in the constructionist sense an unlikely prospect for socially significant sets of emotions.

In addition to defining what terms refer to, the constructionist deference to culture (mis)defines what are in fact particular emotions. The constructionist conception of emotion, by incorporating the explanans of the theory (culture) in the definition of the explanandum (emotion), can at best offer descriptions of emotions, rather than explanations of them (MacKinnon 1994, p. 124), and only descriptions of those emotions which are socially represented in the prevailing culture. Constructionism, therefore, is not simply an account of cultural processes, it is itself captive of cultural preferences.

This last point is frequently overlooked in critical discussions of constructionism, even though it may be the most important. The social representation of emotion is taken to be what emotion *is* in any given social order. But social representations are necessarily distorted and incomplete images (see Farr and Moscovici 1984; Ichheiser 1949). For instance, the representation of emotion under conditions of market capitalism and instrumental rationality ignores precisely the background emotions which are continuous with the operations of the pervasive social institutions, as we shall see in the following chapter. In our day-to-day experiences, therefore, we tend to ignore those emotions which the prevailing cultural conventions do not designate as "emotions." The constructionist approach cannot assist us in uncovering those emotions which are crucial to social processes, such as implicit trust, or bypassed shame, when they are not given social representation in the prevailing culture, along with love and hate, for instance, as emotions.

Much attention has been given to culture by sociologists over the past decade or more. And some researchers have understood emotion to be primarily an aspect or element of culture (McCarthy 1994). But there are good reasons why emotion should not be treated as a cultural phenomenon.

There is no doubt that cultural factors are significant for emotions and the emoting subject's or social actor's experience of them. The particular objects of emotions, the time-frames of emotional experiences, and the way in which emotions are conceptualized are all mediated through culture. But it would be a mistake if, on these grounds, emotion as such was regarded simply as an aspect of culture. It is necessary to be clear about the nature of culture in order to understand why emotion is not reducible to it.

Culture is a self-conscious attribute of human populations which reveals what is particular about the social life of distinct groups or collectivities. The self-consciousness of culture is essential because it acknowledges that culture is always the product of intellectual, moral, aesthetic, and related activities which are necessarily deliberative and intentional in their origins. In its own terms, then, culture is the source of meaning in society. This is because meaning is attached to objects as a result of the uses to which they are put by social actors, and such uses are generated in collectively given understandings or conventions. The etymological root of the term culture is the Latin *colere*, to cultivate. The character of culture described here reflects the self-conscious and alterable qualities of the labors of cultivation.

But cultivation has a context in the cycles of day and night and the seasons, through which culture in its own terms is not supported. Whereas cultivation is performed in tandem with these cycles, culture is defined in opposition to them, in opposition to nature. Culture is a realm in which nature is absent, if not irrelevant. This is mentioned here because at a fundamental level emotion does have a physical basis which modifies the significance of culture in understanding emotional and therefore social processes. Just as the skin which covers human bodies and the capacity for language which ultimately produces human history are natural endowments of humankind, so the emotions which animate human actions, while culturally expressed, are also explicable in terms of the biological processes of evolution which make humankind naturally social.

As Kemper (1978), Scheff (1990), and Smith ([1759] 1982), for example, have shown, the structural relations of circumstance are sufficient to elicit particular emotions in human subjects, and these emotions themselves give meaning to situations irrespective of the prevailing culture. A power relationship which results in the dispossession of a participant also leads to their anger. A relationship in which the esteem of a participant is elevated by the other leads also to a rise in that participant's pride. It is true, certainly, that the conventions of the social group in which these structural relations occur will influence how the anger and pride are acknowledged or expressed. But this is a part and not the whole of the emotion. Culture is an aspect of all social processes, but it is not their totality.

Before anything else, emotions must be understood within the structural relations of power and status which elicit them. This makes emotion a social-structural as much as if not more than a cultural thing. Again, this discussion is not to deny the cultural aspects of emotion but to reassert its non-cultural basis. The argument of this book will demonstrate the way in which a social-structural approach to emotions not only enhances the understanding of emotions but also how it enriches our understanding of social structure.

## The unity of emotions

Throughout this preliminary discussion a unitary conceptualization of emotion has been employed. But emotion is a genus covering enormously diverse and variable species. It is only particular emotions which people are moved by; emotion in general only exists as an imprecise category of thought. In the chapters to follow we shall consider not emotion in general but some particular emotions. Any focus on single or particular emotions must appreciate, as William James ([1890b] 1931, p. 448) cautioned, the "internal shading of emotional feelings" which leads them to "merge endlessly into each other." James thus warns against distinguishing emotions by simply describing them. Such a strategy would give language the task that theory might properly perform. Similarly, it follows that there is no point to explicating emotion through discursive language. We are much better placed, in explaining emotion, to show what emotion does, or rather what particular emotions do, in social relationships. The social sources and consequences of an emotion tell us what that emotion is.

Readers of fiction know what emotions the characters in a story experience when they are told what situations the characters face and what relationships they have with other characters. Particular emotional experiences arise in corresponding relationships. If we are told that Jim, arriving late for work, crashed into his boss's expensive parked car, we will know that Jim is afraid. If we are told that Ann just learned that her sister gave away Ann's new dress, bought to be worn on a special occasion, we will know that Ann is angry. These extremely rudimentary accounts are intelligible because emotional experience has discernible antecedents in the structure or pattern of social relations. Similarly, we would expect Jim to avoid his boss, or approach him or her with caution, for these behaviors are typical of people who experience fear. We would expect Ann to remonstrate with her sister, or to strike out against her in some way, for this is often what angry people do. This is to say that particular emotions dispose persons to commensurate types of action.

The approach indicated in the preceding paragraph suggests that not cultural rules but primarily the structural properties of social interactions determine emotional experiences, and that particular emotional experiences determine inclinations to certain courses of action. Culture plays a role, certainly, in the details but not the gross character of an actor's response to their circumstances. The point to be made here, though, is that emotion is a necessary link between social structure and social actor. The connection is never mechanical, because emotions are normally not behaviorally compelling but inclining (see McDougall [1908] 1948, p. 384). But without the emotions category, accounts of situated actions would be fragmented and incomplete. Emotion is provoked by circumstances and is experienced as transformation of dispositions to act. It is through the subject's active exchange with others that emotional experience is both stimulated in the actor and orientating of their conduct. Emotion is directly implicated in the actors' transformation of their circumstances, as well as the circumstances' transformation of the actors' disposition to act.

This is the view of emotion taken in the chapters which follow. An early expression of such an approach was developed by Adam Smith in *The Theory of Moral Sentiments* ([1759] 1982). Smith acknowledged the novelty of his own approach when he implicitly criticized David Hume, who held that a passion is an "original existence" and has "no reference to any other object" (Hume [1740] 1911, p. 127). Smith, on the other hand, said that:

Philosophers have, of late years, considered chiefly the *tendency of affections*, and have given little attention to the relation which they stand in to the *cause which excites them*. In common life, however, when we judge of any person's conduct, and of the sentiments which directed it, we constantly consider them under both these aspects. (Smith [1759] 1982, p. 18, emphasis added)

That emotions have both antecedents and objects or consequences was also clear to Aristotle. In discussing anger, for instance, he said that emotions (or "affections") must be "divided under three heads . . . the disposition of mind which makes men angry, the persons with whom they are usually angry, and the occasions which give rise to anger" (Aristotle [*c.* 330 BC] 1975, p. 173).

In modern sociology the most sustained, developed, and comprehensive presentation of this form of argument is Theodore Kemper's *A Social*

*Interactional Theory of Emotions* (1978). Kemper's book remains unsurpassed in its clear formulation of the proposition that "a very large class of emotions results from real, imagined, or anticipated outcomes in social relationships" (p. 43) and in its presentation of supporting evidence. If there is a complaint that can be made against Kemper's work it is that it more or less stands alone, and is not part of a growing literature which extends its arguments and applies them to new cases. But the fault here cannot lie with Kemper. These remarks are not designed to depreciate the contribution of others toward the sociological understanding of emotion. The contributions of Thomas Scheff and also Randall Collins, especially, have been of enormous importance in demonstrating the significance of emotion in social processes.

What remains under-represented in the field as a whole, though, is the significance of emotion in large-scale or macroscopic social processes, and the role of emotion in not simply social interactions of a face-to-face nature between individuals, but in the mobilization of collective social actors in historic contexts. Additionally, although less pressing, the neglect of historic textual sources in the sociological discussion of emotion deserves to be corrected. Much of the early treatment of emotion by sociological or sociologically inclined writers is possibly unsophisticated by today's standards. But there is also much which is worthy of retrieval and which would be beneficial for the further development of sociology. Indeed, a new shift of awareness of the importance of emotion in social life requires a reconsideration of the way the content and category of sociological classics are viewed.

It is likely, however, that this latter project cannot be properly begun until a sociology which more fully understands the significance of emotion in social processes is consolidated. For this to occur it will be necessary to get beyond the present stage of developing a "sociology of emotions" and to move beyond the currently dominant social psychological orientation to emotions in sociology. But the relevance of emotion to the wider dimensions and applications of social analysis and theory will have to be demonstrated; it cannot be simply assumed. These remarks on our future prospects are made here not to advertise what is to follow, but to justify and set in context the attempts set out in the following chapters to treat emotions in considerations of macroscopic processes and sociological theory. These chapters are simply steps toward a general sociological acceptance of emotion as a category of explanation.

# 2    Emotion and rationality

The conventional approach holds that emotion is the opposite of reason. But such a view is ultimately subverted by the fact that those who wish to suppress emotion in fully realizing reason are typically engaged by an emotional commitment to the project. Some of the key issues which arise through these currents are discussed in this chapter. Three approaches to the relationship between emotion and reason or rationality are identified: the conventional approach, in which the two are opposed; the critical approach, in which emotion supports rationality by providing it with salience and goal-formation; and the radical approach, in which emotion and rationality are seen to be continuous. Each approach is discussed in what follows.

Max Weber's treatment of rationality as oppositional to emotion represents the conventional approach in the following discussion The critical approach, in which the problems of rationality are solved by emotion, is then discussed. This approach has gained recent support in economic, psychological, and neurological literatures, and these are treated in what follows. While accepting that emotion supports reason, the critical approach is apprehensive about emotion's undermining of instrumental reason. The radical approach, on the other hand, fundamentally qualifies this concern by arguing that instrumental action is founded upon particular emotions. William James provides a version of the radical approach in this chapter. Indeed, while James and Weber apparently hold opposite views concerning the relationship between emotion and rationality, it is shown that they in fact converge. This is because, whereas Weber shows that the actor's control of circumstances is required for rationality, James shows that such control is achieved through the experience of particular emotions.

Finally, it is explained that the conventional opposition between emotion and reason persists because of the cultural discounting of what in the discussion are called "background emotions." These are absolutely necessary for instrumental rationality; nevertheless, these are seldom acknowledged and always regarded as attitudes, customs, or as belonging to some other category which obscures their fundamental emotional nature.

## Introduction

What we know of emotion is characterized by its contrast with reason. The very language through which we refer to emotion, feeling, and affect opposes them to reason, intellect, and rationality. In the conventions which shape our thoughts on the matter, reason and emotion are alternatives: one is defined by what the other is not. But the sharp relief of these conventions does not bear close scrutiny. The actual opposition of emotion and reason is much less durable than the idea of that opposition. Indeed, two other possible relationships between emotion and reason or rationality (the latter terms become interchangeable in these considerations) are much more creditable than the one usually claimed.

In addition to the view that reason and emotion are opposed, there is the idea that emotion supports reason, a view which is widely favored in current specialist literatures. There is also a third possibility, that emotions and reason are continuous with each other, that they are different ways of regarding the same thing. Each of these approaches will be examined in this chapter. Discussion of them allows us to formulate the problem of emotion, and reason, in a new light.

Of the three just mentioned, the notion which continues to have widest currency is the one which claims that emotion undermines reason. Acceptance of this idea is generally taken to lead to another, namely that where possible emotion is to be discounted and suppressed. A history of Western philosophy, which is largely a restatement of these notions, can be traced from Plato (in the *Phaedrus*) to Descartes, and from Kant to the Logical Positivists. Spinoza is typical in not only regarding the intellect as associated with human freedom, but the emotions as associated with human servitude. Even a writer as sympathetic to feelings and emotions as Rousseau was able to insist that "the passage from the state of nature to civil society produces a very remarkable change in man . . . he is forced to . . . consult his reason before listening to his inclinations" ([1762] 1973, pp. 177–8). The vast majority of accounts of rational thought and action avoid positive reference to emotion. Emotion is mentioned only to deny its importance or to warn against its disruptive influence on the proper conduct of human affairs.

This approach – we can continue to call it the conventional approach – makes much of the fact that emotions may be experienced as compulsive forces and at the same time as labile in their manifestation. These dual themes recur in conventional accounts of emotion: emotions may distract persons from their purposes, while at the same time being difficult to make sense of or to grasp firmly. This contrasts fundamentally with the conventional characterization of ideas and thoughts. These latter can be consciously formed and developed, given communicable expression, tested, and improved, and applied in the construction of scientific and moral technologies. Yet even this description of the stark contrasts between emotion and reason does not necessarily lead to the conclusion that they are opposed so much as distinct contributions to a division of labor of human effort.

If emotions distract persons from their purposes, then, at the same time, emotions establish afresh what their purposes are to be. Viewed from this perspective, emotions need not oppose reason so much as give it direction. Emotion and reason, then, are simply different. A classic representation of this alternative view is in the work of the eighteenth-century philosopher David Hume. He held that passion directs the will, and that reason serves the passions ([1740] 1911, pp. 126–7). In more modern terms this is to say that actions are emotionally motivated and executed by means selected with and applied through reason. Emotion is interested, reason disinterested. We shall see that reason unguided by appropriate emotion leads to a disjointedness of purpose. Drawing upon this perspective is a recent literature which regards emotion as rational, or at least as necessary to the enterprise of rationality.

Hume raises a further possibility. He observed that every action of the mind which operates with calmness and tranquility is regarded as reason. At the same time, he distinguished between calm passions and violent passions. Not only are calm passions, therefore, frequently taken to be reason ([1740] 1911, p. 129), but such calm passions are what might be meant by reason ([1740] 1911, p. 147). From the conventional perspective, these two positions are as distinct as an error and what the error is an error of. But Hume's discussion, however it is read, raises the further possibility that emotion does not simply direct reason, but that reason is itself constituted of particular emotions. Against the background of a convention which holds that reason and emotion are opposed, the idea that reason is made up of particular emotions may seem absurd. Yet it is a position which every day is demonstrated to make perfect sense.

In Chaim Potok's (1970) novel *The Promise* a yeshiva student, Abe Greenfield, is taunted and shamed by his Talmud teacher, Rav Kalman, for neglecting class preparation of Talmud by devoting time to revision for a math exam (Potok 1970, pp. 142ff.). Kalman's attacks become too much for Greenfield, who faces Kalman angrily saying that it is he,

Kalman, who wastes time by picking on students. Greenfield's anger carries with it strenuous moral conviction and, standing facing his teacher, he demands an apology from him. But suddenly Greenfield realizes that he alone is standing. He becomes released from his anger, regains the demeanor of his student role, and if not in panic at least in retreat, leaves the room. Reason had returned to Greenfield. But of what does this reason consist?

Outside the class, Greenfield says: "I didn't know what I was saying. My God, what did I do?" (Potok 1970, p. 149). He did not know what he was saying because it was said by the anger which gripped him. His anger is portrayed conventionally, as an external force for which Greenfield could not be responsible. Answering Greenfield's question the narrator says, "You lost your temper" (Potok 1970, p. 149). Literally, Greenfield lost his command over his emotions. Regaining his temper is to regain that command. The dialogue reveals what is the substance of the reassertion of reason over Greenfield's anger.

In response to Greenfield's assertive demand for an apology, Kalman (Potok 1970, p. 148) says: "I did not mean to upset you." The narrator describes what follows:

Abe Greenfield stared at him. I saw him blink his eyes. He seemed to come suddenly awake. He looked quickly around the room and became aware that he was the only one standing. He stared at the eyes that were staring at him. A look of enormous astonishment came over his thin face. (1970, p. 148)

Outside the classroom Greenfield says to the narrator, "What did I do? I just killed myself . . . How can I go home" (1970, p. 149). The regaining of his temper, the return of reason that overcame his anger, was a mix of Greenfield's astonishment at his own boldness and his fear of the consequences of standing up to Kalman. Astonishment and fear, therefore, are the emotional substance of Greenfield's reason.

This scene and its dialogue reveal how important it is to reflect critically on conventional understandings of the relationship between emotion and reason. Different emotions, and the same emotion in different contexts, conduct different relations with reason. Claims about the opposition between emotion and reason must be independently appraised and not simply taken at face-value.

The task of the present chapter is to reveal the role of emotion in rationality. This contrasts with the usual practice of attempting to demonstrate the role of emotion in irrationality. By showing that emotion has a significant purpose in rational thought and action, areas from which it is conventionally excluded, the value of studying emotion in social life in general is strengthened. The focus of discussion will be the treatment of emotion and rationality in the sociology of Max Weber. The work of more recent researchers, as well as that of William James and Georg Simmel, will also be discussed.

## The conventional approach: opposition between rationality and emotion

If there is a single aphorism or credo which summarizes the cultural formation of the modern Western world it would have to be René Descartes' *cogito ergo sum*: I think therefore I am. Indeed, what is remarkable is how well this simple phrase of a seventeenth-century French philosopher captures an entire psychological anthropology and social history. Key aspects of this idea associated with Descartes, and widely accepted since, resonate with elements of the philosophical system of Immanuel Kant, developed a generation later. The concern here is not to elaborate the quite different philosophies of Descartes and Kant. Rather, our attention is focussed only on that part of each which places reason at the center of human being and, consequently, distrusts emotion. Indeed, these ideas are not simply part of philosophical traditions but possess practical currency, and function as second nature in the way in which reason and emotion are understood today, and have been for the previous three centuries.

The idea that human being is uniquely characterized by thought or the activity of thinking places humans clearly apart from non-human animals. However, it does much more than this. It fully locates "responsibility" in the individual person: what one does must be a consequence of what one thinks. This idea is widely taken for granted; but it implies an asociality of human being which is simply erroneous. Indeed, that one even thinks at all is an inter-subjective experience based as much on the communicated experiences of others as on the individual's own internal mental processes.

Our endowments and our purposes are made of the world we inhabit and are fabricated with the involvement of those with whom we share that world. As these change, so the actions and thought of individuals change. Yet in the conventional approach the process of thought, which is taken to be an autonomous capacity of individuals, is seen as the basis of their reasons for action, their decision to act, and their calculations of the success or failure of their actions. The idea, that the defining capacity to think is a proclivity of individual persons, is reinforced by an associated stream of modern Western political thought. This is the idea that by annulling their individuality in collective experience, persons lose their capacity to think and reason. By submerging themselves in crowds persons become subject to a common emotionality of the mass (Le Bon 1895; McClelland 1989).

Descartes was uninterested in crowds, but he was convinced of the subversive influence of emotion on thought. In the *Passions of the Soul* ([1649] 1931), for instance, he held that persons can take no responsibility for their feelings and emotions. This is because these are not things that persons do, but what their bodies do to them. It is on these grounds that he established the division between mind and body, and allocated reason to the mind and emotion to the body. This is the other side of the *cogito*; namely that persons have no control over the emotions which subvert their thoughts and reason. If I am because I think, then I am undone if I feel. The best thing to do with the emotion which subverts reason is suppress it.

In summary: a definition of persons as thinking beings entails that individuals exist apart from others, that emotion disrupts reason, and therefore, if persons are to remain reasonable, that the influence of emotion must be removed from them. Emotion, in this perspective, is understood to arise not from the mind but the body. It is regarded as a compelling force, which leads persons away from the decisions they make, the reasons they have, the choices they take, and is responsible for disrupting the calculations they perform. Each of the highlighted terms characterize thought against emotion.

The commonplace ideas just described do not simply have philosophical origins; they are part of a continuing technical apparatus of much psychology and sociology, and also of everyday conceptions of mind and society. Sigmund Freud, for instance, is widely thought to provide an alternative to this tradition because he paid considerable attention to emotion. But he saw the emotions as part of the *id*, not the *ego*, as part only of the instinctual energy of biological functions, not as contributing to the discernment, memory, judgment, and reasoning which make up personality. Emotion which fails to dissipate and which is inadequately controlled, Freud saw as a force subversive of reason and disruptive of normal personality. And although it is seldom understood in this light, the single most significant text of sociology, Max Weber's *The Protestant Ethic and the Spirit of Capitalism* ([1905a] 1991), is similarly a manual of Cartesian and Kantian principles concerning reason or rationality, emotion, and the opposition between them. Indeed, there is no better way of demonstrating the limitations of this approach to emotion as the subverter of reason than by following Weber's argument and indicating the contradictions to which it leads him.

For Weber, conduct which is rational is that which results from human deliberation. Thus culture, the product of deliberative activities, and not nature, is the locus of rationality. Parallel to this consideration is a distinction between culture and nature in terms of hermeneutic utility, a distinction between that part of "existing concrete reality" which has meaning and significance conferred by human interest on the one hand, and the "meaningless infinity of the world process" on the other (Weber [1904] 1949, pp. 81, 76). For those who are familiar with it, the Kantian orientation will be evident particularly in Weber's notion of rationality and its attendant concepts.

The Kantian sources of Weber's sociology are well known (see Albrow 1990, ch. 2). Less frequently acknowledged is the role of Descartes' *cogito* in the Calvinist rationalization treated by Weber ([1905a] 1991, p. 118), and in Weber's own understanding of the rationalization process. This latter can be discovered in methodological essays written and published by Weber during the period in which *The Protestant Ethic and the Spirit of Capitalism* first appeared. In one of these in particular, "Knies and the Problem of Irrationality" ([1905b] 1975), Weber set out his own position not only on rationality but also emotion. These positions are identical with that which he finds in Calvinism, as related in *The Protestant Ethic and the Spirit of Capitalism*.

Weber's notion of rationality, and his distinction between culture and nature, come together in the proposition that culture is more rational than nature. In "Knies and the Problem of Irrationality," an essay in which many of the methodological principles characteristic of his sociological corpus are first worked out, Weber says that: "because of its susceptibility to a meaningful *interpretation* . . . individual human conduct is in principle intrinsically less 'irrational' than the individual natural event" ([1905b] 1975, p. 125). The interpretability of human action derives from the possibility of ascribing to it motives, intentions, and beliefs (see [1905b] 1975, p. 127). In doing this, action becomes meaningful to the actor; it has a significance not only in the passive sense that there is cognitive discernment, but, more importantly, in the active sense that the actor's own deliberation is experienced as the source of what is rational in the action.

Weber goes on to make exactly this point when he insists that in order for an act to be rational the end must be "clearly conscious and intended" and the means to be applied in achieving that end must be selected on the basis of a "clear knowledge" ([1905b] 1975, p. 186). In other words, rational action is that which follows from the actor's own deliberative considerations. Thus motives, decisions, and calculations are aspects of thought and cognitive processes in general which make action rational. Any interference with the freedom of these deliberations is characterized by Weber as "'external' constraints," which he says may appear as "irresistible 'affect'" ([1905b] 1975, p. 191). Here is emotion, outside of thought and undermining of it. In opposition to the deliberations of rationality is the compulsion of emotion, its irresistibility. Weber's neo-Kantian concept of rationality is connected with a neo-Cartesian conceptualization of emotion.

This characterization of emotion, as inherently irrational because it is compulsive and disruptive of thought and reason, is elaborated in a number of places in the "Knies" essay. For instance, feelings, according to Weber, cannot be defined analytically and must therefore remain cognitively vague because they are "mental experiences 'introjected' into us" ([1905b] 1975, p. 178). But not only are emotions or feelings, according to Weber, vague though compelling, they are fundamentally inchoate: he says that they "cannot be conceptually articulated" (p. 179); that they "are intrinsically unarticulated" (pp. 179–80); that they are "not . . . analytically articulated" (p. 180). And, as if the situation were not clear enough, Weber (p. 182) goes on to say that: "In contrast to mere 'emotional contents,' we ascribe 'value' to an item if and only if it can be the content of a commitment: that is, a consciously articulated positive or negative 'judgment,' something that appears to us to 'demand validity'." Again, we see the free and deliberative qualities of value in the notion of commitment, and their opposite in emotion.

Weber's discussion in the "Knies" paper is tortuous and inconclusive, but the characterization of rationality and emotion in it is consistently developed. Indeed, the position on these matters outlined in this text is to be found in Weber's other works, including his account of "affective action" in *Economy and Society* ([1921a] 1978, p. 25), to which we shall return. It is particularly instructive to consider the treatment of these themes in *The Protestant Ethic and the Spirit of Capitalism*. This is because it will not only become clear that Weber's account of Calvinist rationality conforms with his own understanding of the nature of rational action, but also because the opposition between rationality and emotion which Weber accepts and which he shows to be articulated by Calvinism becomes obviously impossible to maintain.

Weber shows that the ethical creed of the Puritans is a particular apprehension of Descartes' *cogito ergo sum*: "Only a life guided by constant thought could achieve conquest over the state of nature" (Weber [1905a] 1991, p. 118). He goes on to say that: "The Puritan, like every rational type of asceticism, tried to enable a man to maintain and act upon his constant motives, especially those which it taught him itself, against the emotions" ([1905a] 1991, p. 119). Rational action, in realizing motives which are long-held and seriously regarded, must be against the emotions because, as Weber immediately explains, the emotions are spontaneous and impulsive forces which distract a person from their purposes. The implication is that emotion will create disorder in human affairs, whereas rationality will "bring order into the conduct" of persons. This is precisely Weber's understanding of rationality: the realization of individual purpose against impulse and against nature. The "definitely rational character" of "Christian asceticism" is described by Weber ([1905a] 1991, pp. 118–9) in the following terms:

> It had developed a systematic method of rational conduct with the purpose of overcoming the *status naturae*, to free man from the power of irrational impulses and his dependence on the world and on nature. It attempted to subject man to the supremacy of a purposeful will, to bring his actions under constant self-control with a careful consideration of their ethical consequences.

In this account the qualities of purpose, self-control, and forethought not only constitute the substance of rationality but are contrasted with irrational impulse, dependency, and nature. In the Calvinist form of Christian asceticism these latter qualities crystalize as emotion. Here is the full structure of the Cartesian *cogito*.

Weber refers to the "entirely negative attitude of Puritanism to all the sensuous and emotional elements in culture and in religion" ([1905a] 1991, p. 105). He also reports that "Calvin viewed all pure feelings and emotions, no matter how exalted they might seem to be, with suspicion" ([1905a] 1991, p. 114). Indeed, Weber ([1905a] 1991, p. 123) refers to "[Calvinism's] rational suppression of . . . the whole emotional side of religion." In these statements Weber is reporting the conceptions and actions of others. But through his indication that Calvin and the Calvinists were not only suspicious of emotion but suppressed emotion in their construction of a rational program and practice, Weber indicates his own acceptance of such an account of rationality, of emotion, and of the relations between them. In his own voice, Weber ([1905a] 1991, p. 136) refers to "emotional elements" as "anti-rational."

Naturally, the narrow focus and attention to purpose typical of Puritan rationalism would lead to an opposition not only to emotion but to anything which negated or disrupted the application of energy to the achievement of particular outcomes. In line with such a prospect, Weber ([1905a] 1991, p. 168) reports "the Puritan's ferocious hatred of everything which smacked of superstition." It is important to pause a moment at this remark and notice that here a particular emotion, hatred, is in the service of rational asceticism. Earlier in the text, Weber ([1905a] 1991, p. 122) recounts the Puritan's response "toward the sin of one's neighbor," which was "hatred and contempt for him as an enemy of God." The most telling aspect of Weber's discussion in this passage is his description of these feelings not as an emotion but as an "attitude."

The apparent inconsistency of Puritan suppression of emotion on the one hand, and hatred of sin on the other, is not solved by describing such particular emotions as attitudes. Indeed, the concept of attitude has performed a purpose in the development of social psychology similar to that which Weber applies here (see Fishbein and Ajzen 1972; McDougall 1933). The concept of attitude implicitly acknowledges a role for affective or emotional factors in cognitive and purposive, and indeed in rational, processes. But it does so by excluding emotion in its own right from consideration of such processes and therefore leaves unquestioned the conventional view, that reason and emotion are opposed. Weber is correct to acknowledge the importance of emotions in setting goals and forming motives and orientations. But it is inadequate license to treat emotion in general as irrational by describing a particular emotion as an attitude.

What we find in *The Protestant Ethic and the Spirit of Capitalism* is typical of the conventional understanding of emotion. It is held that rational action is undermined by emotion, and that rationality opposes and suppresses emotion. It also emerges that particular emotions or "attitudes" may function to define purposes which become subject to rational realization. Weber, no more than other adherents to the conventional view, does not deal with the obvious question which arises from this characterization of his position: the ultimate impossibility of the rational suppression of emotion in general and the requirement of particular emotions for deliberatively formed motives. Indeed, the obfuscation of the real contribution of emotions in goal-defining practices, by incorporating them in the concept of attitude, reflects the limitations of a general opposition of reason and emotion.

### The critical approach: emotion as a solution to problems rationality cannot solve

Weber's invocation of emotion terms in his characterization of Calvinist attitudes and practices reveals something of the unavoidability of emotion in reasoned conduct. In spite of his intentions and primary analysis, Weber in effect indicates that emotion can not be eliminated from human affairs and also that it has a positive role in clarifying intentions and ordering action. This points to a quite different understanding of the relationship between rationality and emotion than the one Weber assumed and set out to portray. Against the conventional approach, therefore, is a critical perspective which holds that reason and emotion are not necessarily opposed but clearly different faculties, and that their differences allow each to serve in a division of labor in which their distinct capacities contribute to a unified outcome.

The critical view, that reason and emotion are different but mutually supportive, is not entirely new. Its most prominent classical exponent was David Hume, as indicated earlier. After a long period of neglect this position has been developed in a growing recent literature. Representative statements of it are found in philosophy (de Sousa 1990), psychology (Oatley 1992), economics (Frank 1988), and neuroscience (Damasio 1994).

The contribution of emotion to reason, as it is understood in the critical approach, is summarized by Ronald de Sousa (1990, p. xv, emphasis in original) in the following terms: "Despite a common prejudice, reason and emotion are not natural antagonists . . . Emotions are among the mechanisms that control the crucial factor of *salience* among what would otherwise be an unmanageable plethora of objects of attention, interpretation, and strategies of inference and conduct." The critical contention, then, is that knowledge and, by extension, action cannot organize themselves, and that a crucial organizational function is performed by emotions. This clarifies and resolves Weber's apparently anomalous claim concerning the anti-emotional Puritan's hatred of sin.

Within the critical perspective emotion is relocated from a hostile and distant position in the process of human cognition to a supportive and integral one: reason and rationality require emotional guidance. If anything, then, the critical approach is critical of reason and rationality, regarding these as more limited and incomplete than they are understood to be in the conventional perspective. The critical insights regarding the limitations of rationality resonate with the theme of the unreasonableness of rationality, a theme which has a certain currency today.

It is likely that any popular distaste for rationality results from disquiet concerning particular outcomes of specific practices identified as "rational," such as the nuclear arms race, the ascription of supreme value to economic gain, and so on. The point to be made here is that popular perceptions of the unreason of rationality are likely to be formed through a judgment concerning the inappropriateness of a particular purpose or goal. This is essentially the premise of the critical approach. It holds that inappropriate, ambiguous, and competing goals undermine reason and rationality, and also that imperfect, disorganized, and absent knowledge have the same effect. It goes on to indicate that emotion may overcome these limitations of rationality by clarifying or defining goals and by "bridging" information. This is possible because inherent in a goal is an emotion.

The importance of the articulation of appropriate goals or purposes for rational action to occur, and the contribution of emotion to this approbation, are the concerns of Robert Frank's discussion in his *Passions within Reason* (1988). Frank distinguishes two main accounts of rational behavior, which he calls the "present aim theory" and the "self-interest theory" (1988, pp. 67–8). Each of these, he says, is flawed.

The present aim theory holds that whatever serves the realization of an actor's present aim is rational. Thus it conceives of rationality in terms of efficient means–ends relations. But this ignores the possibility of irrational preferences; it ignores the question of the need to define the ends or purpose of an action in order to know whether the action is in fact rational. Frank (1988, p. 68) says that this theory of rationality "permits virtually any behavior to be considered rational merely by asserting that a person prefers it."

The self-interest theory, on the other hand, resolves the problem of the purpose of action by defining rational action as that which serves the actor's interests. This approach therefore rules out self-damaging or irrational preferences. It remains flawed, however, in its inability to discriminate between appropriate and inappropriate means which might be drawn on in satisfying the actor's interests. The view from this theory holds that avoiding undetected cheating, for instance, is irrational: cheating confers advantage, and to avoid using it therefore avoids a means of satisfying self-interest. Frank's point against the self-interest theory of rationality is that moral behavior confers greater advantages than this model of rationality is able to apprehend.

Frank provides ample evidence and argument for the claim that social morality, even though it may prove to be contrary to an actor's immediate interests, nevertheless confers real advantages in the long run. It can be taken as given that dishonest, narrowly selfish, and socially unresponsive behaviors do reduce an actor's opportunities for satisfaction in the medium and long term. The problem of a "commitment" to socially responsive behavior, which opens opportunities for cooperation with others and therefore advantages otherwise denied, is solved by emotion. Frank (1988, p. 237) says that:

> The commitment and self-interest models paint strikingly different pictures not only of human nature, but also of its consequences for material welfare . . . People who love, who feel guilty when they cheat, vengeful when they are wronged, or envious when they get less than their fair share will often behave in ways that reduce their material payoffs. But precisely because of this, they will also enjoy opportunities that would not be available to a purely opportunistic person.

It can be seen from this that Frank's opposition to the self-interest model is in the form of a qualification rather than a rejection. Indeed, this is how he goes on to describe his position (Frank 1988, p. 258).

The "commitment problem" is a problem of appropriateness of goals or purposes of action. The narrowly conceived self-interest theory of rationality defines the self-interested actor from a limited and individualistic perspective. Taking into account an actor's emotional commitments broadens the scope of their opportunities and satisfactions, and therefore redefines the goals or purposes which must be satisfied if an actor's self-interest is to be better understood and more fully realized. Frank's discussion of the relevance of emotion has therefore arguably enhanced the understanding of rational action by expanding the goal or purpose of action to more appropriate dimensions. But it is not clear that it has done this unambiguously, neither is it evident that his discussion has advanced the understanding of emotion to a satisfactory degree.

Frank's uncertainty concerning the relation between what he calls the "commitment model" and the "self-interest theory" – whether they are opposed (1988, p. 237) or are complementary (p. 258) – is not difficult to resolve. His argument against self-interest theory opposes a narrow conception of self-interest, not the concept of self-interest itself. He wishes to show that unselfish and non-opportunistic behavior in the long run will yield greater material benefits for the person who engages in them, and he is therefore arguing for a broader conception of self-interest. The realization of the broader conception of self-interest, Frank shows, is through the emotions which he indicates solve the commitment problem; these are the emotions which set goals for action wider than the purely opportunistic ones, which produce greater benefits, and which are more rational in doing so. Thus emotion provides appropriate or enhanced goals for self-interested action, enlarging its rationality.

Frank has indicated the relevance of emotion to rational goal-formation, through its solution of the commitment problem. But this correction of the account of rationality is not an adequate or complete account of emotion. For instance, the limited and opportunistic goals of lesser or deformed rationality are not free of emotional content. Indeed, fear and shame are likely emotional sources of opportunistic and narrowly selfish behavior (Bowlby 1973; Tomkins 1963), just as other particular emotions will be the sources of more giving and socially committed behavior. The conclusion to be drawn from this is that an understanding of emotion explains both rational and non-rational behaviors. Neither does the commitment problem discussed by Frank alert us to the contributions of emotion to reason and rationality beyond the issue of goal-formation. A more detailed account of reason and rationality will provide a more detailed account of emotion.

At the core of reason is the process of decision-making. Antonio Damasio (1994, p. 165) goes so far as to say that decision-making is the "purpose of reasoning" because reasoning is the business of selecting an appropriate and effective "response option" – a verbal or non-verbal action – to deal with the exigencies of a given situation. It is conventionally assumed that the decider or actor "possesses some logical strategy for producing valid inferences on the basis of which an appropriate response option is selected" (p. 166). This "high-reason" approach holds both that logical inference will provide the best available solution to any problem, and that this will be achieved by the exclusion of emotion from the process (p. 171). Damasio argues that these expectations could never be realized.

The conventional approach assumes that a rational actor would infer which is the best course of action for them from the information they have concerning their circumstances against their desires, expectations, or intentions. In contrast with this scenario, Damasio (1994, pp. 171–2) argues that even the most unimposing set of circumstances and the most modest desires will generate so many possible courses of action that rational calculation would occupy more time than could be available for effective action. Indeed, the time spent in identifying and evaluating each of the logically possible courses of action is likely to remove the possibility of action in any finite time-frame. But there is a further problem which Damasio fails to notice, but which provides even stronger support for his rejection of the "high-reason" account of decision-making.

In any decision-making situation, the weight of alternative possible courses of action will be based on the balance of what might be called a conditional inference: in simple terms, on speculation about what *might* happen. All action is taken in the face of an unknown future. Indeed, any given action changes the conditions of all future actions. This means that the unknowability of the future is not something which might be overcome in time. The problem for calculation is that unknown futures yield no information about themselves and they therefore offer nothing from which a calculation can be made. Damasio's supposition that rational calculation would be an inordinately lengthy procedure must be replaced with the proposition that rational calculation is in fact not possible for most social and interactive situations. The evidence for whether an action will succeed comes only when the action is completed, not when the decision to take it must be made. We shall return to this problem when discussing the radical approach to the relations between rationality and emotion.

These problems of decision-making, concerning logical inference or rational calculation, are solved for human actors by what Damasio (1994, pp. 173–5) calls "somatic markers." Somatic markers are those emotionally borne physical sensations which "tell" those who experience them that a circumstance or event is likely to lead to pleasure or pain, to be favorable or unfavorable. This is because emotion has a necessary physical component, as the conventional view correctly insists. Damasio (p. 159) says that emotional feelings:

offer us the cognition of our visceral and musculo-skeletal state as it becomes affected by preorganized mechanisms and by the cognitive structures we have developed under their influence . . . Feelings offer us a glimpse of what goes on in our flesh, as a momentary image of that flesh is juxtaposed to the images of other objects and situations; in so doing, feelings modify our comprehensive notion of other objects and situations. By dint of juxtaposition, body images give to other images a quality of goodness or badness, of pleasure or pain.

In monitoring and presenting an actor's body images juxtaposed with their circumstances, emotion provides cognitive or decision-making processes with a framework and reference point for reasoning and rationality.

Emotions, according to this argument, indicate which problems reason has to solve, and they assist in delimiting a set of likely solutions. This outcome is possible because of a dual capacity in the nature of emotion itself: emotion combines a mental evaluative process with a dispositional response to that process (Damasio 1994, p. 139; see also Scherer 1984, p. 294). It is not necessary, and frequently unlikely, that the actor will be consciously aware of these emotional sensations. Somatic markers precede thought and reason. These markers or emotional feelings do not replace inference or calculation, according to Damasio, but enhance decision-making by "drastically reduc[ing] the number of options" for consideration. Thus a "partnership" of cognitive and emotional processes make decision-making humanly possible (1994, p. 175).

Key aspects of emotion, which are simply not visible from the conventional perspective, which claims an opposition between reason and emotion, are amplified in the argument concerning the role of somatic markers in decision-making. Damasio (1994, p. 174) says that: "somatic markers are a special instance of feelings generated from secondary emotions. Those emotions and feelings have been connected, by learning, to predicted future outcomes of certain scenarios." This statement explains that emotions can guide reason because they are tutored by experience. Such a perspective is quite at odds with the conventional view, which holds that emotions are innate and indifferent to modification through experience.

Research has long demonstrated that emotions are both deeply embedded in physical structures and also subject to socialization and learning processes (Emde 1984; Lewis and Saarni 1985). As indicated in the preceding quotation, Damasio argues that the emotions which learn from experience and which guide reason are "secondary emotions." The distinction between primary and secondary emotions has a long history and is unavoidable in a general discussion of emotion. This distinction can be drawn with a number of lines, but for Damasio (1994, pp. 131–9) they all point in the direction of whether the emotion can be changed through experience: primary emotions are "preorganized" and secondary emotions modified by learning.

Not all emotions researchers find value in this distinction, and of those who do there is little agreement concerning which are the primary emotions (Kemper 1987; Ortony, Clore, and Collins [1988] 1990, pp. 25–9). Also, Damasio's insistence that only secondary emotions are modified by experience is not an entirely successful boundary-drawing claim concerning the emotional contribution to decision-making through somatic markers. Fear, for instance, is one emotion which features in all typologies of primary or basic emotions. As a primary emotion fear can be simply "triggered" by a stimulus without prior experiential preparation or learning. But the objects of fear, while preorganized in significant cases (every child and many higher mammals fear looming objects), are also frequently learned and therefore vary with experience. Children have to learn to fear traffic, communists, and being late for school. Even though a primary emotion, it is difficult to believe that fear would not function in somatic markers as Damasio describes them, in assisting decision-making in the way he suggests.

It is important to get over this problem, because it is necessary to make it clear that the difference between those emotions which assist rationality and those which undermine it cannot be distinguished with the aid of the distinction between primary and secondary emotions. While the critical perspective understands that emotion can support reason, it does not deny that there are circumstances in which the conventional opposition to emotion, as a saboteur of reason, will not find justification. Somatic markers, and through them emotions, "are essential for rational behaviors," Damasio (1994, p. 192) says, "although they can be pernicious to rational decision-making in certain circumstances by creating an overriding bias against objective facts or even by interfering with support mechanisms of decision-making such as working memory."

The critical perspective holds that emotion is especially inappropriate in decision-making about technical problems (Damasio 1994, pp. 191–2; Oatley 1992, p. 164). These are areas in which calculation must be most clearly regarded as the sole substance of reason, because they are domains in which the purposes of action are resolute and in which the courses of action are procedurally limited by the nature of the tasks. While rejecting the blanket denial of emotion's role in reason and rationality found in the conventional approach, the critical perspective insists on the more limited claim that emotion is disruptive of narrowly technical reason. This is not the last word on the matter, however. There is an argument which claims that emotion has a central role even in technical reason: this we can call the radical argument.

## The radical approach: emotion and rationality as continuous

The limitations of rationality highlighted in the critical approach and the solution offered by this approach of emotional salience were spelled out over a hundred years before the publication of its recent exponents. In an essay provocatively called "The Sentiment of Rationality," William James ([1897a] 1956), the late-nineteenth- and early twentieth-century American psychologist and philosopher, made the following observation: "The absurd abstraction of an intellect verbally formulating all its evidence and carefully estimating the probability thereof by a vulgar fraction by the size of whose denominator and numerator alone it is swayed, is ideally as inept as it is actually impossible" ([1897a] 1956, pp. 92–3). Such an operation is "impossible" in James's account because intellect does not exist except as a category of thought; it is not an independent operation of mind. In reality, says James ([1897a] 1956, p. 92), the whole person is involved in the formation of philosophical opinions just as they are in practical affairs.

James's further claim, made in the context of the remarks just quoted, that intellect, will, taste, and passion all work together, is not a moral injunction holding that aesthetic consideration and emotional commitment, say, should fashion a person's thoughts and that these together should influence their actions. Rather, he is saying that intellect, will, taste, and passion in fact necessarily support each other. From James's perspective, then, reason and emotion are not opposed phenomena but distinct names for aspects of a continuous process. This radical approach to the relationship between rationality and emotion has a number of dimensions.

James begins his account of "The Sentiment of Rationality" by asking how a rational conception might be recognized. It is recognized, he says, by a feeling of rationality. In the first instance this latter is constituted by "the absence of any feeling of irrationality" ([1897a] 1956, pp. 63–4). James acknowledges that, on the face of it, this appears to be a less than satisfactory account, but it is not a vacuous or flippant one. He explains that our strongest feelings are those discharged under impediment or resistance, so that we do not experience a particular pleasure of free breathing, for instance, but intense distress when breathing is prevented. So it is with the feelings of rationality and irrationality: "so any unobstructed tendency to action discharges itself without the production of much cognitive accompaniment, and any perfectly fluent course of thought awakens but little feeling; but when the movement is inhibited, or when the thought meets with difficulties, we experience distress" (James [1897a] 1956, p. 64). Thus James accounts for the lack of intensity in the feeling of rationality in terms of the facilitation of thought associated with it.

With regard to its emotional content, as opposed to its intensity, James understands the "sentiment of rationality" to be a "feeling of the sufficiency of the present moment, of its absoluteness – this absence of all need to explain it, account for it, or justify it . . . As soon, in short, as we are enabled from any cause whatever to think with perfect fluency, the thing we think of seems to us *pro tanto* rational" ([1897a] 1956, p. 64). The "feeling of sufficiency of the present moment," which James regards as the feeling of rationality, has been independently described as an "emotion of security" (de Rivera 1977, pp. 46–7). The context of this latter account is a discussion of the emotional requirements for the occurrence of abstract thinking, in which the emotion of security is implicated as "essential." The continuity between rationality and abstract thinking requires no further comment.

James identifies two general sources of the feeling of sufficiency, and therefore two types of rationality. These bear some relation to Weber's formal and substantive rationalities (Weber 1921, pp. 85–6). The first, which comes from what James calls "the relief of identification," is the source of theoretic rationality ([1897a] 1956, p. 70). Theoretic rationality is not reducible to means–ends relations as is Weber's formal rationality, but, like the latter, functions through a parsimonious principle of simplicity. It brings a feeling of sufficiency in the present by identifying otherwise disparate elements as part of an essential unity. The limitations of this form of rationality are suggested in James's caution that the world "is a complex affair," and therefore cannot be adequately apprehended by principles of simplicity, rational or otherwise.

Theoretic rationality, the operational principle of which being the identification of one thing with another, offers some intellectual comfort, perhaps. But James derisively summarizes its limitations by suggesting that it offers nothing less than the "tranquility of the boor" ([1897a] 1956, p. 71). This dismissive judgment is supported by the claim that whatever human experience consists of, its contrary can be imagined. James argues, then, that theoretic rationality is simply unattainable at a high level because the relation of unity of identity envisioned by it is subverted by the inclination to relations of variety, by the process of "seeing an *other* beside every item of experience" ([1897a] 1956, p. 71, emphasis in original). As Weber's narrowly technical formal rationality is likely to undermine a more broadly based rationality, so is James's theoretic rationality ultimately self-destructive. James notes, in his essay "Reflex Action and Theism" ([1897b] 1956, p. 132), for instance, that, if unmediated, the passion for parsimony will "end by blighting the development of the intellect itself quite as much as that of the feelings or the will." It is practical rationality, then, which James regards as having the greater credibility.

Practical rationality, the rationality which allows persons to deal with the diverse elements and particles of their everyday lives, is, in this regard, like Weber's substantive rationality. James says that a feeling of rationality in this vein can be produced by a mere familiarity with things. Practical rationality, then, does not find a pattern of relations between things in their ultimate identity, as with theoretic rationality, but through acquaintance with their antecedents. Indeed, James ([1897a] 1956, pp. 76–7) notes that this is the singular understanding of rationality in the empiricist tradition.

Empiricism regards sense experience to be the basis of knowledge, and it therefore treats knowledge as the effect of past experience. In a like manner, the empiricist account of rationality focusses on the feeling of ease of thought which derives from the explanation of a thing which refers to its antecedents. James accepts that this is a source of the feeling of rationality insofar as it allows for a fluent movement between things ([1897a] 1956, p. 77). But for an understanding of practical rationality "one particular relation is of greater practical importance than all the rest, [i.e.] the relation of a thing to its consequences" (p. 77). So the first practical prerequisite for the sentiment or emotion of rationality is the "banish[ment of] uncertainty from the future" (p. 77).

It is the ambiguity of the future which is the source of philosophical and practical distress, according to James, even though he observes that the ambiguity of the future is unavoidable ([1897a] 1956, pp. 79–81). Although Weber, for instance, does not acknowledge it, this is the ultimate source of the irrationality of experience, which he also notes ([1905a] 1991, p. 233; [1904] 1949, p. 111), for all experience is had in the absence of knowledge concerning its outcome. The unease which accompanies a sense of futurity is settled by a feeling of expectancy, according to James ([1897a] 1956, pp. 77–8). Thus James locates the sentiment of rationality in the affective or emotional displacement of uncertainty concerning the future. The "emotional effect of expectation" is to enable actors to proceed in their practical affairs (pp. 78–9). Thus James characterizes rationality in terms of the particular emotional configuration which enables the actor to engage their practical affairs.

The "feeling of sufficiency in the present moment," which permits persons to "think with fluency" and to act with purpose, is associated with the feeling of expectation concerning the future. In these ways James characterizes rationality as a property of mind or a quality of action explicable in terms of their emotional qualities. But it is not emotion in general, rather it is particular emotions which constitute the sentiment of rationality. James's conceptualization of rationality in terms of emotional orientations to the future, and his insistence on emotional salience for rationality, is evident in his treatment of the role of emotion in decision-making, to which we now turn. This is an aspect of the question alluded to in the earlier qualification of Damasio's treatment of calculation, when the impossibility of knowing the future was mentioned.

In his essay "The Will to Believe," James ([1897c] 1956, pp. 23–4) notes that in most social situations action is taken in the absence of evidence as to what might be its most appropriate course. The general form of such a circumstance he calls a forced option, a situation in which there is no possibility of not choosing (p. 3). Under these circumstances the absence of evidence regarding a correct course of action means that calculation to aid decision-making is impossible, and an emotional rather than a logical choice or commitment is necessary if action is to occur at all.

In "The Sentiment of Rationality" James ([1897a] 1956, pp. 96–7) develops this point through the case of the "Alpine climber," in which an actor's particular emotional commitment leads to a singular material outcome. To escape serious difficulty the Alpine climber must execute a dangerous leap which they have not performed before. If engaged by the emotions of confidence and hope, the climber is likely to perform a feat which would otherwise be impossible. Fear and mistrust, on the other hand, are likely to lead to hesitation, and this will increase the probability of the climber missing their foothold and falling to their death. Whichever emotion is engaged will be commensurate with a particular outcome, but with contrastingly different consequences.

Philosophers who have considered James's account of forced options typically reject it. One underlying reason for this is that philosophers of a logical disposition tend to regard time as irrelevant (Passmore 1968, p. 271), whereas for James the distinction between the present and the future is essential. Indeed, what James touches on here is identical with the problem of trust, its relationship to time, and the nature of its rationality.

Cooperation with others requires trust, and trust is therefore essential in social relations. But, as Niklas Luhmann (1979, p. 25) says, the decision to trust cannot be based on pertinent knowledge because it is only possible to determine whether an action based on trust was correct by whether the trust was honored or broken. These are events which necessarily occur after the trust has been given. In this sense trust is not rational. Yet there is a further and more compelling sense in which trust is rational. The rationality of trust, Luhmann (p. 88) goes on to indicate, is not in its decision-making form but in its orientating action to meaningful outcomes which enhance understanding and performance. Luhmann acknowledges the emotional nature of trust (pp. 22, 81), but it is precisely as an emotion which overcomes the uncertainty of the future that trust is rational (see also Gambetta 1990). In a remarkably Jamesian turn Luhmann says that: "To show trust is to anticipate the future. It is to behave as though the future were certain [. . .] This problem of time is bridged by trust, paid ahead of time as an advance on success" (1979, pp. 10, 25). Again, a specific emotion contributes to a specific rationality in the absence of a possible contribution by logic or calculation.

The role of emotion in practical rationality, then, is to permit action which would be inhibited if it were to rely on logic or calculation alone. The emotional contribution to rationality is to provide a feeling of certainty concerning the future, which is necessary if action is to occur and the actor to proceed.

James's account of particular emotions as continuous with rationality derived from a conception of persons as interested, purposive, and active agents in their relations with others, generative of the social reality they experience. This focus on action is one which James shares with Weber. But Weber, of course, defines rationality in terms of the absence, indeed the suppression, of emotion. This latter approach is the very opposite of James's. Yet, if we look at the details of Weber's account of rationality, the very conditions are in fact indicated under which James's practical rationality and its emotional substance can be realized.

In the foregoing discussion it was demonstrated that Weber's account of rationality functions in terms of the exclusion of emotion. On the face of it, then, the suggestion that he and William James, who positively defines rationality as the presence of certain emotions, present converging arguments, seems impossible if not absurd. But it will be shown that their views of rationality are remarkably commensurate, even though Weber entertains a limited and erroneous view of emotion.

Weber is *the* theorist of rationality. He explained characteristic features of Western development and a range of technical, institutional, organizational, and social processes in terms of rationality and rationalization. Perhaps as a result of the wide application of the concepts of reason, rationality, and rationalization in his work, Weber's account of rationality may seem ambiguous, even "irredeemably opaque and shifting," as

Steven Lukes has put it (1977, p. 219). Certainly, Weber regards the particular elements of rationality as multiple. But, as we shall see, these are parts of a whole, and the whole is consistent. Additionally, it is consistent in a manner commensurate with James's understanding of the radical continuity of emotion and reason.

Weber regards rationality not as an absolute category but as one which is context dependent. Indeed, he saw rationalism as an "historical concept which covers a whole world of different things" ([1905a] 1991, p. 78), and there is allowance inherent in the concept itself "for widely differing contents" (1921a, p. 998). This means not only that rationality may be present in different degrees in distinct domains of activity, including politics, economics, religion, music, and science and technology, but also that within a given context the differing purposes of actors will generate different rationalities. "Furthermore," as Weber says in his 1920 ([1920] 1991) "Introduction," "each one of these fields may be rationalized in terms of very different ultimate values and ends, and what is rational from one point of view is irrational from another" ([1905a] 1991, p. 26). It might be noticed that James ([1909] 1932, pp. 112–3) also held that rationality occupied different domains, and that its realization in one may be at the expense of its achievement in another.

It is not surprising, then, that coherence in the concept of rationality has sometimes been difficult to grasp. Yet, while acknowledging again that rationalism "may mean very different things" and therefore that there are different "types of rationalism," Weber ([1915a] 1970, p. 293) immediately adds that "ultimately they belong inseparably together" (p. 293). Before we consider the basis of their coherence or unity, it is essential to discuss the varieties of rationality which Weber identifies.

The most general types of rationality are in the forms of systemic arrangement and also logical coherence or consistency. In *The Protestant Ethic and the Spirit of Capitalism*, for instance, Weber ([1905a] 1991, p. 117) indicates that a key feature of rationalization in Calvinism is the systematization of life and works. Elsewhere, Weber says that this is a feature of all rationalization processes in religion ([1915a] 1970, p. 280; [1915b] 1970, p. 327) as much as it is in economics ([1921a] 1978, pp. 71, 348). The form and consequences of systematization are very similar to those of "rationality in the sense of logical or teleological 'consistency'" ([1915b] 1970, p. 324). What Weber here calls the "imperative of consistency" and rational deduction give sense to what otherwise might escape the grasp of the thinker or actor. It is in this way that these two forms of rationality are similar. Systematization relates elements to the unit of which they are a part. This enhances the achievement of the purpose of the unit. So it is with logical coherence. An actor's purpose, and how they might achieve it, becomes clearer to them when logical coherence gives sense to what would otherwise be disparate parts of an unconnected series.

Systematization and logical consistency as forms of rationality are readily understood by William James ([1909] 1932, p. 22) in terms of particular emotions: he refers to the "intellect[ual] . . . passion for generalizing, simplifying and subordinating." Intellect and emotion are not opposed here, but continuous. Yet this view is not so remote from Weber's. He insists that rationality in the sense of logical consistency takes the form of an "intellectual-theoretical or practical-ethical attitude [which] has and always has had power over man" ([1915b] 1970, p. 324). Weber's characterization of the "imperative of consistency" in terms of its attitudinal form and its capacity to constrain indicates that Weber is referring to an emotional force in this rationality. This point deserves emphasis. Although Weber fails to explore the implications of his characterization, the emotional background to consistency as rational is singularly contained in his conceptualization of it.

Rationality as systematization and as logical coherence are rational because they lead to purposiveness of action. Weber also treats purposiveness as a form of rationality in its own right. In his discussion of bureaucracy, for instance, Weber ([1921a] 1978, p. 979) says that: "The only decisive point for us is that in principle a system of rationally debatable 'reasons' stands behind every act of bureaucratic administration, namely, either subsumption under norms, or a weighing of ends and means." The suggestion here is that in the absence of clarity about what reasons there are for acting, in the absence of clarity of purpose, rationality of action becomes entirely problematic. In the passage just quoted Weber refers to both norms and means–ends relations in this context. These can be dealt with in turn.

Purposiveness of action requires the actor's acquisition of an intention in relation to a goal or end, what Weber calls a norm. Rationality of this type is treated by Weber as one of the four ideal-typical forms of action, namely value-rational action. In Weber's ([1921a] 1978, pp. 24–6) general account of it, value-rational action sits between instrumentally rational action and affective or emotional action. Value-rational action shares with emotional action the fact that "the meaning of the action does not lie in the achievement of a result ulterior to it, but in carrying out the specific type of action for its own sake" (p. 25). Weber immediately adds that action which satisfies "a need for revenge, sensual gratification, devotion, contemplative bliss, or for working off emotional tensions," is emotional action, not value-rational action. Value-rational action, being action which is consistent with a principle, shares with emotional action a disregard for the consequences or costs of an action which expresses a conviction.

Value-rational action is distinct from emotional action. It is akin to instrumentally rational action insofar as the ultimate values governing the action are "self-consciously formulat[ed]" by the actor involved. The implication of this claim is that emotional goals, by contrast, are experienced as compelling external forces. Emotion is in the need for revenge, according to Weber, not so much in the revenge itself. Weber's distinction, then, between value-rational and emotional action derives from the view that a person's emotions cannot be subject to the appraisal and deliberation of the person experiencing them, and that choice has no role in emotional experience.

Some emotions are more compelling than others, certainly. But to dismiss the possibility of emotional deliberation and choice suggests prejudice about rather than an adequate understanding of emotion. Indeed, the psychological processes of value attainment and commitment have to be recognized as inextricably complex ones involving judgments, calculations, needs, and affections in such a manner as to make impossible a clear separation of emotional from non-emotional aspects.

That there is a need for purposiveness in rational action, and more than half of Weber's argument concerning it, shows that it is unnecessary to oppose emotion and rationality. The critical and radical approaches to the relation between emotion and rationality demonstrate the contribution of particular emotions to rational action. In spite of his own intentions, Weber's argument concerning purposiveness as a form of rationality also encourages that conclusion.

In addition to norms, means–ends relations are implicated in purposiveness as rationality. As already indicated, the other type of rational action identified in Weber's four ideal types is instrumental or goal rationality. This incorporates the relationship between means and ends, a feature of which is the requirement of calculation, for the efficacy of means to achieve a particular end is always tested in quantifiable efficiencies. Calculation as rationality, Weber ([1905a] 1991, p. 22) says, is "the basis of everything else." Indeed, the importance of formal rules in rational law and administration, for instance, is that it permits calculation (p. 25). Similarly, money and markets rationalize economies because they facilitate calculation, and this generates the impersonality or universality of rationality ([1915b] 1970, p. 331; [1921a] 1978, p. 636).

Calculation as rationality is parallel to logical coherence as rationality. Where means–ends relations provide "the methodical attainment of a definitely given and practical end by means of an increasingly precise calculation of adequate means," premise-conclusion relations provide "an increasing theoretical mastery of reality by means of increasingly precise and abstract concepts" ([1915a] 1970, p. 293). While these are different types of rationality, Weber believes that "ultimately they belong inseparably together" because each gives control: one practical, the other intellectual.

The importance of control to rationality has already been indicated, when Weber was discussed in the context of the conventional approach to the relation between reason and emotion. It has been shown here that all of the modalities of rationality he indicates point in this direction. Rationalization, says Weber ([1919] 1970, p. 139), "means that principally there are no mysterious incalculable forces that come into play, but rather that one can, in principle, master all things by calculation" (see also [1915a] 1970, p. 284). The importance of control to rationality is in rationality as systematization, as logical coherence, as purposiveness, as means-ends relations and as calculability. If another example were needed, Weber's discussion in "Science as a Vocation" of "the rational experiment" could be added, in which it is noted that the "experiment is a means of reliably controlling experience" ([1919] 1970, p. 141). Weber insists that only action which is voluntary and free-willed is rational, because it is action which is not controlled ([1921a] 1978, pp. 23–4). The rational actor is one who controls.

For Weber, the irrational, to which rationality is an oppositional force, is concretely manifest in magic ([1919] 1970, p. 139; [1905a] 1991, pp. 105, 117), eroticism ([1915b] 1970, p. 347), and emotion ([1905a] 1991, p. 136). This is because these are forces which exercise control over persons, and therefore action directed by these forces cannot be rational as it cannot be voluntary and free-willed. The Kantian impetus of Weber's understanding of these matters is perhaps not better expressed than in a passage in his account of Baptist sects. Between a reference to the overcoming of the "passions and subjective interests of the natural man" ([1905a] 1991, p. 148), on the one hand, and the "elimination of magic from the world" (p. 149), on the other, Weber (p. 149) said: "But in so far as Baptism affected the normal workaday world, the idea that God only speaks when the flesh is silent evidently meant an incentive to the deliberate weighing of courses of action and their careful justification in terms of the individual conscience." Here is combined the idea that calculation and clear purpose can proceed only "when the flesh is silent."

Weber's idea of rationality as control is a statement of the conditions under which James's sentiment of rationality might arise or emerge. Remember that, for James, what is of particular importance is the relation of a thing to its consequences, and therefore that rationality is the condition in which uncertainty is banished from the future. This is the emotional end of the mechanical relation described by Weber, of purpose, calculation, and, ultimately, control.

Weber does not have a sense of the emotional dimension of rationality because he regards emotion as undermining of human control. For him, emotion is a singular phenomenon unified by the quality of a force against deliberation. Therefore rationality and emotion are for him opposed. But James recognizes what Weber in fact describes: that there is a human passion for clarity and order, and a need for intellectual frameworks, which he summarizes as the "passion for generalizing, simplifying, and subordinating" (James [1909] 1932, p. 22). In providing the actor with a feeling of control over the future, these passions, emotions, or sentiments engender in the present a feeling of rationality. James does not offer a blanket endorsement of emotion in rationality, as Weber proposes a general rejection of it. James does indicate, though, that particular emotions are implicated in rationality.

## Bases of the separation of reason and emotion

Even if they are not to be fully accepted, there is enough in the critical and radical approaches to show that the conventional distinction between reason and emotion is at least blurred, not sharp, and that the supposed opposition between them is at best difficult to keep in clear focus. In spite of this, the conventional approach to reason and emotion is remarkably durable. It is not sufficient therefore to argue that it is mistaken, it has to be asked why it is so widely believed.

In his account of "The Metropolis and Mental Life," Georg Simmel ([1903] 1971, pp. 328–9) explains that:

Punctuality, calculability, and exactness, which are required by the complications and extensiveness of metropolitan life are not only most intimately connected with its capitalistic and intellectualistic character but also color the content of life and are conducive to the exclusion of those irrational, instinctive, sovereign human traits and impulses which originally seek to determine the form of life from within instead of receiving it from the outside in a general, schematically precise form.

Here, Simmel is indicating that the instrumental orientations of urban and market society simply displace emotion as a motivating force. In capitalist society the imperatives of human conduct are outside the individual's subjective, that is emotional, states, and in the external demands of the market.

Simmel argues that with the rise of a money-based economy, relationships between persons have become impersonal and intellectual, and therefore that within such relationships there is indifference to the individuality of each and a focus on "something objectively perceivable" ([1903] 1971, p. 326). Thus, "instead of reacting emotionally, the metropolitan type reacts primarily in a rational manner, thus creating a mental predominance through the intensification of consciousness, which in turn is caused by it" (p. 326). This argument is rather like Weber's in its key features. Market rationality leads to a calculativeness of thought which simply displaces emotion; rationality drives out irrationality. But Simmel makes clear what is sometimes obscure in Weber: it is instrumentalism, born of capitalistic market relations, which separates emotion from reason.

There is a crucial detail in Simmel's argument, however, which makes it quite unlike Weber's. For Simmel, the displacement of emotion by rationality is not the end of emotion, and the source of the rational orientation is not simply the market but the emotional pattern the market promotes. Simmel's claims in this area are by no means fully developed but they are explicit. Simmel says that the "psychological foundation, upon which the metropolitan individuality is erected, is the intensification of emotional life due to the swift and continuous shift of external and internal stimuli" ([1903] 1971, p. 325). The tempo and diversity of civic and market exchanges proportionately stimulate the emotions. Such a prospect contains not only thrills but dangers. The metropolitan type, as a consequence, "creates a protective organ for itself against the profound disruption with which the fluctuations and discontinuities of the external milieu threaten it" (p. 326).

Simmel's argument is not simply that rational calculability and exactness form a "protective organ" against the disturbingly intense emotional life which would otherwise ensue. It is also that the protective organ of rationality is itself covered with an emotional cloak, what Simmel calls the "blasé outlook" and the "blasé attitude" ([1903] 1971, p. 329). The emotional dimensions of this are clear in Simmel's description of it as "a feeling of [one's] own valuelessness." This feeling, he says, exists in the form of a "peculiar adaptive phenomenon . . . in which the nerves reveal their final possibility of adjusting themselves to the content and form of metropolitan life by renouncing the response to them" (p. 330). For Simmel, then, rationality arises in the control of emotion. In containing emotion, it is guided by an alienated emotion of distance, remoteness, and indifference to excitement and pleasure, namely the emotions expressed through the blasé feeling.

The explanation of the separation of reason from emotion in Simmel's account contains three elements. First, an instrumental orientation, through which activity is directed to the realization of some externally given object or end, separates thought and emotion. Second, it does this through its association with an emotion which is an antidote to all other emotions, experienced as the blasé feeling. Third, the social basis of such an orientation is market society. We shall consider each of these in turn.

The significance of the social institution of the market to the separation of reason and emotion is frequently acknowledged. In such accounts, the ascendence of the market and its association with reason or rationality is taken to lead also to the depreciation, even stigmatization of emotion, if not its elimination. Agnes Heller (1979) develops such an argument in explaining that in the "bourgeois world-epoch" a dual structure emerges in which the "domain of the market is the world of instrumental rationality, [and] the domain of the family is the world of emotional 'inwardness'" (p. 185). Any given individual may unite these distinct domains in their own life experience, but at the same time there is an institutional basis for one or the other domain to predominate. Such is the social basis for a separation of reason and emotion under the conditions of modern capitalism.

Heller's account addresses matters raised earlier in discussion, namely that emotions do function in rational processes but are seldom acknowledged to be emotions (we saw them become attitudes); and that the emotions which are acknowledged as such constitute a limited range of emotions (only certain emotions are regarded as emotions). We shall return to the question of instrumental rationality and its suppression of emotion below. At this point the market-sponsored narrowing of the category of emotion will be considered.

The capitalistic conversion of labor-power into a commodity and the consequent separation of the sphere of paid work from the domestic sphere have had a profound impact on the social conventions concerning what constitutes an emotion. The transformation of the pre-capitalistic family, a site of productive activity and collectively relevant symbolic performance, into the family of market society, an exclusive realm of non-instrumental affectivity or "emotional inwardness," has transformed also what is covered by the category of emotion. Under the latter conditions, the category of emotion includes mainly, although, as we shall see, not exclusively, the nurturing emotions. At the same time, because the activities to which such emotions are attached draw little market value, so emotion itself is regarded as being of little worth.

Heller (1979, p. 211) draws the obvious conclusion that the "contradiction between rational thinking and the inner life of feeling in the bourgeois era also appears in the form of the division of labor between the sexes." The identification of reason with the male and emotion with the female has drawn enough attention to render its statement commonplace. But there is another aspect to the social basis of the distinction between reason and emotion which takes us away from the sexual division of labor and turns the gender associations to mere cultural symbols. Heller (p. 209) notes that in market society persons are free to create their own inner life. But the institutional and cultural resources available to them in doing so are shaped by the priorities of the larger social system.

Thus reason narrowed to market rationality is matched by emotions of isolated subjectivity. Heller notes that it "is in the name of reason that polemics have been undertaken against alienated feelings, and in the name of feelings against the alienated reason; only, the alienation of reason and feeling are part of the same process" (p. 209). The forms of alienated emotions found in capitalist society are described by Heller (p. 209) as "the inner life of feeling 'wrapped in itself' that turns its back to the tasks of the world . . . the unfettered exercise of egoist passions . . . false sentimentality or sentimental convention." While the conventional approach to the relations between rationality and emotion typically supposes that emotion is suppressed by reason, Heller's account indicates instead transformations of what the category of emotion denotes under the force of market conditions.

In capitalist society the cultivation of emotion is entirely possible. Yet the social representation of emotion in this context reflects rather than challenges conventional assumptions. A commitment to develop the emotional side of life typically incorporates a rejection of the determination of intellectual considerations. This may appear to turn the conventional tables, which privilege the ascendence of reason over emotion. But in fact this approach preserves the conventional division between reason and emotion, and the conventional distortion of each. Thus Carl Jung's commitment to irrationalism ("Nothing disturbs feeling, however, so much as thinking") is not a rejection of alienated instrumental rationality so much as a retreat to alienated emotionalism. The earlier Romantic surrender to emotion and its rejection of reason similarly maintained the dichotomy between the two (Toulmin 1990, p. 148). The Jungian flavor of a growing current literature, both popular and specialist, understands emotion as covering only nurturing and personal, what Heller calls "inward," feelings.

Conceptualizations of emotion in non- or early-capitalist literatures indicate a much broader range of types of feeling than those associated with emotion under conditions of market rationality. In Adam Smith ([1759] 1982), for example, the emotions include "moral sentiments," which were the source of justice and beneficence, the sense of duty, approbation and disapprobation, in fact the full range of conduct, both social and unsocial, sympathetic and selfish. Similarly, Alexis de Tocqueville ([1835] 1945) in the second volume of *Democracy in America*,

Books II and IV, addressed the "intense passions" which animated American public life and preserved liberty. In these early writers, emotion simply does not conform to the narrow range of subjective and personal feelings we associate with the term today.

The referents of the term emotion cover a broader range in "pre-conventional" discussions, because in these the separation of reason and emotion is not fundamental. Rather, reason and emotion are simply different, not opposed. A typical statement is that of Francis Bacon ([1605] 1977, p. 120), who, in distinguishing two faculties of the human mind, says that: "the one respecting his Understanding and Reason, and the other his Will, Appetite, and Affection: whereof the former produceth Position or Decree, and the latter Action or Execution . . . the face towards Reason hath the print of Truth, but the face towards Action hath the print of Good." The difference between reason and emotion in the "pre-conventional" approach is not between rationality and irrationality, but between what we now call ideas and action.

Yet, while this distinction is readily drawn, it is, to the "pre-conventional" approach, the combination of these distinct faculties which in practice is the basis of what we today understand as rationality. Adam Ferguson ([1767] 1966, p. 29), for example, says that in practical and therefore in social activities:

the understanding appears to borrow very much from the passions; and there is a felicity of conduct in human affairs, in which it is difficult to distinguish the promptitude of the head from the ardor and sensibility of the heart. Where both are united, they constitute that superiority of mind, the frequency of which among men, in particular ages and nations, much more than the progress they have made in speculation, or in the practice of mechanical and liberal arts, should determine the rate of their genius, and assign the palm of distinction and honour.

In this context, the scope of emotion is not merely personal, individual, and introspective or "inner," but social, political, and moral.

Rationality appears to become fundamentally separated from emotion when the purposes of action are limited to those of pervasive institutions. Pervasive institutions are those which color the operations of all others. Under these circumstances action is entirely instrumental in realizing purposes which will not yield to modification in the conduct of the action itself, but which is fixed by some principle external to the action. An obvious pervasive institution of this type is the market in capitalist society. In Weber's words, the "market community as such is the most impersonal relationship of practical life into which humans can enter with one another." He goes on to say that:

The reason for the impersonality of the market is its matter-of-factness, its orientation to the commodity and only to that. Where the market is allowed to follow its own autonomous tendencies, its participants do not look toward the persons of each other but only toward the commodity; there are no obligations of brotherliness or reverence, and none of those spontaneous human relations that are sustained by personal unions. They all would just obstruct the free development of the bare market relationship, and its specific interests serve, in their turn, to weaken the sentiments on which these obstructions rest. Market behavior is influenced by rational, purposive pursuit of interests. (Weber [1921a] 1978, p. 636)

Under conditions of market rationality, then, any action which functions in terms of goals or purposes extrinsic to a market exchange is non-instrumental and irrational.

This allows us to complete the conceptualization of emotion sponsored by capitalist rationality. In addition to the nurturing and inward emotions already discussed are those strong feelings which introduce orientations toward persons rather than commodities, and therefore turn aside the pursuit of market interests. Love, hate, fear, and anger are typical examples of such emotions. Their salient characteristic is that they introduce purposes extrinsic to the socially pervasive institution. As just indicated, the dominant pervasive institution of capitalist society is the market. But in other systems, other institutions will define the content of instrumental rationality and therefore also the concept of emotion.

It is necessary to regard the correlative conceptualization of emotion in instrumental rationality as incomplete because, while it ostensibly expels emotion in general, instrumentalism always relies on under-conceptualized emotions in particular. The instrumental rationality of market competition, for instance, cannot do without emotions, which are background to the impersonal pursuit of commodities, and as background are simply assumed, taken for granted, and unacknowledged. And if acknowledged, they are regarded not as emotions, the latter being a category already conceptualized as disruptive of instrumental rationality, but as attitudes, components of culture, and so on. Yet the technical enterprise of commodity exchange requires of those human actors involved in it a number of emotions, which include commitment to the purposes at hand, loyalty to the employing organization, joy in success to encourage more success, and dissatisfaction at failure to encourage success, trust in those with whom cooperation is necessary, envy of competitors to spur the pursuit of interests, and greed to encourage aggrandizement.

A failure to acknowledge the presence, let alone the salience, of such particular background emotions in instrumentally rational pursuits is unavoidable in the context of the characterization of emotion under market conditions which has been described here. It was revealed in the earlier discussion of the critical approach to the relation between rationality and emotion that one of the leading functions of emotion is to set goals or purposes for action, both mental and practical. Thus advocates of the critical approach regard the precondition for (a foregrounded) emotion to be an actor's ambiguity of purpose (see Oatley 1992, pp. 164–5, 175). It follows, then, as Keith Oatley (p. 164), for instance, says, that emotion is likely to be irrational in the service of a technical problem. But this is simply to say that technical tasks have their own purposes: the introduction of an extrinsic purpose will interfere with the execution of a technical task.

Oatley's account leaves out the fact that the human execution of a technical task requires facilitating purposes to achieve the technical intention. This general point was implicit in the earlier description of the background emotions required for the instrumental rationality of commodity exchange in markets. In order to perform instrumental tasks effectively, human actors must not only be committed to the purposes intrinsic to them, but also committed to avoiding extrinsic and distracting purposes. Thus in addition to the particular facilitating emotions which function to motivate instrumental action, such as pride in one's expertise and skill, satisfaction in one's work, distaste for waste of materials and time, and so on, there is also a need for emotional distance from potentially disruptive emotions which a wider involvement with others might bring. That is to say that in instrumental rationality there is a need for what Simmel called the blasé feeling. All of these emotions remain necessary in but background to instrumental rationality, seldom acknowledged as emotions, and, if referred to at all, likely to be labeled as attitudes.

The failure to distinguish between emotion which is foregrounded and emotion which is backgrounded leads to the entirely arbitrary and ultimately absurd view that emotion is only disruptive of rational pursuits, indeed any pursuit. It is especially ironic that Gilbert Ryle, who was devoted to challenging the Cartesian legacy in philosophy, supposes that: "we do not . . . act purposively because we experience feelings; we experience feelings . . . because we are inhibited from acting purposively" (1949, p. 106). This is the view from the perspective of instrumental rationality; only those feelings which introduce purposes extrinsic to technical goals are characterized as emotions. Those feelings continuous with the technical tasks are thus by definition something other than emotion.

While the conventional opposition between rationality and emotion is impossible to defend, its persistence is supported by social representations of both reason and emotion. These representations emerge through the dominance of market instrumentalism, which, in coloring the conventional understanding of rationality, also limits the conventional conception of emotion, as we have seen. To leave unquestioned these conventional understandings or conceptualizations of rationality and emotion is to leave each of them and the relations between them distorted.

The representation of emotion under conditions of instrumental rationality ignores precisely the backgrounded emotions which are continuous with the operations of pervasive social institutions. Conventional representations of emotion are blind to these emotions. These emotions render especially absurd the idea that reason and emotion are opposed.

# 3    Class and resentment

Class systems are typically explained in terms of the unequal distribution of material resources and of power inequalities based on unequal material conditions. A difficulty arises, however, when appropriate material conditions fail to give rise to correspondingly expected class actions. In this chapter an account of class resentment more completely links class conditions and actions. Not only does an emotions category therefore expand the competence of class theory, but a macroscopic conceptualization of emotion is also outlined in the discussion.

The chapter begins with a brief account of the way in which resentment has been presented in sociological thought. There is also a statement of the problems of class theory. The importance of emotion to social action is indicated, and of resentment to class action. Then follows an exposition of the neglected account of class antagonism in terms of "resentment against inequality" developed by the English sociologist T. H. Marshall. Marshall's discussion is shown to be important but incomplete, and Marshall's account is broadened in various ways.

One important element of this is to show that actions of a class nature arise not simply from the inequalities between classes, but also within them. Especially important in this latter category are inequalities resulting from the differential movements of real-income groups through the different phases of the business or trade cycle. It is shown that experiences of class resentment vary in terms of ascendence or descendence through trade-cycle movements. Additionally, it is shown that the organizational context of class actors has significant impact on the strength, direction, and outcome of resentment. These, in turn, have significant consequences for difference in class processes.

Finally, it is argued that a macroscopic conceptualization of emotion is possible when not only the experience of emotional feelings, but also the social context in which these arise, is understood as a key element of the emotion itself. Emotion is a social thing, and it is not only formed in but can be conceptualized as a social relationship.

## Introduction

The purpose of this chapter is to expand the consideration of emotion to a macroscopic conceptualization. This will be done by indicating the place of one particular emotion, resentment, in class structure and by showing what significance it has for class processes. Class rather than some other aspect of social structure is treated here because, while the class literature is well developed, it is now recognized that there is an impasse in class analysis, which the presentation of emotion to be developed in this chapter can overcome. The following discussion will be directed to the importance of emotion in social processes, and the significance of resentment in class formation.

Unlike most emotions, resentment has a visible standing in sociology through its representation in the work of Max Scheler, and the earlier discussion of Friedrich Nietzsche. This is a mixed blessing for any account of resentment: through this earlier recruitment, resentment now wears a uniform which may not properly fit. The structural basis of resentment was explored in Max Scheler's classic study *Ressentiment*, first published in 1912. The scope of the present discussion differs from that of Scheler's study in three fundamental ways.

First, Scheler used the term *ressentiment* in a limited or at least specialized sense drawn from the Nietzschian dichotomous states of being, as either power or impotence: *ressentiment* is the condemnation of what one secretly craves but cannot achieve. In the Nietzschian tradition resentment is regarded as a necessarily self-destructive form of anger which, in reinforcing a passivity in those subject to it, functions anesthetically to deaden the pain of injury (Nietzsche [1887] 1992, p. 563). There is no doubt that resentment may take the form Nietzsche describes, but to insist that this is the only form which is possible is to essentialize and not properly to analyze resentment. Resentment is debilitating in the Nietzschian sense when those who experience it are also bereft of resources, and therefore unable to turn their resentment into action.

In the present discussion resentment is understood in a non-Nietzschian sense in which the possibility of action is not defined away by fiat. Rather, resentment is taken to be the emotional apprehension of undeserved advantage (Marshall [1938] 1973, pp. 168–70; Ortony, Clore, and Collins 1988, pp. 99–100; Runciman 1972, pp. 3–9; Solomon 1991, pp. 247–8). The action or inaction of those experiencing resentment is a separate and distinct matter. A fuller discussion of Nietzschian resentment is conducted in chapter 6 later. There is an element of the Nietzschian notion which is important to retain, however. This is the special place given to unacknowledged resentment as an explosive force in social relations, which thus removes it from the plane of consciousness, a point we shall return to later.

The second way in which the following discussion departs from Scheler's account is that Scheler conceptualized social structure at the level of social roles. In this he anticipated elements of Robert Merton's account of social structure and anomie, and is acknowledged by the latter for having done so (Merton 1968, pp. 209–10). While including role-related categories such as reference-group behavior, the notion of social structure in the present discussion is more broadly conceived of than Scheler's, to include class systems. Finally, Scheler understood emotion psychologically, as referring to internal states. The treatment of resentment in the present volume is predicated upon the social dimensions of the emotion.

Emotion and social class occupy ostensibly quite different existential and theoretical domains. Persons have emotions but belong to classes: emotions are psycho-physiological phenomena of microsociological or social psychological concern, whereas classes are socio-economic phenomena of macrosociological or political and economic concern. But the clear separation between social perception and social structure can no longer be sustained. Class theorists have begun to recognize the limitations of structural accounts which cannot show, for instance, why class members do not always act in a manner indicated by material conditions.

In a conventional statement of Marx's theory of class, for example, any failure to engage in class action when theoretically given appropriate material conditions obtain is explained in terms of "false consciousness." False consciousness, according to Frederick Engels's ([1893] 1965, p. 459) classic definition, is a state in which the "real motive forces impelling [class actors] remain unknown to [them]." False consciousness, then, is a failure of persons to comprehend the situation in which they are involved. In this sense, false consciousness refers to an inadequacy of social knowledge. False consciousness, according to this standard account, leads to a failure to act appropriately in terms of a class actor's real interests.

The term false consciousness has fallen into relative disuse in Marxisant writing. Perhaps this is because of a recognition that it is a residual category which therefore does not explain what it refers to but instead implicitly acknowledges a weakness in the theoretical account of action to which it belongs. Nevertheless, the need persists for an account of social behavior which acknowledges not only the material background of action but also the orientations of the actors involved. And the frankly cognitive dimension of false consciousness has been carried over into subsequent attempts to solve the problem of failures of class action.

A growing awareness of the importance of actors' orientations to structural processes is responsible for the application of rational choice theory to questions of class formation and action (Carling 1991; Elster 1985; Przeworski 1985; Roemer 1982). In a real sense, rational choice theory, which among other things points to the rational basis for actors not to join in collective action (Barbalet 1991a), stands as an alternative to the theory of false consciousness. The two approaches are melded together in Analytic Marxism, which, in Jon Elster's (1985, pp. 346–7) words, regards "(positive) class consciousness as the ability to overcome the free rider problem in realizing class interest." But it is precisely the formalism and excessively cognitive assumptions of rational choice theory, and other cognitive approaches, which limit their value to sociological analysis (Hindess 1988; Wood 1989; see also Collins 1981, pp. 990–4).

Even if social action does result from the individual actors' calculus of their interests, the emotional basis of interest remains crucial (Geiger 1969, p. 202). It will be shown that emotion is essential to social processes not only in being central to identity and affiliation, in which its role is frequently acknowledged, but also in being the necessary basis of social action and in being responsible for the form which action takes.

A feature of accounts of social phenomena based on actors' orientations and proclivities, whether they be their rational choices or their emotions, is a methodological commitment to somehow reduce macroscopic and collective phenomena to aggregations of microscopic or individual elements (Collins 1981; Hechter 1983; Kemper and Collins 1990). It is true that there is a sense in which explanation *per se* is reductionist insofar as it necessarily indicates the significance of certain things, and therefore the insignificance of other things, in the occurrence of an event. But *a priori* denials of the integrity of one social domain (the macro) and assumptions of the authentic facticity of another (the micro) are neither justified nor necessary in understanding the impact of emotion on social structure, as we shall see.

In order to show that emotion influences class formation and class action, it is not required that social-class phenomena be reduced to individual-level interactions. It will be shown that emotions have a macrosociological presence in their own right, or, more specifically, that emotion inheres simultaneously in individuals and in the social structures and relationships in which individuals are embedded. Such a conceptualization not only broadens our understanding of emotion, but helps to resolve some continuing problems of social structure, including class structure and formation. In particular, emotion connects different phases of social structure through time. Emotion arises in the pattern of structured relationships, and forms the basis of action, which then consolidates or modifies social structures at some later time.

The following discussion will show that as emotions are crucial for social action, in class systems the role of class resentment in particular is signal. Yet class inequality is not a sufficient basis for class resentment. It will be shown that other aspects of social structure contribute to the relational basis of resentment, and that these therefore tend to make complex the relationship between class inequalities on the one hand, and resentment of them, on the other.

### Class and class resentment

Structural accounts of class, which function in terms of categories of economic forces, can readily point to the social bases of conditions and opportunities for action. But they cannot explain the absence of class formation or action, given the basis of class structure. There is a frequent complaint, which goes back to Max Weber, that structural or economic theories of class ignore the importance of consciousness and culture in the generation of class conditions. Approaches based on these latter factors, however, are themselves limited by the fact that the relevance to class action of cognitions and values cannot be specified through cognitive and cultural accounts of class inequality. This is because meaning, in which cognitive and cultural factors are realized, attaches to objects only as a consequence of how actor's expectations and understandings lead those objects to be used. Thus meaning arises in and through action, it does not produce it. It follows that in addition to class structure, on the one hand, and the meanings which class actors possess, on the other, it is necessary that those participating in social action discern or evaluate salient aspects of their circumstances or situation and are energized to act on them.

The two last-mentioned functions, of evaluation of impinging circumstance and preparedness to act on such evaluations, are performed – often below the threshold of awareness (and therefore of consciousness) – by emotion. Resources, knowledge, and meaning, relating to structure, cognition, and culture respectively, are not sufficient bases of action. Human agency or practice becomes possible through emotion because emotion links conditions and opportunities in action. This occurs through a process described by the psychologist Klaus Scherer (1984, p. 296) as the "constant evaluation of external and internal stimuli in terms of their relevance for the organism and the preparation of behavioral reactions which may be required as a response to those stimuli." Emotion, then, is precisely the experience of readiness for action.

The relationship between emotion and action is complex and subject to wide differences of interpretation and theoretical representation. In a simplifying gesture, one writer has suggested that modern psychology has "resisted the time-honored conclusion that emotions are intrinsically motivating, that they are, in fact, the main human motive" because of the "problems such a conclusion would create for current reinforcement theory" (Ainslie 1985, p. 358). There is no doubt that learning theory diminishes the significance of emotion in mental and social processes; but it is too narrow and simple directly to link emotion and action through motivation.

Motivation is a category ready at hand in psychological explanation, and one which appears to point in the direction of action from the starting point of emotion. Nevertheless, as one writer has cautioned, the concept of motive is a joker in the psychologist's pack (Heller 1979, pp. 46–50). Indeed, it is necessary to regard the linking of emotion to action, through motivation, with caution. This is because motives, as C. Wright Mills ([1940] 1967) has shown, are part of the linguistic apparatus of a social actor's self-justification. This is to say that motives are best understood as elements of the social rhetoric of verbal action, rather than the wellsprings of social action in general. The self-consciousness required for consistent accounts of action in terms of motive are simply not available for the contribution of emotion to social action. Sociological attempts to provide complex accounts of the emotional bases of action, while diverse, are impressive because they have tended to avoid the temptation to collapse emotion into motivation (Collins 1990; Heise 1979; Scheff 1990).

Emotions are implicated in action through their evaluation of the actor's circumstance and their contribution to the preparedness to act. Emotions achieve this through the feelings and associated states they induce in those subject to them. The emotions which influence class forces cannot be understood merely at the level of idiosyncratic experience influencing individual psyches, either isolated or serial. It is necessary to conceptualize class-relevant emotions at the level of the structure of social relationships. Indeed, it is essential to understand that in general terms emotion does not simply exist as internal states of individual persons, but in the relationships between individuals and in the interaction between individuals and their social situations. This is not simply to say that social conditions precipitate emotions. Rather, it is to say that emotions may be understood as social relationships, so that anger, for example, is the dispositional orientation to a challenge posed by another (de Rivera 1977; de Rivera and Grinkis 1986). In this account, emotion is not reduced to the feeling experienced by the subject, but is understood as the interaction in which the feeling arises and through which it is transformed as the interaction itself unfolds. Considerations such as these encourage a conceptualization of emotion at a macroscopic level.

It will be shown that it is the structure of class relations themselves which tend to determine the emotions which individual class members feel. While the relationship between class and emotion is not direct or simple, the emotional tone of class members can be explained in terms of the pattern of class relations. This in turn disposes social collectivities to particular types of action, or the absence of action, which feeds back into the pattern of class relations. What is being proposed is not a simple loop. It will be shown that class structure has a complexity frequently ignored, and that the features most commonly pointed to, such as property and wealth, the contradiction between forces and relations of production, and so on, though necessary, are in themselves insufficient bases for the emotions relevant to class action or inaction.

Many different emotions are generated in class systems, of course. But one emotion in particular, resentment, is crucial in influencing the processes of class systems. The phenomenology of resentment will be dealt with in greater detail in chapter 6. It is sufficient to say here that resentment is a feeling that another has gained unfair advantage (Ortony, Clore, and Collins 1988, pp. 99–100). Social actors experience resentment when an external agency denies them opportunities or valued resources (including status) which would otherwise be available to them. Class systems are structurally based on chronic asymmetries of power and reward, which nevertheless remain stable. While structural contradiction is a necessary feature of class systems, antagonism or conflict are contingent and sporadic. What converts structural contradiction to class antagonism significantly includes the feeling of resentment which leads the members of social classes to action. Such action derives from or is directed toward unfair advantages, which are implicit in class inequalities.

There will be a good deal of common-sense acceptance of the proposition that it is class resentment, the feeling of indignation against inequality, which is necessary for class antagonism to occur. But the concept of class resentment is largely absent from the writings of class theorists. In one notable case, the possibility of using the concept of resentment was rejected out of hand. Max Weber, for instance, in his discussion of "Class, Status, Party," refers dismissively to Friedrich Nietzsche's account of resentment as being irrelevant to considerations of status group formation (Weber [1921a] 1978, pp. 934–5). And Weber failed to appreciate the wider relevance of resentment in his consideration of class struggle.

In his discussion of class struggle, Weber indicated that "the struggle in which class situations are effective" had historically shifted from "consumption credit" to "the determination of the price of labor" (Weber [1921a] 1978, pp. 930–1). In neither of these did Weber consider the role of resentment. The place of resentment in modern class systems will be examined shortly.

The important role of resentment in class struggle over consumption credit had been noted by R. H. Tawney, in his classic study *Religion and the Rise of Capitalism* ([1926] 1948). Tawney argued that during the medieval period, "in a society of small masters and peasant farmers," wages were of little significance (p. 50). But loans, borrowing, and lending, within these classes, were common occurrences of high salience. Indeed, during this historical period, loans were made "largely for consumption, not production." Tawney goes on to say that: "The farmer whose harvest fails or whose beasts die, or the artisan who loses money, must have credit . . . and his distress is [therefore] the money-lender's opportunity" (pp. 50–1). It was in the provision of such credit, Tawney says, "that oppression was easiest and its results most pitiable" (p. 57). Tawney described here the material conditions of resentment, as he was fully aware (p. 51). His purpose is not to outline the bases of class struggle, but to point to the source of popular resentment against usury. In indicating the latter, however, he gestures toward the former.

The English historical sociologist T. H. Marshall is exceptional in explicitly treating modern class conflict in terms of class resentment. This aspect of Marshall's work has not been noticed in the secondary literature, nor is it highlighted by Marshall himself. Nevertheless, unlike most theorists of social class, Marshall holds that the propensity for class conflict derives from the level of a particular emotion, resentment. This is a real departure from the great majority of class theories, which explain class conflict in structural or cognitive terms associated with interests or consciousness.

Marshall does not discuss his material in terms of the development of a theory of emotion. He does, however, contribute to our understanding of the social nature and manifestation of an emotion, class resentment, and its consequences for social structural processes. In developing arguments about the nature of social conflict and also the consequences of institutional developments in the welfare state, Marshall indicates significant sources of class resentment and its consequences for macro-structural configurations and processes. Marshall's arguments can therefore be seen as setting the ground for a sociological consideration of class resentment. Further discussion of some of the limitations of Marshall's approach will broaden the account of class resentment and class structure.

### Class inequality and resentment

In an early paper on the nature of class conflict, Marshall argued that class antagonism has an affective source in "resentment against inequality"

([1938] 1973, p. 168). While Marshall indicated that there is an emotional basis for social conflict, he did not follow the inclination of the earlier emotionalists, such as Gabriel Tarde (1890) or Gustave Le Bon (1895), to treat shared mobilizing emotions as either psychological or pathological and irrational. Feelings of resentment against inequality are simply assumed under given social circumstances. Marshall specified the latter in terms of three distinct processes: comparison, frustration, and oppression. Comparison, Marshall said, "is the main force creating social levels" ([1938] 1973, p. 168). It does this, he continued, "by perfecting the individual's awareness of himself and the group's consciousness of its own character." According to Marshall, comparison, by itself, leads to isolation rather than conflict because it tends to break rather than make contacts. Nevertheless, comparison can inflame a situation of conflict should it occur.

Frustration arises "wherever privilege creates inequality of opportunity" (Marshall [1938] 1973, p. 169). The role of frustration in conflict, and more directly in intensifying class resentment, is that it "imput[es] to the superior class responsibility for the injustice under which the inferior suffers" (pp. 168–9). Finally, oppression, which Marshall (p. 170) described as "conflict between two parties engaged in unequal co-operation," identifies the "group of persons wielding power" against whom the struggle may be waged.

According to Marshall, the resentment which individuals feel resides in the structured relations of the creation and reproduction of "social levels," of opportunity structures generated by privilege, and the "[oppressive] institutions of a stratified society" (Marshall [1938] 1973, p. 170). Each of these have consequences for the individuals implicated in them, especially consequences for emotional experience, but none of them can be described or understood in terms of non-relational individual characteristics. Interaction between individuals (as opposed to structural relations) may account for certain inequalities but not social levels, certain advantages but not privilege, and some unequal exchanges but not oppression.

In a later paper Marshall ([1956] 1973, p. 137) returned to the issue of class resentment. On this occasion he indicated the economic and political changes which had occurred up to the middle of the century as being responsible for a decline in class conflict through changes in the processes of comparison, frustration, and oppression:

There is first . . . the rise in the level of consumption as a whole and the compressing of the scale . . . it is less likely that differences in standard of living will produce self-conscious, antagonized social groups. There is second the aspect of the rights of citizenship . . . which carries with it rights to freedom, to political power and to welfare. And there is thirdly the structural change in the economy which makes the distribution of property less decisively determinant of the distribution of power . . . (p. 137)

The particulars of this argument are less important than the fact that Marshall placed the issue of social emotion in a clear politico-economic framework. The structure of social relations is important because it determines the level of class resentment. The level of class resentment is important because it determines the level of class conflict. Here, an emotion has both a basis in social relations and a social efficacy in changing those relations.

Marshall's discussion has clear relevance for an attempt to conceptualize emotion at the level of the structure of social relations. As persons in the same social situation will share a common awareness of their situation, other things being equal, *mutatis mutandis*, they will have a common emotional or evaluative reaction to it. In this sense emotion can be said to inhere in social relations.

Important as Marshall's argument is, it cannot be regarded as complete, and a number of objections may be raised against it. Two minor difficulties can be dealt with here before moving on to two larger issues. One problem with Marshall's account, and with any account which focusses upon groups rather than individuals, is that the actual emotional experience of any given person at any given time will not correspond with the analogous "macro-emotion." Without denying the importance of unique biographical influences as sources of emotional experiences, and therefore of individual differences, this problem of "response specificity" is not as significant for macro-conceptualizations of emotion as it is for more conventional modes of behavioral research (Scherer, Wallbott, and Summerfield 1986, pp. 8–9).

It is the psychological approach itself which generates the problematic nature of response specificity by individuating and decontextualizing social behavior. The unique and idiosyncratic reactions of individuals to events are magnified by a slice-of-time focus, which emphasizes the distinct reactions of particular individuals to a given situation, as opposed to the common currents which run through an experience shared by associated individuals. The relationship of a person with an event or situation changes. What is first felt will be different from later feelings as the subject sees things in different lights, partly illuminated by the differential involvement of others. More structural or macrosociological accounts, because they tend to be historical and focussed on change over time, appreciate the force of emergent patterns. As a person's reaction to a situation at one time will be different from their reaction at another time, a methodology considering only the feelings of singular persons at only a particular time will yield quite different results than one considering a number of persons or an interactive collectivity over a period of time.

A more serious objection to Marshall's account is that he sees class resentment as a one-way feeling. In his statement, class resentment is felt only by members of the subordinate class and is directed against the superordinate class. There is no reason, however, why there should not be superordinate class resentment against the opportunities it forgoes through action by the subordinate class. Indeed, a number of significant historical events can be seen as cases in point. For example, the thoroughness and severity with which the Conservative Thatcher government crushed the British mining union during the 1984–5 coal-industry strike can be explained partly in terms of resentment generated in the humiliating defeat of Conservative Prime Minister Edward Heath's government by the miners' union in the 1970s. Class resentment is a phenomenon of class systems and can therefore affect any class.

This example raises a further issue. The Thatcher government was much harsher than the Heath government in its treatment of striking miners and their union. Similarly, the hostility of the miners against the Thatcher government was much more intense than it had been against the Heath government (Green 1990). Here is an instance of the dynamic effects of mutual resentment which a Marshallian analysis must fail to grasp. Such resentment, however, is a crucial feature of situations of class conflict and of social conflict generally, including interpersonal hostilities. Key features of the latter were described in Erving Goffman's (1967, pp. 239–58) account of character contests. These are a special kind of moral game in which offense or provocation leads to actions commensurate with self-understanding of character. Character contests, then, may terminate in an apology, expand into a duel, and possibly spiral into a feud.

The escalation of hostility through mutual resentment has been analyzed in a different context by Thomas Scheff (1990, pp. 76–78) as triple spirals of shame and anger. He argued that unacknowledged shame arising from rejection leads to anger (a sequel which is self-repeating), and that in social interactions this occurs both within and between the interactants (hence the triple spiral). The shame/anger sequence is not confined to face-to-face exchanges but occurs in collective behavior, including international relations between nation-states.

Apart from the obvious relevance of this account to the discussion here of macroscopic class resentment, Scheff points to a feature of socially effective emotion frequently overlooked, and quite ignored by Marshall. That is, the emotions centrally implicated in social action operate at an unacknowledged and therefore non-conscious level. According to

Marshall, resentment is experienced consciously. In fact, however, resentment need not be mediated by thought in order to be implicated in action; on the contrary.

Two additional problems of Marshall's account will be dealt with in the following order to develop a more comprehensive understanding of class resentment. First, his class model is insufficiently complex. This is not a peculiarity of Marshall's treatment but is common in the class literature. Class systems are defined in terms of structures of inequality understood in the relations of production or exchange, or as points on an ordinal scale of wealth, earnings, or some other measure of economic standing. Thus the units of class inequality are seen as secular vectors. But in addition to these factors there is a cyclical relationship between capital and labor through the trade or business cycle. Although frequently ignored in treatments of class inequality, we shall see that the cyclical relations impact significantly on class resentment. A second major problem is that Marshall's account simply assumes a cultural context which is not a constant feature of class systems.

## Trade cycle and resentment

The trade or business cycle is seldom viewed as a significant sociological aspect of class, precisely because it does not affect the secular structure of class systems. Although the trade cycle is clearly a phenomenon of class society, and functions to reorganize both capital and labor, trade cycles introduce relationships between sub-class groups (based on occupation, industry, or economic sector) which can be defined in purely quantitative terms of real income. Trade-cycle movements introduce unequally distributed costs and opportunities for income. The subsequent material changes which occur through trade-cycle movements have significant consequences for the nature and the distribution of resentment.

Marshall treated the resentment-forming process of comparison in terms of inter-class comparison. When consideration of the trade cycle is introduced, however, the units of comparison change. As the real income of persons goes up or down at varying rates through the movement of the trade cycle, so comparisons are drawn between different economic groups from within the same class, in addition to those between different classes. Comparisons are also made between a group's present situation and its past situation in the trade cycle. The degree and focus of class resentment varies in terms of these changes as much as in terms of more direct class comparisons. Indeed, in many ways, these are more salient as their impact on emotional patterns can be more direct and forceful. The point here is that when trade-cycle considerations are introduced, the articulation between the domain of structural resources and social emotion is more complex and variable than Marshall suggests.

Very little has been written on the sociology of the trade cycle and emotion, and trade-cycle data are generally collected in terms of economic variables and seldom applied to social or emotional categories. Michael Kalecki's ([1943] 1972) sociology of business confidence is not directly relevant to the discussion here. A less well known work, but highly relevant to our purposes, is a paper by Joseph Bensman and Arthur Vidich, "Business Cycles, Class and Personality" (1962).

Bensman and Vidich (1962, pp. 33–4) argued that three possible classifications are created by the balance of rising and declining opportunities for income and costs which occur through the progression of a trade cycle. Ascendent groups accumulate an unearned increment in the upward movement of the trade cycle through a rise in income which is faster than the rise in costs. In the downward movement of the cycle they suffer a decline in income at a slower rate than the decline in costs. Descendent groups are those whose costs rise faster than their incomes during the trade cycle's upward movement or whose incomes decline at a faster rate than the decline in costs during the downward movement of the cycle. A third category, the economically unaffected group, is of less interest to our argument and will not be dealt with here.

The group which is ascendent with respect to the average movement of the trade cycle will not experience a feeling of resentment at all. Because this group enjoys an expansion of income opportunity at a rate faster than the general price rise, the predominant sentiment or emotion which derives from comparison with its own previous position and with other groups will be optimism, aggressive self-assurance, and an orientation to the future (Bensman and Vidich 1962, p. 36). These structural conditions which undermine or prevent feelings of resentment obtain for significant sections of the working class, especially those working in expanding industries with new investment.

This effect is demonstrated in the British research on the "affluent worker" (Goldthorpe *et al.* 1968a, 1968b, 1969; Zweig 1961), which discovered a lack of class commitment and low class resentment among industrial workers in England during the late 1960s. By the early 1970s, however, a quite different image of English labor emerged as a consequence of the intensification of industrial conflict and the reassertion of class politics (Crouch 1978). The "affluent-worker" studies have been criticized on mainly methodological grounds (Mackenzie 1974). What has not been appreciated in this debate is that the economic upswing in Britain, which began after the slump of 1955–8 and continued more or less until 1966–7, did in fact lead to a reduction in the class resentment of industrial workers in manufacturing. This situation was reversed, though, as the decline in the economic cycle took hold in the late 1960s and early 1970s.

The emotional consequences of membership in descending groups varies with the position they occupied in the preceding cycle. Groups displaced by ascendent groups from once favorable economic positions will be orientated to the past and develop an emotional pattern congruent with status defensiveness. In particular, a pattern of resentment will develop in such groups which is directed to those perceived as threatening their area of ascendency (Bensman and Vidich 1962, pp. 37–9). Thus white-collar workers may resent unionized blue-collar workers, and manual workers resent welfare recipients.

Such a pattern of resentment was discussed by W. G. Runciman in a study which explored "the relation between the inequalities in a society and the feelings of acquiescence or resentment to which they give rise" (Runciman 1972, p. 3). He showed that in the post-Second World War period English non-manual workers were resentful of "the diminution of what they saw as their legitimate differential advantages" (p. 95). This situation arose through an improvement in the standard of living of manual workers. The non-manual workers, according to Runciman, did not regard the upward movement of manual workers in itself as illegitimate. Nor was the situation of non-manual workers close to that of manual workers: the advantages of superannuation, promotion, hours, and conditions were heavily in favor of non-manual workers (p. 97). Rather, the resentment of non-manual toward manual workers derived from an inability of the former to enjoy corresponding new advantages and, therefore, an inability to maintain their relative position apart from manual workers.

Quite different emotional patterns emerge in groups who were in economically unfavored positions prior to their present descent in the average movement of the trade cycle. Bensman and Vidich (1962, p. 40) described this group as having a "psychology of noncommitment to both present and past . . . of resenting and rejecting the total framework of society." Actions that arise in such groups are likely to "seek political solutions to economic problems and to make broad attacks on the framework of constituted society" (p. 40). Intense totalizing resentment of this type has been found in socially marginal agrarian groups who are threatened further by disruptive economic changes brought either by the industrialization of agriculture or by unfavorable terms of trade for rural products. Such groups often turn to political radicalism, described by Erik Allardt (1970), for instance, as "backwoods communism" (see also Gallie 1983, pp. 206–23).

Such political action is not inevitable, however, because the resentment felt by this type of group may be sublimated. The contribution of this group to religions which promise divine intervention today and a new world tomorrow is extensive. Here religiosity can be understood as an expression of sublimated resentment. Bensman and Vidich (1962, p. 41) showed that this group's resentment also displays secular sublimations in its fascination with cruelty, crime, and perverse sexuality, an interest readily served by sections of the mass media.

The influences of trade-cycle movements on emotion in general and resentment in particular are highly significant. The class nature of the trade cycle shows that the class structure and its impact on emotion can be rendered more complex than allowed by Marshall's account of class inequality and class resentment. Within a single class, a number of groups can be defined in terms of their trade-cycle generated opportunities for income and costs. The pattern of resentment in the class is therefore more closely associated with the pattern of ascending and descending prospects of real-income groups than it is with the wider patterns of inequality between classes. Thus the movement of the components of class resentment means that class mobilization is typically partial and phasal, and seldom uniform or total. The difficulties of class mobilization canvassed in much of the literature of class theory may well be explained in terms of the uneven pattern of class resentment through trade-cycle movements.

One reason why trade-cycle considerations are too frequently left out of class analyses is that the movement of the trade cycle does not change the class structure itself. Yet by introducing relatively small and short-term changes in the economic power relations between a diversity of sub-class groups, it impacts significantly and diversely on the emotional patterns of social actors.

### Culture and resentment

As with mere class structure, the trade-cycle bases of emotion are structurally defined. This point leads us to a second major problem with Marshall's account of social emotion, which indicates that a broader approach is required. Marshall's discussion carries with it assumptions about the political and cultural domains which are not general and therefore need to be made specific in order to be qualified as context and application change. In particular, Marshall wrote about Britain from the 1930s to the 1950s. The orientation of the British labor movement during this period was collectivist, as were the political and civic cultures in which it operated. Under these conditions feelings of resentment generated by class experiences would have a clear propensity for political mobilization. But this is not a universal feature of class systems or of class resentment.

It is instructive to contrast Marshall's ([1938] 1973) ready assumption that resentment leads to class antagonism with the account of the hidden injuries of class presented by Richard Sennett and Jonathan Cobb based on American, in fact Bostonian, data from the 1960s. Sennett and Cobb described a situation in which working-class men, through their subordination in class relations, are divided within themselves as to who they are and what are their just deserts. Sennett and Cobb ([1972] 1983, p. 118) described this as an existential problem which "subjects a man internally to a cross-fire of conflicting demands for fraternity and individual assertion of his own worth."

Sennett and Cobb develop a number of themes in their book, but perhaps the key notion is that of the sacrificial contract in which workers make what they consider to be sacrifices for others, especially family members, with the implicit expectation that a sacrifice is given in return for respect or gratitude. Yet the family members for whom sacrifices are made have seldom asked for them. They are therefore not committed to an exchange or contract, which often has real costs for them and possibly only dubious benefits. Sennett and Cobb ([1972] 1983, pp. 134–5) go on to say that:

> The theme of giving oneself, and receiving ingratitude in return, stretches beyond the home to the more general awareness working men have of their class position in America. There is a feeling that the anxieties they have taken upon themselves, the tensions they have to bear, ought to give them the right to demand that society give something in return . . . But ingratitude is the return they feel from society, too, a refusal to acknowledge that their sacrifices finally create a claim on the respect of others.

The resentments generated in the frustrated sacrificial contract has a clear basis in class relations, but their consequences are individuating and isolating. They lead to self-blame and shame rather than to a mobilization with others in action directed toward aspects of the class relationship itself.

Here is a situation in which the circumstances an individual faces, of an unequal distribution of material resources and opportunities for dignity, have their origin in the class system. But an individual's subjective experience of these circumstances is self-doubt. The resentment generated in individuated class subordination is not generalized against the class forces responsible for subordination and powerlessness. Instead, resentment is directed against those who are perceived as gaining rewards without having made sacrifices, such as welfare recipients, and those who disdain the rewards the economy can provide for them, such as radical students (Sennett and Cobb [1972] 1983, pp. 137–9).

But simply to say that these are effects of an individualistic culture is to beg the question. "Culture" implies a shared cognitive and evaluational structure or pattern, whereas "social structure" implies a structure of relationships in which individuals or groups are variously implicated (Merton 1968, p. 216). One conclusion of the present chapter is that the fundamental distinction generally drawn between culture and social structure as autonomous realms is not justified.

In usual treatments, culture is regarded as an integrated whole and is understood as the basis of a cohesive pattern of life and practices. Such a view thus tends to ignore not only the discontinuities within but also the organizational and political sources of life patterns and practices about which contestation is continuous and uneven. The circularity of cultural explanation, suggested by Barrington Moore (1967, p. 486), is made graphic when he says that:

To maintain and transmit a value system, human beings are punched, bullied, sent to jail, thrown into concentration camps, cajoled, bribed, made into heroes, encouraged to read newspapers, stood up against a wall and shot, and sometimes even taught sociology. To speak of cultural inertia is to overlook the concrete interests and privileges that are served by . . . the entire complicated process of transmitting culture from one generation to the next.

The many and various relational, organizational and institutional forces which not only transmit but also constitute the particulars of a culture are not always indicated in accounts of class structure. Yet, as Rick Fantasia (1988, p. 71) demonstrated in his discussion of managerial practices, the explanations of the "acquiescent, individualistic character of American workers" which are most successful acknowledge the role of "the massive structures and resources devoted to controlling collective impulses." Thus, it would be difficult to account for the individualistic culture in which Sennett and Cobb's subjects operate without some reference to such things as the structure of the political party system (including the degree of party discipline within it, and the nature of its links with social and economic interests), and the place of unions in the nation's political economy and legal system, and the degree and scope of unionization in the workforce. As Ira Katznelson (1981), for instance, has shown, the political life and ethos of American workers derives from local organization, ethnic identity, and patronage. These are the mainsprings of a cultural formation quite unlike the one Marshall describes.

Having qualified the concept of culture, the fact remains that individuals in some social milieux but not in others perceive their situation to be their own responsibility. In the former, the resentments generated by class forces are individualized in terms similar to those described by Sennett and Cobb as the sacrificial contract. It is important to recognize the significance of those organizational forces and powers, summarized as "culture," in defining what Marshall describes as the unit of comparison and the nature of the oppressor; these forces and powers are likely to vary much more widely than variation in the pattern of class inequality.

It has been shown that the experience of resentment, its intensity, and the objects toward which it is directed, do arise from the processes of comparison, frustration, and oppression which Marshall identified. What we have seen in the foregoing discussion is that as the details of these processes which structure resentment change, so the force, direction, and consequences of resentment are also altered. Here is clear evidence of the social-relational nature of emotion, and of resentment in particular.

## The social dimension of emotion

In the preceding discussion it has been possible to account for an emotion, class resentment, in terms of social-structural factors. Normally, emotion is conceptualized as an individual level phenomenon, as an empirical psycho-physiological experience of individual persons. The preceding account does not deny this latter possibility; on the contrary. It does propose, though, that emotion be seen as having a basis or grounding in social relations as well as in the reality of individual experience.

Emotion is well understood as individual experience, as a state of being affected by an event. To put it this way, positing emotional experience as event dependent allows us to see that emotion is always situated and therefore has a context. The social context of the emotion-provoking experience is usually not included in the understanding of the emotion, and the abstraction of emotion at the level of individual experience is the one most developed in the literature. But each of these elements of emotion, the experiential and the contextual, is necessary in any adequate conceptualization of emotion as a social phenomenon.

Let us go back a step: emotion understood as an experience has to be seen as involving the person and not simply as an isolatable aspect or attribute of a person's body or psychology. Howard Leventhal (1984, pp. 271–2) made the latter point when he said that:

emotion as an experience . . . is private and can only be studied through indicators. The indicators for emotion are verbal and instrumental responses, expressive responses, and autonomic responses. All three types of indicator response are used in the study of emotion. None of the three types of response is itself "the emotion," as "the emotion" is a hypothetical construct.

The notion that emotion is a hypothetical construct follows from the fact that emotion cannot be reduced to its indicators. The various conceptualizations of emotion in life and in science derive from the frameworks in which the indicators of emotion are placed. These vary with the context and purpose of those involved. Thus the definitions of emotion are necessarily culturally diverse, both across societies and within them.

As already indicated, the type of experience which constitutes an emotion is a continuous flow of evaluative responses to situations. These responses are in various ways associated with preparation for action, and it is for this reason that emotion is generally associated with changes in bodily sensation or physiological processes, psychological state, and physical gesture or expression. The experiential nature of emotion, however, does not mean that the person subject to an emotional experience will necessarily be aware of it. In spite of the suggestion by Marshall, and also by Sennett and Cobb, that class resentment is inevitably conscious, one need not be affected consciously by an event in order to experience it. Indeed, many significant emotions function below the threshold of awareness (Scheff 1988, pp. 397–8). What is important in an emotional experience is that it registers in the processes constitutive of the person, which is more than but includes the proposition that emotional experience introduces physical and psychological changes in the subject of the experience.

By their nature, experiences are transient, and emotion frequently is defined as short lived. Whether or not emotional experience in fact is short lived depends on the context, the aspect of emotion which is generally ignored in psychological accounts. It is of interest that emotion has been distinguished from sentiment, for instance, on the grounds that one is of short duration and the other long lasting (Gordon 1981, pp. 566–7; Kemper 1978, pp. 47–8). In these cases, the characteristic duration of a sentiment might be explained by relational patterns which are assumed to persist over time. These later function to repeatedly or continuously stimulate what would otherwise be simply described as a (short-lived) emotional experience. While the need to distinguish between emotion and sentiment is not necessary in the discussion of this chapter, the underpinning point of the distinction supports the argument presented earlier. This is one which holds that emotions are distinguishable in terms of the types of emotional contexts which obtain.

The situation or context in which emotion is experienced can be conceptualized as an aspect of the emotion itself when emotion is understood as a dimension of the relations between persons or social agents rather than as a merely empirical individual psychological or physiological state. These different levels of social reality are distinguished by processes of abstraction through which are established the specificities and the boundaries of the objects with which we interact intellectually and practically (Ollman 1993, p. 25; see also Lauderdale, McLaughlin, and Oliverio 1990). Abstracting at the level of the individual person in face-to-face interaction gives rise to a particular classification of sets of relationships, namely the social psychological perspective, and creates a mode for explaining them. Abstracting at the level of social relationships or structures gives rise to the macro-perspective and another mode of explanation, peculiar to it.

The present chapter has shown that when emotion is conceptualized at the level of class relations, it can be seen as a particular type of experience having a complex relationship with social structure. First, emotion arises from or inheres in the structural relations of society. It has been shown that these are more complex than class theories assume, and should include not only class inequality but also trade- or business-cycle movements and cultural patterns. Second, emotion is the basis of or gives rise to action, which varies with the nature and distribution of the emotional pattern. Third, these actions affect the social structure by either reinforcing current outcomes or leading to modifications in the relations between social actors. Thus emotion can be viewed as having both a social ontology and a social efficacy, and, through being a source of social action, as linking phases of social structure as they change through time.

The assumption that the bases of social action are both cognitive and conscious, summarized in the generic category of "class consciousness," has low explanatory yield and is rejected in the preceding argument. The position developed in this chapter therefore has some affinity with the work of Friedrich Nietzsche, insofar as he developed a critique of "false consciousness" in his analysis of the social significance of deception and self-deception, and insofar as his conceptualization of resentment implies social outcomes (Berger and Luckmann 1969, p. 19; Nietzsche [1887] 1992). Nevertheless, the understanding of resentment used here is not Nietzschian, a point more fully developed in chapter 6. But even more important, resentment, and emotion in general, are not here displaced from a social-structural context. Rather, emotion functions in a macro-sociological framework in which it is given a social-relational form and structural effect.

# 4    Action and confidence

Confidence is conventionally not thought of as an emotion. Indeed, the cognitive dimension of it is widely held to be much higher than the feeling dimension. But all action, it is argued in this chapter, is based upon that confidence which apprehends a possible future. This is where the conventions become unstuck. Futures, as states of affairs which have not yet occurred, cannot be known. The cognitive dimension of confidence is therefore best understood not in terms of what the actor is directed toward, but in terms of the actor's "self-knowledge." But, as William James reminds us, persons know themselves through the emotions self-examination or self-awareness arouse or provoke ([1890a] 1931, p. 305). Confidence is one such emotion: its cognitive aspects encompass information of self-understanding; without this, action could not occur.

After an account is given of confidence as an emotion, and of its object, future time, this chapter moves to a discussion of the significance of confidence for the theory of action. In this exposition the contribution of Keynes's account of investment confidence is highlighted. This is an appropriate point of departure for a treatment of the case of business confidence. This latter is engaged in the chapter to demonstrate further possibilities to be drawn from a focus on the emotional nature of confidence. There are a number of formal and empirical problems associated with the phenomenon of business confidence, which, it is shown, can be overcome when its emotional aspects are foregrounded. Thus the contribution of the emotion of confidence to action is demonstrated in the chapter in an entirely macroscopic setting.

## Introduction

Confidence, according to Georg Simmel, is "one of the most important synthetic forces within society" (Simmel [1906] 1964, p. 318). Simmel says this because, as "a hypothesis regarding future behavior," confidence is "certain enough to serve as a basis for practical conduct." In overcoming the uncertainty, indeed the unknowability of the future, confidence is a basic foundation of action. Yet Simmel's enthusiasm for confidence has not been noticeably shared by other sociologists. This is because sociology is generally less comfortable with feelings and emotions, such as confidence, than it is with categories of calculation or culture such as interests or values. In addition, sociology is generally time-blind. Thus confidence has not been given the importance Simmel correctly indicated it deserves.

The purpose of this chapter is to discuss the necessary contribution of confidence to an understanding of social action. It is also to show that a recognition of the role of confidence in social action introduces both time and emotion into the theory of action.

The term confidence has different meanings in different contexts. It can refer to a person's trust in another, as when one is confident of another's ability to perform a particular task. In addition, confidence can refer to a person's judgment of certainty about a future event or outcome, as in the confidence one has in not needing to take an umbrella on a clear day. The term can also refer to confidence in oneself, indicating a willingness to act. Indeed, the other two are derivative forms of this notion of self-confidence. It is this latter form of confidence which is the subject of the discussion to follow.

Whereas self-confidence is primarily relevant for action, confidence in another and in one's judgment are principally constructions of belief. In this latter case, confidence stands with trust and faith as expressions of belief differentiated by the amount of evidence on which each is based. Faith requires no evidence or very little evidence, trust gets by with inconclusive evidence, and confidence requires substantial evidence (Hart 1990, p. 187). At the same time, the strength of feelings attached to faith, trust, and confidence varies inversely with the amount of evidence required to sustain them: a high intensity of feelings attach to faith, while confidence stands in contrast as a low feeling state.

This picture is somewhat modified when self-confidence is the focus of consideration. Self-confidence is predicated less on knowledge as factual information and more on a form of self-understanding, which generally operates unself-consciously, or, to use a phrase of the previous chapter, below the threshold of awareness. This self-understanding of confidence promotes a willingness to action. A paradoxical but crucial element here is that action necessarily goes beyond the temporal present into the future at the time of the onset of the action; or, to put the same point more realistically, action brings a possible future into the ever present. The future is in principle unknown, and therefore evidence about it is simply unavailable. The efficacious "evidence" or "knowledge" of self-confidence is a feeling about the actor's own capacities to approximate what they set out to achieve. This feeling is essential for an actor to engage the unknowable future, which all action entails.

## Confidence

While there is likely to be agreement that it is meaningful to refer to a feeling of confidence, the suggestion that confidence is an emotion may not appear to be immediately self-evident. Part of the reason for this is that both in common-sense understandings and in sections of the relevant literature (Gordon 1981) there is an association of emotion with strong bodily arousal, psychic turmoil, and erratic or disorganized behavior. On this basis, gentler, more positive, and less visceral feelings become affects or sentiments. Yet this understanding of the term, in which fear and anger are emotions but joy and satisfaction – and confidence – are not, misconstrues the nature and consequences of both sets of experiences, and arbitrarily distinguishes between them (Leeper 1948).

At the same time, there is no agreement in the literature concerning the classification of different emotions, nor of the distinction between emotions and other affective states. Indeed, the terms emotion, affect, feeling, and sentiment are frequently used in the relevant literature to cover identical phenomena. While there is no consensus on what is an emotion, there is, nevertheless, sufficient overlap in the various definitions of it for research and communication between researchers to take place.

There is widespread agreement that emotion typically includes a subjective component of feelings, a physiological component of arousal or bodily sensation, and an impulsive or motor component of expressive gesture. Each of these obtain for the experience of confidence. The feeling of confidence has characteristic content and tone which is both experienced subjectively (one knows when one feels confident) and expressed behaviorally (others can see that one is confident). Those who feel confident are likely also to report bodily sensations of muscular control, deep and even breathing, and other sensations of well-being.

In addition to feeling, sensation, and expression, emotion typically includes cognitive and motivational components. Given the reservations concerning motive and motivation indicated in the previous chapter, the concept of disposition rather than motivation will be used here. The difference between these is not simply semantic. The preferred concept of disposition does not imply a conscious awareness on the part of human subjects, in the way that motivation does. Emotional experience therefore includes a cognitive element of evaluation or appraisal of the situation in which the experience occurs in terms of its relevance to the subject, and also a dispositional element in which there is preparation of behavioral reactions to the situation the subject faces. These two components have been described as the functions of emotion (Scherer 1984, p. 296). Not all accounts of emotion refer to both functions.

Theories which focus on the ways in which persons manage their emotions, for instance, recognize cognitive appraisal in emotion, but tend to ignore disposition or motivation (Hochschild 1990, p. 119). Others, though, while acknowledging that emotions are amenable to social suppression or enhancement, emphasize that emotion involves a transformation in the subject's relation with the world through the experience, as Joseph de Rivera (1977) puts it, of "being moved." While an emotional impulse to act in a particular way may be constrained by judgment, this behavioral preparation, which is a component of emotion, is generally not merely acknowledged but emphasized in phenomenological and also positivist accounts of emotion (Collins 1981; de Rivera 1977; Kemper 1978; Scheff 1988).

The cognitive and dispositional components of emotion can both be demonstrated for confidence, as the discussion which follows will indicate in detail. The cognitive element of confidence involves images or projections of self and beliefs concerning the future. The dispositional aspect concerns inclinations to act on those images, projections, and beliefs.

Having indicated something of the nature of emotion and of the emotional nature of confidence, it is anomalous to now note that the term "confidence" seldom appears in emotions lexicons, and confidence is largely ignored in the emotions literature. This absence of confidence, however, is more apparent than real, as we shall see.

A statement of the nature of confidence can begin by situating it in terms of its logical relationship with certain other emotions. While confidence is not discussed by Charles Darwin ([1872] 1965), for instance, in his germinal and comprehensive classification of emotions, it can be shown to function in opposition to two sets of emotions with which he did deal.

Darwin ([1872] 1965, pp. 176–95) grouped together the emotions of low spirits, anxiety, grief, dejection, and despair. These emotions have in common an association with inactivity. Persons subject to them, Darwin said, "no longer wish for action, but remain motionless and passive" (p. 176). Confidence stands in sharp contrast to the emotions of low spirits in being an emotion without which action could not take place. Anxiety, grief, dejection, and despair lead to uncertainty, and this curtails inclinations toward action. These emotions also lead to isolation from others, and this limits opportunities and resources for action. Confidence, on the other hand, is an emotion of assured expectation which is not only the basis of but a positive encouragement to action.

Confidence is also the opposite of another group of emotions which Darwin treated, namely those of shame, shyness, and modesty ([1872] 1965, pp. 309–46). These have in common the fact that they are emotions of self-attention. Self-attention is not simply asocial self-reflection but "thinking what others think of us" (p. 325). Thus Darwin saw these emotions not simply as bases of self-censure but rather of social control, and he saw that these are emotions which frequently arise out of "breaches of conventional rules of conduct" (p. 345). The emotions of self-attention function to enforce social conformity, as Norbert Elias ([1939] 1978) and Thomas Scheff (1988) have more recently shown, and as we shall see in chapter 5. They therefore serve to curtail and narrow the range of action. Confidence, on the other hand, serves an opposite function. Confidence is the feeling which encourages one to go one's own way: confidence is a feeling state of self-projection.

Confidence can thus be characterized by the two attributes just indicated. Assured expectation and self-projection are connected insofar as they are together essential for, indeed the necessary affective basis of, human agency. Human agency, the ability to make a difference in the world, is only possible through action in which the actor projects his or her capacities into an extensive relationship. The function of confidence, then, is to promote social action. It does so by virtue of its object, which is the future. But before this latter aspect of it can be elucidated, it is necessary to say something of the social basis of confidence.

Self-projected assured expectation may be treated as a psychological state, but it does not simply arise in the mind. It has a basis, rather, in a particular experience of social relationships. The feeling of confidence arises in the subject of a relationship in which the participant receives acceptance and recognition. In all likelihood, the greater the degree of acceptance and recognition accorded to an actor in a social relationship, the higher that actor's feeling of confidence, and the more inclined that actor will be to engage in future interactions.

This perspective on confidence is captured by Randall Collins's notion of "emotional energy," which, he says, is generated in a person through their being "successfully accepted into an interaction" and manifest in "what we commonly call confidence, warmth and enthusiasm" (1981, pp. 1001–2). Thomas Scheff (1988, p. 396) has similarly indicated that "when we are accepted as we present ourselves, we usually feel rewarded by the pleasant emotions of pride and fellow feeling." The context of this remark is that rejection, on the other hand, usually leads to the painful emotions of shame, embarrassment, and humiliation. There is clear agreement in these authors about the relational basis of confidence. It is also clear that different terms are used to cover the same referent. A momentarily digression on this latter point is necessary for clarification.

Collins's "emotional energy" and Scheff's "pride" are in this context both confidence variants. Given this possibility, of different words for the same emotion, it might be asked whether a term more neutral than confidence, such as Collins's emotional energy, might be preferable. There are important reasons, however, why these terms in particular cannot be collapsed together. First, it must be remembered that the emotions which Darwin associated with inactivity and with self-attention, for instance, which are here counterpoised against confidence, are not themselves without energy. In addition, confidence has a clear object to which it is directed, it is not merely energy, undirected and differentiated only by degree. As we shall see, confidence is directed to the future, which is its object. Pride and confidence are distinguished by the fact that the object of pride is the actor's past behavior, whereas the object of confidence is the actor's prospective behavior. These overlap as positive self-evaluations of capacities, but in quite different time-planes.

On the more general point of overlapping terms, Andrew Ortony and his associates have indicated this limitation of vocabularies of emotion by distinguishing between emotion tokens, which are natural-language words for emotional states, and emotion types, which are emotions themselves "characterized in terms of their cognitive eliciting conditions" (Ortony, Clore, and Collins [1988] 1990, p. 173). In this chapter the term confidence refers to the emotion type of self-projected assured expectation.

It was mentioned earlier that feelings of confidence arise from acceptance and recognition in social relationships. The level of confidence experienced by a participant in social interaction is affected not simply by relational acceptance. In addition, the type and amount of resources which the actor has access to, as a result of the relationship into which they are accepted, is central to the formation of confidence (Collins 1981, p. 1002; Lewin [1942] 1973, p. 108). This aspect of it refers to a further dimension of confidence, namely the fact that confidence is an emotion through which a possible future is brought into the present. Resources are important not because they are drawn upon all the time, for they may not be; they are important because access to them assures their availability at some future time (see Westergaard and Resler 1976, pp. 142–3).

What distinguishes confidence from most other emotions is that whereas the objects of many emotions are discrete others (including "other" aspects of self), the object of confidence is a temporal state or plane: the future. Confidence, in bringing a possible future into the present, provides a sense of certainty to what is essentially unknowable, so that assured action with regard to it may be engaged. The importance of this point cannot be underestimated. All action functions in terms of outcomes which have not occurred at the time the action itself is undertaken. As the future is in principle unknowable, it is not possible for actors to operate in terms of calculations based on information about it. In this sense, calculative reason necessarily gives way to emotion as the basis of action (Barbalet 1996a).

The problem of the unknowability of the future was referred to in chapter 2. It was noted there that as any given action changes the conditions of all future actions, the unknowability of the future is not overcome in time. This problem, although seldom described in these terms, is arguably the most pervasive to be found in human societies. Social organization arises as a means of holding the future accountable by increasing the predictability of events and processes. But its success in doing so is necessarily imperfect. Organizations have varying but always limited capacities to control and therefore regulate their members and their environments. Similarly, organizations cannot insulate themselves from the impact of changes in an (imperfectly controlled) environment, and therefore can never fully manage disruptive internal developments. Ultimately, then, the future remains unknown; and that which achieves its engagement is never only information or calculation, but necessarily a feeling of confidence.

Thus it is the time perspective so crucial to it which makes confidence a central affect or emotion for praxis. This is because all human action occurs in time, drawing upon a past which cannot be undone and facing a future which cannot be known (Robinson 1964, pp. 73–4). It is precisely the time perspective integral to confidence which makes it the affective basis of action and agency. As Kurt Lewin ([1942] 1973) demonstrated, in his discussion of hope and morale, the more constrained the time perspective, the lower the range of activity and initiative; and the more expansive the time perspective, the higher the inclination to action.

Most accounts of time in sociology point to serial time, and especially its social construction (Elias 1992; Nowotony 1994). But confidence as an emotional apprehension of the future introduces a quite different concept of time, namely temporality or the difference between the past and the future as a constitutive element of social relations.

In summary, then, the emotion of confidence can be treated in the following way. It can be characterized as self-projected assured expectation; it functions to promote social action; it arises in (or is caused by) relations of acceptance and recognition; and its object is the future. The veracity of this conceptualization of confidence can be demonstrated by comparing it with another.

It was mentioned earlier that confidence is largely ignored in the emotions literature. Two notable exceptions are the discussions of confidence as an emotion by Joseph de Rivera (1977, pp. 45–51) and also by Theodore Kemper (1978, pp. 73–7). In many ways these two accounts run parallel to the one presented here. For instance, de Rivera says that confidence functions "to enable a person to assert his own particular view of reality" (1977, p. 46), and that confidence arises out of "being wanted" (p. 48; see also p. 50). Our accounts differ, however, on the way in which the object of confidence is characterized. According to de Rivera (pp. 44–5) depression, anxiety, confidence, and security constitute a set of emotions in which "there is no apparent other and the object of the affect seems to be the person's self."

A convincing case was made by de Rivera that whereas love, desire, anger, and fear, for instance, involve emotional transformations which implicate a person in relation to another, depression, anxiety, confidence, and security involve emotional transformations in which the other is not apparent, and "the self is the object for the movements of an implicit other" (1977, p. 48). Without taking issue with this characterization, we can describe differently that to which confidence, and the emotions associated with it by de Rivera, refers. Depression, anxiety, confidence, and security are each particular appropriations of time in the way that love, desire, and anger simply are not. This is the approach which Kemper endorses. He describes security, depression, anxiety, and confidence as "anticipatory emotions" which function in terms of a positive or negative "orientation towards the future" (Kemper 1978, p. 72).

While the function or consequence of depression, for instance, is for one to give up an active involvement in affairs, and the function of anxiety is for one to cling defensively on to one's current reality, as de Rivera (1977, pp. 46, 47) said, it does not follow that the object of these emotions is best conceived of as "the self." What depression, anxiety, confidence, and security have in common is that each is an emotion in which the self bears a particular relation with different temporal states. These emotions are not simply in time, as love, desire, and anger may be, their very objects are temporal states. Whereas depression is a morbid remorse over past events, anxiety is a fearful anticipation of future events; whereas security is a feeling of comfort in the present, confidence is a feeling of assurance about the future.

The explicit introduction of temporality into the account of action through the concept of confidence as an emotion overcomes a problem in classic action theory almost wholly overlooked in the literature. As action brings a possible future into the present, and as the future is unknown and therefore information about it unavailable, reason as calculation cannot provide the basis for action. All action is ultimately founded on the actor's feeling of confidence in their capacities and the effectiveness of those capacities. The actor's confidence is a necessary source of action; without it, action simply would not occur.

This characterization of action is quite unlike that found in classic statements. Unlike Max Weber's ([1921a] 1978, p. 25) ideal-type "affectual action," for instance, in which emotion is central, the notion of action developed here does not propose a type, confident action. Rather, it is held that confidence underlies all action as its affective basis. Weber's notion of rational action, in which calculation is characteristic, is fundamentally flawed from the perspective of confidence as the basis of action. Similarly, Vilfredo Pareto's observation that much action is non-logical superficially shares something with the position developed here. But Pareto assumes that sentiment, affect, and emotion, in determining the course of action, inhibit the actor's use of logic and calculation (see Finer 1976, passim). The position developed here, on the other hand, holds that the emotion of confidence is the unavoidable basis of action. As action is necessarily future oriented, calculation is significantly unavailable if not irrelevant in the ultimate determination of its course.

## Confidence and the theory of action

The implicit critique here of conventional theories of action through an elaboration of the place of confidence in action is analogous to a similar discussion in the work of the British economist John Maynard Keynes. Norbert Wiley (1983, p. 31) reminds us that the theory of action in Talcott Parsons, developed in *The Structure of Social Action* ([1937] 1968), which has dominated – and continues to shape – sociological discussion, drew upon the "neoclassicism of Alfred Marshall and Vilfredo Pareto, just as neoclassicism was undergoing major surgery at the hands of Keynes." Parsons did not read Keynes until 1953 (Parsons [1970] 1977, p. 44). And when he did read Keynes, it was to integrate his economic theory into a functional model of the social system, not to develop the theory of action (Parsons [1953] 1991). The pattern variables of Parsonian theory point in the direction of affective neutrality, as we saw in chapter 1. A restatement of Keynes's theory of action will show that it has much to offer a sociological structure of social action: it includes future time and the emotion confidence as central to an understanding of action.

The emotional nature of confidence, and its fundamental importance to action, are treated by Keynes in *The General Theory of Employment,*

*Interest and Money* ([1936] 1981). His comments on the practical importance of confidence and its theoretical neglect (pp. 148–9) are in the context of a discussion of the relevance of confidence for economic processes. In particular, confidence is indicated because of its influence on the schedule of the marginal efficiency of capital. Keynes refined this latter concept precisely to demonstrate the importance of confidence to economic action.

The technical details of Keynes's approach to the marginal efficiency of capital (MEC) are not relevant here. The important thing, to which Keynes ([1936] 1981, p. 135) drew attention, is the understanding of the MEC in terms of an expectation of yield. It is in this that the state of confidence is crucial to capitalist reproduction through the propensity to invest. Keynes's point is that the "state of confidence is . . . one of the major factors determining the [schedule of the MEC], which is the same thing as the investment demand-schedule" (p. 149).

The role indicated for the schedule of the MEC, through which Keynes said confidence functions, is to provide a "theoretical link between to-day and tomorrow" ([1936] 1981, p. 145). It does this because, more thoroughly and directly than the rate of interest (which is more a measure of current prospects), the schedule of the MEC conveys an expectation of future prospects for investments made at the present time, and thus through it "the expectation of the future influences the present" (p. 145).

Keynes therefore anticipated our preceding discussion of the nature of confidence, in which the future was shown to be the object of confidence. It will become clear that he also anticipated the idea that confidence functions as a necessary precondition for action. These two aspects of confidence are brought together by Keynes in what amounts to a prolegomenon to a reconstruction of the theory of action, recognizing its emotional basis and displacing the conventional rational-cognitive approach.

Keynes said that in forming expectations weight is given more to facts about which we feel confident than to matters about which there is uncertainty. In general, then, there is a tendency to project from present facts to future outcomes ([1936] 1981, p. 148). The paradox indicated here is that while confidence brings a possible future into the present, it does so through a psychological mechanism in which the reverse projection, of the present into the future, occurs. The facts about which we feel most confident are those pertaining to an existing situation, and these, therefore enter "into the formation of our long term expectations" (p. 148). Keynes's point is that it is in this way that economic actors face uncertainty, with a constructed, indeed fabricated, rationality, based on projection rather than on calculation.

This insight, concerning the extra-rational basis of action, is expanded in Keynes's discussion of speculation on the stock market. Such reasonable, but only pseudo-rational, projections as Keynes describes are institutionalized in stock markets ([1936] 1981, pp. 151–3). This institutionalization occurs by virtue of the fact that the market offers a daily revaluation of stock, and this permits the daily revision of a commitment to invest.

Later in the same chapter Keynes refers to "the characteristic of human nature that a large proportion of our positive activities depend on spontaneous optimism rather than on a mathematical expectation, whether moral or hedonistic or economic." He immediately goes on to say that "most . . . of our decisions to do something positive . . . can only be taken as a result of animal spirits – of a spontaneous urge to action rather than inaction, and not as the outcome of a weighted average of quantitative benefits multiplied by quantitative probabilities" ([1936] 1981, p. 161). Thus Keynes acknowledged and gave support to the notion that action has a significant emotional basis.

The importance of emotion and the insufficiency of calculation is further stressed by Keynes when he says that:

human decisions affecting the future, whether personal or political or economic, cannot depend on strict mathematical expectation, since the basis for making such calculation does not exist; and that it is our innate urge to activity which makes the wheels go round, our rational selves choosing between the alternatives as best we are able, calculating where we can, but often falling back for our motive on whim or sentiment or chance. ([1936] 1981, pp. 162–3)

This account is the obverse of the "rational-actor" model of conventional economic analysis, in which calculations on the basis of precise information are assumed. By treating the dimension of time prospectively and not merely retrospectively, Keynes did not simply introduce a new variable into economic analysis; he changed its foundations. The extent to which he did this is still incompletely appreciated.

Like most economics, most sociology is quite timeless. Both disciplines have largely failed to situate their subjects, market behavior or social interaction, in time. In fact, they each actively take their subjects outside of time through functionalist and synchronic modes of analysis. Anthony Giddens, for instance, recently attempted to introduce time into sociological analysis. But his understanding of time is geographic and historical. His concerns include the quality of the experience of time and its commodification in differential spatial arrangements; and also past time as a resource for action in present time (Giddens 1984, pp. 45–51, 110–58). Indeed, when social science deals with time it is most frequently historical. The constitution of past time, including phenomenological processes through memory (Game 1991, pp. 90–111), occupies most current sociological writing about time. But what weighs on all social systems and what all social action must deal with is the unavoidability of an unknowable future.

Keynes's focus on the future led to fundamental theoretical developments, predicated on a new understanding of action. These included revisions in the theory of money, which go well beyond the conventional idea, taken up by Talcott Parsons ([1963] 1969, p. 360), for instance, that money is simply a measure of value and has no utility of its own. For Keynes the distinguishing feature of money is its liquidity, its ability to change in or out of a particular asset without loss. Thus money is a hedge against uncertainty. Connectedly, it is not inconsistent to hold money for speculative reasons: money allows its owner to control the future. For Keynes, then, money is not a measure of value but a store of value, a notion of some sociological significance (Smelt 1980, pp. 216–19). Keynes's perspective on capital formation or investment indicates even more directly the importance of a focus on future time and necessarily introduces the centrality of confidence as an emotion, as we have seen.

Investment decisions are about future consequences of present actions. As the future is necessarily uncertain, and as all action is future-making, action is necessarily based on interpretation rather than precision, relevant information is limited, and calculation is therefore difficult when not impossible (Keynes [1936] 1981, pp. 149–50). Keynes's attitude was clear in his reference to the "dark forces of time and ignorance that envelope our future" (p. 155). At the root of investment action is not rational calculation, then, but uncertainty mediated by the feeling of confidence, mediated by what Keynes, following Descartes, called "animal spirits."

In this regard Keynes's account of investment represents an alternative to and an advancement on Weber's famous statement in which emotion has a place only in a "*panic* on the stock exchange" (Weber [1921a] 1978, p. 6, emphasis added). Keynes, at least, understood that emotion has a crucial role in the normal operations of the stock market and associated activities.

While Keynes and Weber had different views of the role of emotion in the operation of stock markets, they did agree that emotion is an "irrational" force. Keynes's association of emotion with the irrational requires no special explanation; the convention is in the very language he used. But it is necessary to make the point that there is a growing awareness that the conventional disjuncture, indeed opposition, between reason and emotion is exaggerated and associated with a number of confusions, as we saw in chapter 2 (see also Fricker, 1991; Leeper 1948; McGill 1954). Emotion is a source of evaluation of circumstances that, while not based on reason (as calculation), is not necessarily irrational. Emotion is a fundamental means of evaluating the significance of a relationship for the subject of that relationship.

Keynes did understand the significance of emotion to action, and he was aware of the central role of confidence in it. It is unfortunate indeed that Parsons ignored Keynes in his influential construction of the structure of social action. But it should not be assumed that the Keynes described here is well known to economists, even if neglected by sociologists. The *General Theory* ([1936] 1981) is largely understood by economists as a source of economic management policies concerned with public spending, interest rates, and taxation. The incapacity of these to stem the problems of national governments and their economies subject to decidedly international market forces from the 1970s has led to the discrediting of Keynesian macro-economics and the rejection of the *General Theory*. It would therefore be doubly unfortunate if endeavors to reconstitute the theory of action again had no recourse to Keynes's contribution, because the *General Theory* no longer served the narrow interpretations of economic practitioners.

Keynes's important account of it assumed that not much could be said about business confidence *a priori*, and that only summary generalizations of "the actual observation of markets and business psychology" ([1936] 1981, p. 149) were possible. No doubt this follows from his assumption that emotions are no more than "animal spirits," base as well as basic, perhaps beyond rational comprehension, and, anyway, unyielding to abstract analysis. While Keynesian economics assumes that confidence may be maintained by certain government rituals (Wiley 1983, p. 45), Keynes left the systematics of confidence undeveloped. It will be shown in what follows that the systematics of confidence can be developed, even in a macro-economic setting, and that this is possible by further drawing upon the emotional nature of confidence outlined in the preceding section of this chapter.

### The case of business confidence

The position developed here claims that action and therefore inaction derive from the degree to which actors feel confident about their capacities to realize an unknowable future. There is no suggestion that this feeling is conscious, although it is argued in the first section of this chapter (but not by Keynes) that it correlates with the extent of acceptance in and level of standing of previous interactions. Thus confidence is not merely a subjective sentiment but an emotion with a clearly social basis.

This perspective encourages not only a reinterpretation of conventional action theory and current accounts of social and political action, but also encourages a reinterpretation of the literatures of alienation, anomie, depoliticization, and the end of ideology. In the situations referred to by these categories, inaction can be understood to derive from the detraction from or prevention of confidence by the inculcation of functional equivalents to the antithetical emotions Darwin described as low spirits, anxiety, dejection, and despair.

An application of the approach developed here to the case of business confidence will be outlined in what follows. There are a number of reasons for this choice of confirming demonstration. First, the case of business confidence is continuous with the preceding discussion of Keynes. Whereas Keynes denied the possibility of a systematized account of business confidence, it will be shown that such a thing is possible when confidence is treated as an emotion in the manner set out in the first part of this chapter.

A second reason is that economic relations, much more than social or political relations, are widely held to be based on non-emotional action or, ostensibly, are the least influenced by emotional factors. Robert Frank (1988) and Robert Lane (1991) have recently demonstrated that emotion is integral to economic processes, but neither directly addresses the question treated here of the emotional basis of economic action itself. Finally, a discussion of business confidence demonstrates the importance of the argument concerning emotions not merely for individual-level interactions but for collective relationships at the macroscopic level, and therefore demonstrates the significance of the approach for the full span of sociological analysis and theorizing.

The component units of macro-economics are not reducible to those which function in the micro-economic sphere. Economies as a whole, in which aggregate investment propensities function, cannot be explained through the proclivities of individual investors. The tendency, which has become current in sociology, to reduce macro-phenomena to micro-components, while not universal (Turner 1987), sustains the inclination to keep sociological analyses of emotion exclusively in the realm of social psychology. Yet if emotion is understood in terms of social relationships, then the relationship between not human individuals but social collectivities gives rise to macro- or social emotions, which can be analyzed macrosociologically.

Business confidence is precisely the affective dimension and motor of group relations to economic opportunities. These are the opportunities of industrial sectors or economies as a whole. As George Katona (1979) has shown, in his development of a macropsychology, aggregative or macroscopic regularities of economic confidence and behavior can be demonstrated where fluctuation and noise characterize individual attitudes and behavior.

Yet business confidence is not a group or collective emotion in the sense that it leads to joint or group action; it is an emotion of the business community which leads to common action. Common action is the action of individuals, subject to the same conditions, which is parallel or serial rather than collective. Common action within collectivities may occur in conjunction with competition between their individual members. Group or joint action, on the other hand, tends to override individual competition. Max Weber ([1921a] 1978, p. 636) referred to the impersonality of the market, through which individuals orient not to others but to the commodity. Analogously, business confidence is an emotion concerning the relation between individual investors as members of a business community, on the one hand, and their future returns in terms of the performance of the economy as a whole, on the other.

Convention holds that business confidence varies in terms of structural factors (inversely with government intervention), or cognitive factors (directly with perception of market opportunities). It will be shown that neither of these are general possibilities. Any demonstration of such propositions will be an artifact or consequence of a consideration of insufficient cases. It will be shown that investment confidence can be explained by the nature of the relationship between the business community and another collective actor, the political state.

The last-mentioned proposition is in need of qualification, of course. Investment presupposes not only the actor's confidence, but also trust in the cooperative capabilities of others (Luhmann 1979), and the organizational coherence of collective or corporate actors based upon the loyalty of their members (Hirschman 1970). But in this discussion of the affective basis of action it is not necessary to develop the concepts of trust and loyalty. This is because trust is a particular form of confidence, and so is loyalty. Trust is the confident expectation of the intentions of others; and loyalty, the confidence that trust between others can be maintained over the long term (Barbalet 1996a). Thus while confidence, trust, and loyalty relate to action, cooperation, and organization, respectively, action – and therefore confidence – acquires a global or total character through the constitution of cooperation in cooperative action and organization in organizational action.

It must also be acknowledged that collective actors, in addition to business and the state, such as unions, the scientific and technological communities, and the financial sector, to name only the most obvious, necessarily impact on business confidence. But each of these factors is typically mediated by government regulation. In this context, then, they take on a second-order character. Thus, to confine discussion to only the two principal actors is sufficient to indicate the basis of confidence in the relationships of acceptance and recognition between business and government.

Michael Kalecki's ([1943] 1972) classic sociology of full employment and business confidence indicates an inverse structural relation between business confidence and government economic activity. As government spending increases, so business confidence decreases. Kalecki (p. 423), not unlike Keynes, held that if the state of confidence should deteriorate, private investment will decline, with a consequent fall in output and employment. Thus, the level of employment in a market economy largely depends on "the so-called state of confidence."

Kalecki noted that this arrangement provides capitalists with an indirect but nevertheless powerful control over government policy: "everything which may shake the state of confidence must be carefully avoided because it would cause an economic crisis" ([1943] 1972, p. 423). Once the government understands that it can increase employment by its own purchases, however, "this powerful controlling device loses its effectiveness" (p. 423). Business is thus fundamentally opposed to budget deficits used by government to intervene in the economy. Kalecki concluded that the "social function of the doctrine of 'sound finance' is to make the level of employment dependent on the 'state of confidence'" (p. 423).

A reduction of business confidence, according to this argument, is a consequence of government spending, including capital investment. This latter generates in the business community a fear of "crowding out." Investment dollars spent by government are not available to business. In addition, business feels that government investment robs the business community of opportunities for initiative in economic development (Kalecki [1943] 1972, pp. 423–44). Government expenditure on social services also leads to a reduction in business confidence because such expenditure subsidizes mass consumption. In this instance business loses confidence because state social services render labor less reliant on employment for subsistence and therefore more independent of industrial control (p. 424). Government policy directed toward full employment further reduces business confidence because such policy renders the threat of dismissal ineffective as a means of labor discipline (pp. 424–5).

Kalecki's argument can be summarized in terms of a depiction of the bases or sources of confidence in social relationships, as already outlined. Government spending lowers the recognition and acceptance of business spending, and thus diminishes business initiative, and therefore the sense of certainty concerning the level of future returns on current investment. Thus Kalecki places confidence in the context of macro-social relations.

Kalecki, however, unlike Keynes, took confidence to be a matter of doctrine, not an emotion. Keynes, nevertheless, anticipated a key element of Kalecki's argument when he noted that "the delicate balance of spontaneous optimism" is easily upset, and therefore that "the *fear* of a Labour Government or a New Deal depresses enterprise" (Keynes [1936] 1981, p. 162, emphasis added). But Kalecki's failure to appreciate the emotional nature of the business community's reactions to government conduct, whether fear or confidence, narrows the scope of his formulation of the relations between confidence and state activity.

Before indicating the limitations of Kalecki's approach, it has to be acknowledged that his account of the structural relationship between business confidence and government spending seems to hold true for the major capitalist economies of the West today. But because he treated state expenditure, rather than acceptance and recognition, as the independent variable, his formulation is without general application. Indeed, a reverse structural relationship, in which government spending enhances business confidence, obtains for a number of significant cases, including nineteenth-century American and European economies, and developing economies in general.

During periods of early industrialization, for instance, state subsidies, credits, guaranteed prices, and profits, and more direct forms of state investment frequently encourage rather than undermine private business confidence or investment action. This has been documented for Russia (Gerschenkron 1965, pp. 16–20, 46–9), Japan (Lockwood 1954, pp. 246–8, 503–9, 571–92), and other economies (Aitken 1959; Shonfield 1965). And it should not be assumed that this is an exclusively Old World, or even Third World, phenomenon.

The economic activity of American governments, both federal and state, was not only significant but highly visible during the eighteenth and nineteenth centuries. Its clear purpose was to encourage business confidence in investment and capital formation.

Alexander Hamilton's public credit bills of the 1790s, for instance, in lowering the interest rate on government debt, reduced the market rate of interest and thereby cheapened the capital costs of investment. In his insightful assessment of this, the nineteenth-century historian Richard Hildreth said:

The great secret of the beneficial operation of the funding system was the re-establishment of confidence; for commercial confidence, though political economists may have omitted to enumerate it among the elements of production, is just as much one of those elements as labor, land, or capital – a due infusion of it increasing in a most remarkable degree the productive activity of those other elements, and the want of it paralyzing their power to a corresponding extent. By the restoration of confidence . . . the funding system actually added to the labor, land, and capital of the country a much greater value than the amount of the debt thereby charged upon them. (1856, p. 276, quoted in Bruchey 1965, p. 112)

Although constitutionally weak in its powers, the federal government did not confine its interventionist activities to raising revenue. During the period 1813–37, for instance, the US federal government was active in canal building, and in subsidizing various enterprises including steamships, telegraph lines, and the import of railroad iron (Bruchey 1965, pp. 122–3).

State governments were much more able than the federal government to extend their activities into industry. From the period after the Revolution to the middle of the nineteenth century, state governments created thousands of business corporations. Bruchey reports that of the 2,333 corporations chartered by special act in Pennsylvania during the period 1790–1860, 64.17 percent were in the transport industry, 11.14 percent in insurance, 7.72 percent in manufacturing, 7.2 percent in banking, 6.0 percent in gas and water, and 3.77 percent in miscellaneous categories (1965, pp. 128–9). In addition, state governments invested public moneys in the securities of corporations, offered other direct financial assistance, guaranteed corporation bonds, granted monopoly rights, tax exemptions, and provided other benefits.

Economic historians recognize that under conditions of capital shortages and market uncertainties, government spending encourages private investment and capital formation – encourages, that is, business confidence. When the economic infrastructure is undeveloped, state expenditure on public works increases profits and enhances the attractiveness of private investment. In these historical cases, then, government spending and business confidence are related to each other in a manner which contradicts Kalecki's account. Depending upon the historical level of development of a national economy, then, a postulated structural relationship between government spending and business confidence, in the form presented by Kalecki, tends to contradiction: spending enhances confidence in immature economies, but undermines it in mature economies.

It can be seen from the preceding discussion that the economic historical and emotional accounts of confidence agree that government expenditure does not in fact uni-directionally determine business confidence. The difference between these two general accounts, however, is that the emotions account, but not the economic account, regards the level of state expenditure to be dependent on or a function of government acceptance and recognition of business. This formulation yields to possibilities which the economic account must fail to grasp.

Two relatively recent sets of US government policy indicate that state economic expenditure itself is less significant in affecting confidence than how such policies relate to a more general pattern of government acceptance and recognition of business. For instance, the United States federal government's 1989 legislative guarantee of Savings and Loans losses (at an estimated cost of $157 billion) constitutes a state expenditure without positive economic purpose, but which encouraged a feeling of confidence in the business community (Adams 1989; Pizzo, Fricker, and Muolo 1989). Pollution-control legislation, on the other hand, which addresses a problem with demonstrable economic costs (Ridker 1967; Smith 1976) and with limited consequences for budget deficits, seriously undermines the sense of assured expectation in the business community.

While these two cases are anomalous to economic analysis, they can be explained by the treatment of confidence as an emotion. The Savings and Loans bail-out encouraged business to feel that its interests and purposes were not ignored but sympathetically understood by government. Pollution control, on the other hand, has the effect of generating a feeling in the business community of government regulation indifferent to the needs of profit-making, managerial sensibilities, and the prevailing values of business.

These remarks return us to the general relevance of the perspective of confidence as an emotion for the understanding of economic activity. While the object of confidence is a future return on market investment, the basis or source of confidence is in the relationship business enters into with government, from which its sense of acceptance and recognition arises.

This account provides a context for and gives sense to the observation made by the political scientist Charles Lindblom, for instance, when he insists that:

One of the great misconceptions of conventional economic theory is that businessmen are induced to perform their functions by purchase of their goods and services, as though the vast productive tasks performed in market-oriented systems could be motivated solely by exchange relations between buyers and sellers. On so slender a foundation no great productive system can be established. What is required in addition is a set of government provided inducements in the form of market and political benefits. And because market demands themselves do not spontaneously spring up, they too have to be nurtured by government. (1977, p. 173)

Lindblom took this perspective beyond the limited idea that the state has a role in economic development or transformation (Rueschemeyer and

Evans 1985, pp. 44–6) to the wider notion that governments in all market economies, and not simply emergent ones, must continually induce business confidence in order for enterprise to operate (Lindblom 1977, pp. 173, 176).

In their relationship, government entices the economic participation of business, through investment action, by inducing feelings of acceptance. In developing economies this is typically achieved by public investment in infrastructure and in the foundation of key industries to generate markets for private investors. In developed economies, on the other hand, taxation and monetary policy, infrastructural subsidies, and the regulation of labor, enhance or encourage a state of confidence, which reflects a feeling that government accepts the legitimacy of business activity and profit-making.

A focus on the affective dimensions of business confidence points to the macro-socially situated relational sources of the feeling of self-projected assured expectation required for action in investment markets.

## Conclusion

The importance of confidence to action and to the theory of action has been explained in this chapter in terms of its emotional nature. The characterization of the emotion of confidence as self-projected assured expectation is associated in the preceding discussion with its function in promoting social action, in its source in relations of acceptance and recognition, and in the future as its object. These components of confidence operate for collective as well as for individual actors.

As all action brings a possible future into the present, the concept of time, or more properly temporality, and especially future time, is necessarily introduced into the analysis in this account. By definition, the future cannot be known and therefore actors cannot have available to them information which might form the basis of calculations for the orientation of action. Instead, action is necessarily based on the feeling of confidence actors have in their capacities for successfully engaging the future. It is precisely the uncertainty of the future which renders calculation with regard to it impossible. The "rational actor" model of economic and social analysis is thus shown to be not only empirically flawed, but heuristically misleading.

The social basis of confidence has been located in the actor's acceptance in previous relationships and the resources to which such relationships have given access. While the broad mechanisms of this general set of processes are not in themselves problematic, future research needs to be directed in this area to more clearly indicate their finer details. This would not only more firmly ground the sociology of confidence but also provide a basis for a sociological understanding of overconfidence. This latter has not been discussed here, but has to be seen as an aspect of the issues dealt with in this chapter as it is associated with failures of action (see Lynd 1958, pp. 43–4).

The contribution of Keynes to an understanding of the role of confidence in action, the temporality of action, and the emotional nature of confidence have also been outlined in the preceding discussion. Keynes's arguments were not complete and not entirely sociological – it is unreasonable to expect that they should be – but they are sufficiently important to the theory of action to require restatement here. That they are so little known has necessitated the degree of elaboration they have received.

The treatment of business confidence, informed by an understanding of the emotional nature of confidence and especially its relational basis, demonstrated that it is not simply market opportunities which determine investment action. The business community's relationship with the political state is a source of confidence which informs expectations regarding future returns on current expenditure.

This latter argument, while apparently remote from the earlier discussion of confidence as an emotion at the root of action, in fact demonstrates the force of this perspective. It indicates that the structure of social action not only implicates emotion as a key element, but also that its emotional basis stretches from the social individual to the collective action.

# 5    Conformity and shame

The oldest explanations of human behavior are moral, not social; and one of the oldest forms of moral exhortation mobilizes the emotion of shame. It is a measure of our times that, together with a popular perception of declining morality, a popular view is that experience of shame is oppressive. Shame is able to play a role in these different formulations because it is unavoidably a social emotion. Shame operates in terms of a supposition of another's regard for self, of taking on the view of another. In this way, shame pulls those who experience it in line with social expectations.

It will be shown in this chapter that shame has played a continuing role in explanations of social conformity. The chapter begins by considering various statements of just this point in writers from the eighteenth century to the present. It is shown that while Adam Smith misunderstands the capacity of shame to stem envy, he nevertheless developed a fully sociological account of shame's contribution to social conformity. In fact, he was the first to do so. Charles Darwin's discussion of shame is also recounted in this chapter. The links between these accounts and the sociological account of shame by the American sociologist Thomas Scheff is also discussed.

But not all theories of conformity function in terms of shame, and some writers have held that shame is of historical interest only, that it is today a declining emotion. These positions are also critically discussed in this chapter. The position adopted in the following pages is not that shame no longer has a place in the emotional repertoire of social actors, but that the context is changing in which the experience of shame occurs. A discussion of the social bases of shame, on which the chapter concludes, indicates four types of shame experience which differ in terms of distinct social preconditions. Each of these, it is shown, bears a distinct relationship with conforming behavior.

## Introduction

Through a consideration of the emotion of shame, the categories of the subjective self and the objective other, the internal world of individual psychology and the interactive world of social relationships, become inextricably linked. With shame, self is necessarily qualified by the other; the individual is unavoidably social.

The literature on shame extends back in time to the opening sections of the first book of the Bible. Here, shame functions to limit transgressive behavior. The interest in shame continues today. The idea that shame is toxic, for instance, propagated by the Recovery Movement, among others, is predicated on a critical re-evaluation of the nature and consequences of adherence to external norms, and on the service shame provides to conforming behavior. Indeed, the role of shame in processes of social conformity is of enduring interest in sociology.

The concern of this chapter is to review those arguments which explain social processes in terms of shame. In doing this, the idea of shame as a thoroughly social emotion will be reinforced. It will also be shown that a sociological account of shame can distinguish different types of shame experience.

There is always some resistance to the idea that social analysis can be conducted through emotions categories. But we should be aware that one of the earliest theories of modern society operated precisely in terms of emotion, although only partially in terms of shame. Indeed, that is its limitation.

## Sympathy and Adam Smith

Although he is predominantly remembered as the theorist of self-interest, the eighteenth-century philosopher Adam Smith argued that social processes cannot be explained exclusively in terms of orientations to utility, or what he called self-love. This is because, in addition to self-interest persons have a natural inclination toward "fellow-feeling" or sympathy. Sympathy is not itself an emotion or passion, according to Smith, but the vehicle which conveys our feelings for others.

In summary, Smith held that the relations of market society are harmonized and stabilized by the interaction of self-love and sympathy. Whereas self-love produces self-interested individual actions which aggregate to a collective aggrandizement, sympathy moderates the injurious consequences of self-interested actions. This is an elegant formulation, certainly, but Smith overstated sympathy's capacity to balance self-love.

The category of sympathy continued to play an important role in liberal theory after Smith. John Stuart Mill, for instance, argued that a fundamental tenet of utilitarian morality is the propensity in human nature for sympathy ([1863] 1960, pp. 29, 31). It was only with the arrival of the twentieth century that liberalism was prepared to acknowledge that the socially important work of sympathy must be performed by the state if it is to be done at all (Hobhouse 1911, pp. 158–60). This realization did not merely transform liberalism but effectively undermined it.

Smith himself was not blind to the need for socially protective state action, and therefore to the limitations of sympathy in maintaining the conditions for moral behavior among large sections of the population. In his discussion of the division of labor, in *The Wealth of Nations*, Smith notes that a lifelong specialization in "performing a few simple operations" enhances the worker's dexterity at the cost of his intellectual and moral capacities ([1776] 1979, p. 782). Smith goes on to say that "in every improved and civilized society" the mass of the population will become "incapable of . . . conceiving any generous, noble, or tender sentiment, and consequently of forming any just judgment concerning many even of the ordinary duties of private life . . . unless government takes some pains to prevent it" (p. 782).

Whereas Smith implies that the division of labor may be corrosive of sympathy, Karl Marx, in an early manuscript in which Smith occupies a good deal of attention, offers a different explanation. Marx holds, rather, that it is money which undermines the "bonds of society" on which sympathy is based ([1844] 1967, p. 130). This perspective resonates with what has become a sociological commonplace: that market relations destroy the veracity and efficacy of emotional factors in social relations.

Max Weber, for instance, explained that the market community is based on entirely impersonal relations which undermine and exclude emotion, a pattern which is repeated in bureaucratic organization, and which, Weber held, constitutes an aspect of the "peculiarity of modern culture" (Weber [1921a] 1978, pp. 636, 975). The difficulty with Weber's argument, and others like it, is that they forget, as Smith did not, that self-interest, central to market and administrative structures, itself has a significant emotional component.

Where there is self-interest in market society, and competitive relationships, there is also envy. There can be no dispute about the emotional nature of envy. Market society modifies the context and therefore the form and possibly the experience of emotion, as we saw in chapter 2. But the conclusion that modernity implies affective-neutrality, to use Parsons's term, reflects a fundamental confusion. It is particularly relevant to mention envy in this context because it is envy which potentially displaces sympathy in the social world which Smith describes, and almost removes it from Smith's argument.

In *The Theory of Moral Sentiments* (hereafter *TMS*) Smith refers to envy, along with anger, hatred, malice, and revenge, as affections which "drive men from one another, and which tend, as it were, to break the bonds of human society." Yet it is envy alone which is singled out as the "odious and detestable passion" (Smith [1759] 1982, p. 243). This is because, in the context of market society, envy in particular poses a fundamental threat to sympathy, according to Smith. Smith indicates this assessment when he says that persons can "readily" sympathize with others, only so long as they "are not prejudiced by envy" (p. 42).

In market society, competition leads people to emulate others, and the likelihood that persons will feel envy toward others is therefore high. Smith was aware that envy is an unavoidable aspect of the emotional life of market actors, but he believed that it would not predominate. After acknowledging in *TMS* that envy does undermine sympathy, Smith immediately added that envy, when it arose, would itself be undermined by shame ([1759] 1982, pp. 44, 45–6). It is proper that shame be brought into the argument, but Smith's suppositions regarding the capacity of shame to limit envy, and thus preserve sympathy, cannot be accepted.

Envy is not thought of today as a shameful thing. All claims on resources by social actors are given animus by their desire for such things. Envy is simply the emotional form of a desire for benefits which others are believed to possess. It is for this reason that envy is so common between market actors. Markets readily facilitate impersonal processes of possession, and envy does not therefore necessarily reflect negatively on the character of those who do the envying (unless the envy is excessive: but any excess reflects badly on character). However, in order to understand Smith's supposition that shame would prevent envy, it is necessary to remember that Smith was writing at a time when Scotland was still an agrarian society, even though in the early stages of a transforming industrial revolution. In agrarian or peasant societies envy is necessarily viewed differently than it is in market societies.

Peasant societies are hierarchically organized, with many aspects of social exchange and distribution fixed by ascriptive qualities. Under these circumstances, desire, acquisition, and possession are subject to sanctions and limitations which are alien to market societies. While the structure of the emotion of envy is the same in both peasant and market societies, its consequences are quite different, and it is therefore regarded differently in the two types of society. In peasant or traditional society, envy is seen as an emotion of transgression, and associated with the "evil eye." Indeed, the original meaning of the term envy is malice or ill-will. Clearly, under these circumstances, it is likely that envy would be shameful, as Smith assumes.

The transition from the shameful-envy of peasant society to the competitive-envy of modern society is clear in Francis Bacon's essay "Of Envy," written in 1625. At this time English society and economy were being changed through the introduction of commercial agriculture and American treasure. Bacon ([1625] 1911, pp. 52–7) notes the early association of envy with malignant desire, regards it as an essentially undesirable passion, and ascribes to it a vehemence which is equivalent to that of love. Yet despite the traditional sanctions against it, envy has become a dominant and worrisome emotion in Bacon's time. More words are devoted to envy by Bacon than to practically any of the other topics of his *Essays*. Had Smith taken note of Bacon's discussion, he might have come to realize that changes in the significance of envy made the shame of it a weakening defence for sympathy against envy.

### Smith's hidden shame

While shame of envy is less likely in market society than Smith believed, shame itself might function to maintain conformity and order in a society based on self-love but in which sympathy is eroded. Sympathy is self's interest in the fortune of others, whereas shame derives from an interest in how others regard self. Although he saw a particular role for shame in the maintenance of social order, in terms of its supposed support for sympathy against envy, Smith failed to acknowledge the general role of shame in social processes – although he came very close to it.

Just five years before Smith first published *The Theory of Moral Sentiments*, Jean-Jacques Rousseau, in his "Discourse on the Origin of Inequality," observed that with the advent of private property and the social inequality it produces, modern society is riven with "rivalry and competition . . . conflicting interests . . . [and desires] of profiting at the expense of others" (Rousseau [1754] 1973, p. 87). Under these conditions, he goes on to say, "social man lives constantly outside himself, and only knows how to live in the opinion of others, so that he seems to receive the consciousness of his own existence merely from the judgment of others concerning him" (p. 104). Rousseau uses this point to moralize on the shallowness and ignobility of post-savage humanity. But the fact that social persons live in the opinion of others does suggest a possible basis of constraint on individual action which might maintain the order of a society potentially destroyed by competitive envy. While Rousseau did not develop this point, Smith in fact does so only a few years later.

In the third part of *TMS* Smith is concerned with "the Foundation of our Judgments concerning our own Sentiments and Conduct, and of the

Sense of Duty" ([1759] 1982, p. 109). His argument concerning the basis of right conduct is sociological, original, and profound:

> We suppose ourselves the spectators of our own behavior, and endeavor to imagine what effect it would, in this light, produce upon us. This is the only looking-glass by which we can, in some measure, with the eyes of other people, scrutinize the propriety of our own conduct. If in this view it pleases us, we are tolerably satisfied . . . if we are doubtful about it, we are often, upon that very account, more anxious to gain their approbation, and . . . we are altogether distracted at the thoughts of their censure, which then strikes us with double severity. (p. 109)

Smith demonstrates in this statement that social harmony and order are maintained, not by the subject's feelings for others, but by the subject's feelings concerning how they are regarded by others: the opposite pull of pride and shame keep the rope of social restraint tight.

The terms pride and shame are not used by Smith in the passage just quoted, although these emotions are clearly the referents of his discussion. The failure to identify the pleasures and anxieties which he does refer to, as pride and shame respectively, is probably a consequence of his assuming that this account functions entirely in terms of self-love and sympathy.

Although he does not explicitly offer such an explanation, it is possible that Smith could have regarded the propensity of persons to take pleasure in praise and to feel pain in condemnation as an aspect of self-love. Similarly, the sensibility of persons to be affected by their perceptions of the feelings of others about them was seen by Smith as an instance of sympathy. This is also how Smith scholars have understood his discussion of internal judgment (Campbell 1981, p. 101; Schneider 1948, pp. xix–xx). While he did endeavor to explain social order and social constraints on individuals in terms of sympathy, Smith, in the discussion just referred to, in fact lay the foundation for an explanation of social conformity in terms of pride and shame, without indicating that he had done so and without being acknowledged for having done so by others.

We shall see later that Smith's argument concerning the social monitoring of self through feelings of pride and shame is replicated by the early American sociologist Charles Horton Cooley. Indeed, the "looking glass" metaphor used by Smith is also central to Cooley's account of social perception and conformity. Yet Cooley fails to acknowledge or even mention Smith. Instead, he claims that William James was the source and inspiration of his appreciation of the social functions of pride and shame. This failure to put Smith in his rightful place as the originator of the argument concerning the role of shame in social conformity is current in all the literature on the topic, including the most recent.

An element of the argument which would be used by subsequent writers to explain how shame maintains moral order in modern societies was also discovered by Smith, but not incorporated into his discussion of the role of the approbation of others, both positive and negative, in the self's disposition.

The importance of a developed division of labor in the social structure of shame was indicated nearly 200 years after Smith by Norbert Elias when he wrote: "As the interdependence of men increases with the increasing division of labor, everyone becomes increasingly dependent on everyone else, those of high social rank on those socially inferior or weaker. The latter become so much the equals of the former that they, the social superior, feel shame even before their inferiors" (Elias [1939] 1978, p. 138). Prior to the rise of market or bourgeois society, the "control of impulses," as Elias quaintly describes the refinements of civilization associated with natural functions – eating, nose-blowing, spitting, bedroom behavior, relations between the sexes – was externally imposed "by those of high social rank on their social inferiors or, at most, their social equals" (p. 137). With the extension of the division of labor, and its consequent psychological leveling, each person might experience shame through the supposed regard of any other, irrespective of rank. The conformity of all to a general moral order can in principle now, with an advanced division of labor, be achieved through ostensibly internal processes: the regard of others in the generation of pride and shame.

### Darwin and internal processes

There is a conundrum for those, like Elias and other writers, who wish to argue that emotions, and shame in particular, is significant in social relations. Seventeenth- and eighteenth-century philosophers, such as Baruch Spinoza, Thomas Hobbes, David Hume, and Adam Smith, might have been comfortable explaining affairs in terms of emotions. But the modernizing processes which were the backdrop to their theorizing moved emotion from the public realm of relations between persons to the personal and private spheres of life. Max Weber's description of this process in relation to economy and organization was indicated earlier. Theodor Geiger (1969, pp. 225–7) has shown how similar processes operated in the modernization of law. To this consensus, that capitalist economy and organization removes emotion from social life, the weight of Karl Marx and Friedrich Engels can be added. They tell us that with the rise of the bourgeoisie the only ties between persons are "naked self-interest," and that the "most heavenly ecstasies of religious fervor, of chivalrous enthusiasm, of philistine sentimentalism [have been drowned] in the icy waters of egotistical calculation" (Marx and Engels [1848] 1970, p. 38).

There seems to be almost universal agreement that under modernizing conditions emotion is dispelled from social organization and process, internalized, and made the exclusive province of personal and private experience. Georg Simmel summarizes the situation exactly:

Instead of reacting emotionally, the metropolitan type reacts primarily in a rational manner . . . Money economy and the domination of the intellect stand in the closest relationship to one another . . . All emotional relationships between persons rest on their individuality, whereas intellectual relationships deal with persons . . . [as] something objectively perceivable. (Simmel [1903] 1971, p. 326)

Thus, by the beginning of the twentieth century the role of emotion in human affairs and social relations is widely seen to have been enormously diminished. The quintessentially modern conceptualization of emotion, commensurate with this understanding of its asocial role and interior nature, was expertly articulated by the nineteenth-century biologist Charles Darwin.

Darwin is best known for the theory of evolution, spelled out in *Of the Origin of Species by Means of Natural Selection*, first published in 1859. Although it is hardly ever mentioned in general discussions of his work, in 1872 Darwin published a book, the subject of which had occupied his researches and attention since 1840, namely *The Expression of the Emotions in Man and Animals*. The primary purpose of this work was to add support to the theory of evolution, to demonstrate – against the opinion of earlier and contemporary authors – that humans share the means of emotional expression with their non-human progenitors, and that the "habits of all animals have been gradually evolved" (Darwin [1872] 1965, pp. 10, 12). The reference to "habits" here is of signal importance, because it indicates that not only are skeletal structures, for instance, characteristic of distinct species and indicate evolutionary connections between them, but that so too do patterns of behavior, including emotional behavior.

In *Expression*, Darwin locates emotion within the individual who experiences it. He has no interest in classifying the relational circumstances of the individual's life and interactions which give rise to a particular emotion. The significance of emotion for Darwin is in its physical expression. He accepted the essentially modern assumption that an individual's appearance reveals their standing and character, and their emotional disposition. In this way emotion is regarded as a personal attribute and, although private, publicly expressive of feelings. For Darwin, the physiological nature of emotional expression meant that it functions involuntarily and therefore cannot be repressed. Emotional expression thus offers public evidence of private states. The idea that an emotion would have a "self-contained meaning" (Sennett 1974, p. 21, see also pp. 171–3), in the sense that emotion expresses a personal and private experience, is thus entirely modern. Emotional experiences might indeed be regarded as fundamentally private, because they pertain to the inner mechanisms of the emoting subject's own body.

Internal and self-contained emotion is given its fullest account by Darwin. In his discussion of grief, for instance, Darwin indicates that "the circulation becomes languid; the face pale; the muscles flaccid; the eyelids droop; the head hangs on the contracted chest; the lips, cheeks, and lower jaw all sink downwards from their own weight" (Darwin [1872] 1965, p. 176). In considering how these expressions of grief occur, Darwin is not concerned with the subject's exterior relations. "The expression of grief," Darwin (p. 185) says, is "due to the contraction of the grief-muscles." It is these latter which cause the obliquity of the eyebrows, the depression of the corners of the mouth, and so on, which he describes as characteristic of grief.

It is almost incidental that this series of causes and effects occur "involuntarily . . . whenever certain transitory emotions pass through our minds" ([1872] 1965, p. 195). The cause of the transitory emotion of grief, which might be located outside the individual even though central to the onset of a grief-emotion episode – such as a young woman "nursing her baby who was at the point of death" (p. 186) – is apparently without interest for Darwin, and quite unsystematically treated. Darwin simply failed to pay attention to the social bases and consequences of grief in particular and emotions in general, and almost exclusively focussed on the physiological aspects of expression.

Darwin treated anger in exactly the same manner as he did grief. He says that under moderate anger:

the action of the heart is a little increased, the color heightened, and the eyes become bright. The respiration is likewise a little hurried; and as all the muscles serving for this function act in association, the wings of the nostrils are somewhat raised to allow for a free indraught of air . . . The mouth is commonly compressed, and there is almost always a frown on the brow. (Darwin [1972] 1965, p. 244)

Again, when the social context is mentioned, it is incidentally and unsystematically regarded. Darwin says that one who has "suffered or expect[s] to suffer a wilful injury" from another will readily "dislike" him, and that this feeling could rise to "hatred" and then to "rage" (p. 237). For instance, a dispute over a loan, an accusation of theft, and an unfair sharing of a payment are all indicated as possible precipitants of anger (pp. 246–7). But these suggestions are offered without classifying the situations in which anger occurs, or indicating general categories of social relations to match the general statement Darwin developed of the physiological processes implicated in the expression of anger.

It is, therefore, of particular interest that Darwin not only provided a detailed physical analysis of shame in the manner of his discussion of grief and anger described here, but also a general account of the social basis of the emotion. The discussion of the emotions of self-attention – shame, shyness, and modesty – is principally in terms of blushing, and much of the relevant chapter is occupied with the physiological and evolutionary aspects of that theme. But Darwin, uniquely in the *Expression*, went on to outline a general account of the social-relational context and basis of shame/blushing.

Darwin said that:

> It is not the simple act of reflecting on our own appearance, but the thinking what others think of us, which excites a blush. In absolute solitude the most sensitive person would be quite indifferent about his appearance. We feel blame or disapprobation more acutely than approbation; and consequently depreciatory remarks or ridicule, whether of our appearance or conduct, causes us to blush much more readily than does praise. ([1872] 1965, p. 325)

Thus in his treatment of shame Darwin showed that self-attention is not simply asocial self-reflection, but is rather "thinking what others think of us." Thus the internal emotion shame, as Darwin saw it, is explained by him in an entirely social field: it is the self-perception of another's apprehension of the subject which is at the root of shame. Darwin saw shame not simply as a base of self-censure but of social control, and therefore as an emotion which frequently arises out of "breaches of conventional rules of conduct" (p. 345). Here is a second dimension of Darwin's sociological insight, namely that shame is important in its impact on social behavior in the direction of conformity with conventions. In spite of the methodology and orientation he employed in his study of emotions and expression, Darwin could not avoid a clear formulation of the social basis and consequences of shame.

### Scheff and silent shame

More recently, Thomas Scheff has acknowledged the sociological significance of Darwin's account of blushing and the emotions of self-attention. Indeed, he has restated Darwin's position to indicate that the latter showed that "shame is *the* social emotion, arising as it does out of the monitoring of one's own actions by viewing one's self from the standpoint of others" (Scheff 1988, p. 398, emphasis in original). Scheff qualifies the details of Darwin's findings when he says that shyness and modesty can be regarded as variants or cognates of shame, and that "blushing is only one of several visible markers of overt shame, and therefore is not a primary concept for a theory of social influence" (p. 398). He also shows that other writers, in addition to Darwin, have recognized the significance of social perception for social conformity. One writer in particular to whom Scheff refers in this context is Charles Horton Cooley.

Through the concept of the "looking-glass self," Cooley ([1922] 1964, pp. 184–5) holds that social monitoring of self is virtually continuous, and that it always contains an evaluative element, necessarily giving rise to either pride or shame. Scheff does not disagree with Cooley on these points, on the contrary, but he does argue that together these propositions raise a puzzle. Scheff conjectures a resolution to this puzzle and, in demonstrating its validity, makes a significant contribution to the understanding of shame and conformity. Scheff says that: "If social monitoring of self is almost continuous, and if it gives rise to pride or shame, why do we see so few manifestations of either emotion in adult life? Among possible answers is that the pride or shame is there, but has such low visibility that we do not notice it" (1988, p. 399). The concept of low-visibility shame is not immediately self-evident, and Scheff offers an explication of it before demonstrating its validity.

An aspect of the discussion of grief in the work of the psychologist Silvan Tomkins is in this respect analogous to Scheff's characterization of low-visibility shame. Tomkins argues that all persons suffer distress daily, and that crying is therefore ubiquitous. Nevertheless, "nothing seems less common that an adult cry" (Tomkins 1963, p. 56; quoted in Scheff 1988, p. 399). But Tomkins shows that adults do cry, as adults. The adult cry is brief, muted, fractured, and partial, substituted by other physical and vocal actions, and often masked by expressions of anger. This is to say that the adult cry is a cry modified and transformed (see Tomkins 1963, pp. 56–65). The low visibility of the adult cry, Scheff concludes, is "because its manifestations have been disguised or ignored" (Scheff 1988, p. 399).

The imputation in Scheff's discussion is that shame, too, is disguised and ignored. The likelihood of low-visibility shame is enhanced by an additional factor. In modern society, says Scheff, "the emotions of shame and pride often seem to themselves arouse shame" (1988, p. 400). Scheff is encouraged to accept this proposition because it explains Darwin's observation that both pride and shame can cause blushing. The correctness of the idea that pride and shame arouse shame is given independent support by the fact that in modern society there is a premium on the idea that the self is the proprietor of the capacities one exercises. On this basis it is likely that defects of self revealed by shame will be denied: a shame of shame produces a masking of shame, which leads to its low visibility and its being readily ignored.

Scheff demonstrates the low visibility of shame through a discussion of the psychological research of Helen Block Lewis ([1971] 1974) and the conformity studies conducted by Solomon Asch (1956). He shows that through a careful analysis of over a hundred clinical encounters Lewis was able to demonstrate that most of the shame episodes between participants were invisible to them. She was also able to show that in spite of the lack of awareness of shame on the part of those involved in clinical exchanges in which shame was present but unacknowledged, verbal and non-verbal or behavioral shame-markers were nevertheless manifest (Scheff 1988, p. 401).

Scheff went on to demonstrate the veracity of the concept of low-visibility shame in social conformity through an analysis of Asch's report of his conformity experiments. Scheff shows that the subjects who agreed with a majority view concerning the alleged truth of an obviously false proposition did so under the pressure of shame unacknowledged and unrecognized, that is, as a result of low-visibility shame (Scheff 1988, pp. 402–5).

The significance of Scheff's arguments, first, that shame is primary in social organization as a mechanism for conformity, and, second, that it may be experienced below the threshold of awareness, are of enormous importance to an understanding of the significance of emotion in society. With regard to the second of these arguments, it has to be said that the widespread assumption that emotions have to be consciously experienced in order to be effective is not borne out by Scheff's discussion of shame. Indeed, it is not contradictory to say that persons may not be clear about their emotions, and also that persons may deny their emotions. The supposition that a person must be conscious of an emotion in order that they experience it, and be moved by it, is therefore discredited by Scheff's conclusions.

The details of Scheff's position will be treated in the following. At this point an independent argument will be proposed which holds that the feeling of an emotion is not essential for emotional experience to occur.

Emotion can be described in terms of five discrete elements or components: only one of these is the subjective component of feeling; the others are a physiological component of arousal or bodily sensation, an impulsive or motor component of expressive gesture, a cognitive component of evaluation or appraisal of stimuli and situation, and a dispositional or motivational component of readiness for and intentionality in action (Scherer 1984, p. 294). Emotion links a person's conditions and their opportunities for action by a process described by Klaus Scherer as "the constant evaluation of external and internal stimuli in terms of their relevance for the [person] and the preparation of behavioral reactions which may be required as a response to those stimuli" (p. 296). It does not follow that such emotional evaluation and emotional preparation of behavioral reactions are necessarily felt in any conscious way by those who experience them. That is to say that for emotion to influence behavior it is not required to be consciously experienced.

Consciousness of a feeling is associated with an ability of a person to give such feeling verbal or linguistic expression. Yet much emotional activity is mediated by areas of the brain unconnected with language functions (Gazzaniga 1985). Much of the time, therefore, many people simply do not know what moves them: they may be inarticulate about feelings which they have, and they may have no clear feelings of the emotions which influence their dispositions. In such circumstances, self-monitoring of dispositions and actions will be low and therefore there will be a relative reduction in the control a person may exercise over their emotional desires and conduct. The converse is also readily supported; in feeling an emotion, actors are able to reflect on their motives and circumstances (Damasio 1994, pp. 133, 145, 159–60; McDougall [1908] 1948, p. 384). As a matter of fact, though, and for the reasons just indicated, much social behavior is unreflective, even though informed by emotional dispositions.

Shame, as an emotion, achieves the function, described by Scherer in the preceding, of assessing a person's circumstances and preparing their response to it, by forming an impression of what others (might) think of them. A positive evaluation of pride or a negative evaluation of shame has behavioral consequences in the form of a generalized outcome of conforming behavior. It is simply not required that this process be mediated by the consciousness of the social agent. There is nothing contradictory in the proposition that actors experience an emotion, such as shame, and be moved by that experience, without being conscious of a feeling of shame.

Without recourse to the physiological argument indicated here, Scheff has shown that shame, which is generative of conformity, is likely to be of low visibility to all the participants in the social relationships involved.

### The decline of shame?

The question arises of whether Scheff has solved the problem of understanding shame at a time when it no longer matters. The idea that ours is a post-shame society presents itself from a number of sources. Perhaps this characterization of society, as post-shame, substantiates the idea of a post-modern society by referring to a means of discipline associated with modernity, but which is no longer prevalent in social perception and control. It is therefore appropriate to ask whether shame continues to function in the maintenance of social conformity.

The argument against the continuing salience of shame in the maintenance of social conformity can be summarized by reference to particular trends in contemporary behavior and how they are understood. But before we deal with social behavior, the prevalence of a theory of social conformity, which functions without recourse to emotion in general or shame in particular, also might be taken to suggest that the authors treated here have inflated the relevance of shame in understanding social conformity. In particular, the "disciplinary" sources of social order should be considered in relation to the argument concerning shame as the basis of social conformity.

Given the extensive use to which Michel Foucault's understanding of social power and order has been put, it is appropriate to consider its relationship with the argument concerning shame. In *Discipline and Punish* ([1975] 1977) and the first volume of *The History of Sexuality* ([1976] 1978), Foucault argues that the administrative regime of institutions and specialist knowledge are two sides of a single process of control of physical human bodies. The infrastructure of social order is thus generated and maintained by a disciplinary power which includes both systems of surveillance and scientific discourses of knowledge.

The obvious appeal of Foucault's approach is that it acknowledges the extent to which Weber's iron cage of the future has been realized, the importance of the knowledge base of power in administration and profession, and the corporeal focus of life. But in his exclusive focus on administrative and cognitive techniques of control Foucault creates an impression that social life is wholly explicable in terms of the external manipulation of subjects by means of power.

This raises a number of considerations which together would contribute to a critique of Foucault's account, and not simply from the perspective that shame has a role in the maintenance of social conformity. But the need to articulate such a critique is averted here because of the quality of the dissatisfaction with which Foucault himself came to regard the position briefly outlined here.

In the second and third volumes of *The History of Sexuality*, *The Use of Pleasure* ([1984a] 1985) and *The Care of the Self* ([1984b] 1987) respectively, Foucault moves from the treatment of subjectivity as a function of external power to subjectivity as an independent sphere of human being. In *The Use of Pleasure*, Foucault acknowledges the limitations of his approach up until this work. He suggests a corrective focus which recognizes that the success of techniques of power require a precondition in the relation of subjects to themselves. He argues that it is "appropriate to look for the forms and modalities of the relation to self by which the individual constitutes and recognizes himself *qua* subject" (Foucault [1984a] 1985, p. 6).

This perspective opens the possibility of recognizing both that social conformity cannot be explained by reference merely to the instruments of conformity, and that the mechanisms of conformity include the actor's relation to self, possibly including emotions generated through processes of social perception. Foucault does not refer to pride and shame here, and his later discussion of honor and shame ([1984a] 1985, pp. 204–14) is disappointing for our purposes. What can be concluded, though, is that the popular currency of Foucault's work on disciplinary power offers no purchase against the continuing veracity of the role of shame in social conformity.

A point more telling against the focus on shame than the example of Foucault's account of disciplinary power is possibly the discussion of Rom Harré, which explicitly holds that "shame is everywhere giving place to embarrassment as the major affective instrument of conformity" (1990, p. 181). This is held to be so because of the apparent "collapse of the distinction between manners and morality" (p. 203). The significance of this, Harré immediately adds, is that:

Relativism in matters of ethics would be expressed as conventionalism, which is as much as to say that morality is just the manners and customs of this or that tribe. Bodily modesty, then, becomes a locally variant set of conventions, not a virtue deeply embedded in the very quality of womanhood. The collapse of the distinction between manners and morality would explain the recency of an interest in embarrassment and a decline of attention to shame. (p. 203)

For Harré, embarrassment is the emotion associated with a violation of convention or breach of manners, whereas shame is the emotion associated with failure of character.

The distinction between manners and morality as analogs of embarrassment and shame is ingenious, but misses the point that both are what Darwin called emotions of self-assessment. It is in this area that the apparent decline of shame, and embarrassment as well, for that matter, is in fact to be located. Without necessarily disagreeing with Harré's characterization, it can be said that shame is an emotion of negative assessment of self, whereas embarrassment is an emotion of negative assessment of one's behavior and other peripheral attributes of self. The anecdotal evidence typically drawn into discussions of this type is used to support the suggestion that both shame and embarrassment are in decline.

Day-time television talk shows provide what has been taken to be cultural evidence of an absence of shame, embarrassment, or guilt on the part of participants concerning a range of beliefs, practices, and events. These programs, which have in common a confessional format, encourage participants to make public what in earlier times or other contexts would have been subject to the sanction of shame. That participants are rewarded with publicity for revealing sanctionable facts about themselves encourages further the conclusion that shame, embarrassment, and even guilt are in serious decline. The confusion displayed in these programs is not simply of morality but also of manners.

In addition to such public displays of shamelessness, evidence for the social decline of shame might be deduced from the expansion of the Recovery Movement which began in the 1980s. The Recovery Movement can be characterized as a voluntaristic rejection of shame as a toxic influence in the lives of ordinary persons (Bradshaw 1988; Fossum and Mason 1986). Through this trend there has been a growing reversal in popular discourse of the idea that shame is a positive moral force. Shame is depicted by Recovery exponents not as the moral rod that it was thought to be, but as a vicious stick, which if not broken will damage the person subject to it, and their relations with others.

No matter how limited a contribution these examples make to an argument concerning the decline of shame, it is clear in all this that a re-evaluation of the popular meaning of the term is occurring. It is less clear what these developments imply for the salience of the emotion of shame for social control. Certainly, the apparent rejection in conventional ideology of shame as a positive force of social conformity is continuous with the idea that personal autonomy requires the separation of the individual from external determination, including social processes. But the unrealizable desire for asocial being, in order to achieve individual self-realization, does not imply that the emotion of low-visibility shame is any less central to processes of social perception and social conformity.

The contention to be outlined here is that the issue arising from the idea that shame is toxic is not so much the decline of shame, but rather that certain social changes have affected both conventional rules of conduct and the experience of one's own self. It is worth recalling that Darwin ([1872] 1965) said that shame frequently arises out of "breaches of conventional rules of conduct." And in Scheff's terms, "shame is *the* social emotion, arising as it does out of the monitoring of one's own actions by viewing one's self from the standpoint of others" (1980, p. 398, emphasis in original). It is precisely changes in conventions and self-forming experiences that are responsible for the apparent decline of shame today. The suggestion here is that there has been a transformation of the social context in which shame is experienced.

Rather than treat changes in conventional rules of conduct, a topic needing little attention, changes in the experience of self, and their impact on the experience of shame, will be discussed. The subjective reality of self arises in and is sustained by social processes and relationships which change within an individual's life-cycle. These social processes and relationships are themselves subject to change over historical time. A frequently noted aspect of self in modern urban settings is its fragmentary nature: Georg Simmel ([1903] 1971), Ferdinand Tönnies ([1887] 1963), and Lewis Wirth ([1938] 1957), for instance, have each contributed to the formation of a widely accepted template for understanding the modern self as comprising a number of components which potentially may be disarticulated.

The self-forming experiences which occur in modern society are described in this literature as impersonal, superficial, transitory, and segmental. Wirth tellingly says that "by virtue of his different interests arising out of different aspects of social life, the individual acquires membership in widely divergent groups, each of which functions only with reference to a certain segment of his personality" (Wirth [1938] 1957, p. 57). Indeed, the concept of self becomes problematic under these circumstances because the experience of self tends to a degree of contextual variability. The ultimate outcome, increasingly taken as a real option, is that the self, rather than simply forming the core of being which persons are subjectively aware of, becomes a conscious project of their own activity. This reflexively created self was noted as a possibility by Simmel ([1903] 1971, p. 336), and has more recently been discussed at length by Anthony Giddens (1991) as an accomplished reality.

The fragmentary, reflexively created self impacts on the experience of shame in a number of ways. With the freedom, insecurity, and isolation of the late-modern self, one's view of oneself – even from the standpoint of others – is likely to be less focussed than it would have been when the social formation of self gave rise to a more solid and unitary product. Also, in the fragmentation of the self, experiences of shame may arise through the standpoint of another which is a disarticulated aspect of self. In this latter case the shame is narcissistic, and does not necessarily contribute to social conformity but is symptomatic of individual pathology. The clinical condition of narcissism arises when the self fails to form social relationships with others but treats them as objects which can be used to satisfy unconnected desires of the self. Narcissistic shame, then, is more a short-circuit and less a social sanction. We shall return to this question later.

The evidence therefore does not lead to the conclusion that shame has declined; it simply does not address that issue. Nor does the evidence indicate that shame is no longer implicated in conforming processes. What has emerged in late modernity, though, is a partial loss of coherence in what it is that is conformed with, and the rising prospect of an increase in self-referential or narcissistic shame. In conclusion, therefore, it is necessary to situate these comments in a discussion of the social basis of shame and the social source of its various forms.

## The social basis and forms of shame

While the classic writers on pride and shame were able to draw a straight line between social perception and conformity, more recently it has become necessary to acknowledge the variety of shames, and the potentially problematic relationship some of these might bear to social conformity. Scheff, for instance, indicates that while feelings of shame typically lead to social conformity, rigid conformity and even rage may result from an experience of shame in which the feeling aspect of the emotion is bypassed (Scheff 1988, pp. 396–7, 401–2, 404).

The difficulty with Scheff's explanation of shame variation, however, is that, in drawing on the work of Helen Block Lewis, it emphasizes psychological rather than sociological statements of cause. This has the consequence of pointing only to a relationship between an actor and their own affective processes, and underplays the social relationships in which emotions are formed and experienced. The concept of bypassed shame, used by Scheff to explain the shame–rage spiral, and the form of the argument in which it functions, he takes directly from Lewis ([1971] 1974). This final section of the present chapter will outline an alternative sociological explanation of the cause of shame, and of the different types of shame and their social consequences. But before proceeding it is necessary to indicate the presuppositions of Lewis's approach. These inform Scheff's argument, but he does not spell them out.

Lewis distinguishes between at least three types of shame. The first is one in which the feeling of shame is experienced, and accepted by the subject. The other two are versions of denied shame. What Lewis describes as overt shame is characterized by the fact that the "shame affect is overt or available to consciousness but the person experiencing it either will not or cannot identify it" (Lewis [1971] 1974, p. 196). In the third type of shame (the second type of denied shame) the shame affect is unavailable to the subject, and the feeling of shame is bypassed (p. 197). Scheff's point is that denied shame, and especially bypassed shame is the source of hostility and rage, rather than a direct source of social conformity; Lewis makes no such distinction.

For Lewis, shame is an emotion which "helps to maintain the sense of separate identity, by making the self the focus of experience" ([1971]

1974, p. 25). It does this, she says, by bringing into "focal awareness both the self and the 'other', with the imagery that the 'other' rejects the self." The imagery of rejection is important for Lewis's argument because it means that in shame the "other" is experienced as a source of hostility, and this almost always simultaneously evokes hostility against the rejecting other (p. 41). Thus hostility, rather than conformity, is the likely consequence of shame experience in Lewis's account.

Lewis argues that under normal circumstances the feeling of shame, including the sense of hostility which, by hypothesis, accompanies it, is experienced and then discharged. The quality of Lewis's thinking on this theme and her concerns are clear: "Shame reactions, taken lightly, dissipate of their own accord. The self recedes into its more automatic background position and resumes its more taken-for-granted functioning" ([1971] 1974, p. 27, see also p. 276). In the case of overt and bypassed shame, on the other hand, the feeling of shame, the shame affect, is respectively unidentified or not experienced. In these cases the feeling of shame cannot be discharged. A consequence of this is that neurotic symptoms form, the expressions of which include humiliated fury and shame-rage (pp. 197–8, 275, 276).

Lewis's argument is based precisely on the Freudian version of Cartesianism which holds that emotion not mediated by mind torments the body. Lewis says that in "undertaking this study . . . I have depended on . . . Freud's discovery that unresolved conflict between the passions and the internal forces which forbid them can generate neurotic symptoms" ([1971] 1974, p. 7). It is not being claimed that Lewis and Scheff are wrong to identify forms of shame more associated with rage than conformity. What is being rejected here is the mind–body dualism and the Freudian metaphysic that supports this particular version of the argument. A quite different approach, more sociological in its method of treating shame, in fact covers the Lewis–Scheff ground and more.

Discussion up to this point has accepted the phenomenological account of shame, captured in the image of a looking-glass self. In these terms shame is a negative social perception of one's self, the seeing of one's self from the standpoint of others. It has been demonstrated that this is how the concept of shame is indicated in Smith, Elias, Darwin, Cooley, Scheff, and Lewis, among others. But the general form of the social relationship out of which this perception, and the accompanying emotion, arises has yet to be made explicit. A lead in the right direction was offered by Adam Smith.

After stating that it is "with the eyes of other people" that social actors "scrutinize the propriety of [their] own conduct" (Smith [1759] 1982, p. 112), Smith goes on to say that: "If we are conscious that we do not deserve to be so favorably thought of, and that if the truth were known, we should be regarded with very different sentiments, our satisfaction is far from complete" (pp. 114–5). This statement approaches a causal account of shame, in which the particular nature of the relations between actors determines the emotion. It is suggested in this passage that shame is caused by a social actor receiving a higher level of regard from the other than is warranted.

An explicit causal theory of shame, which operates in similar terms, has been developed by Theodore Kemper (1978, pp. 59–62). Kemper argues that shame arises in social interactions or relationships in which one actor is accorded excess status by an other. The strength of Kemper's treatment of shame is not simply his appreciation of a need to situate shame in a general causal and not merely phenomenological account, but in its capacity sociologically to differentiate distinct forms of shame.

In social relationships, an actor who meets standards of competence or achievement typically wins the regard of others for doing so. In this sense, such an actor acquires status. It is possible that actors may claim more status than is their due. Alternatively, others may accord higher levels of status to an actor than is warranted. In each of these cases the resulting receipt of excess status will typically give rise to an emotional experience of shame (Kemper 1978, p. 59). By distinguishing between whether self or other is the agent of excess status, Kemper is able to account for different types of shame.

When self is the agent of excess status, that is, when status is falsely claimed by a social actor, then introjected shame, in Kemper's terms, results (1978, p. 61). This is the shame which is colored by embarrassment and humiliation. It arises when an actor (potentially) exposes their failings of competence or character, or otherwise lays a false claim to the good opinion of others. The consequences of this type of shame for the actor's behavior are multiple, according to Kemper (p. 59). The actor may accept a lower status; they may withdraw from interaction, nullifying the status exchange; or they may offer compensation in order to regain lost status.

A quite different set of possibilities is put in place when the other is the agent of an actor's excess status, when status is given in excess of its desert. The resulting emotion is still shame, but under these circumstances, what Kemper calls extrojected shame takes the form of anger and hostility expressed toward the other (Kemper 1978, p. 62). This is because it is the other's unrealistic evaluation of the subject's competence or achievements which generates the tension between "what one is and what one receives credit for" (p. 62).

Kemper is thus able clearly to distinguish different specific types or expressions of shame on the basis of whether self or other is the agent of

Table 5.1 *Social typology of shame*

|  | Agency | |
|---|---|---|
|  | Self | Other |
| External default | Situational shame | Aggressive shame |
| Internal default | Narcissistic shame | Deferential shame |

excess status. Building on Kemper's argument, we can add other variables, in addition to that of the source of agency, in developing a sociological typology of shame. In particular, the suggestion that the experience of shame is effected by the prevailing normative structure and also by self-forming experiences, mentioned in the preceding section of this chapter when considering the alleged decline of shame, constitute two such variables. These can be summarized as variables relating to the basis of default in shame, as either external or internal, respectively. When these are added to the variables which Kemper discusses, four distinct sets of possibilities of shame responses can be identified. These can be simply represented in tabular form (see Table 5.1).

Kemper dichotomized shame experience in terms of whether self or other is responsible for an excess of status accruing to self. In addition to these variables, shame experience may arise as a consequence of a failure of social rules or norms of behavior from preventing an ascription of excess of status. This is called here an external source of default. In addition, an excess of status may be accorded as a result of unsubstantiated self-conceptions or some other aspect of the formation of self. This is called here an internal source of default. An account based on these four variables offers a complex characterization by distinguishing four distinct types of shame. The circumstance of each cell of the shame table presented here (see Table 5.1) can be dealt with in turn.

The most common possibility, represented by the upper-left cell of the table, is one in which self claims status under false pretenses through a contravention of a social convention or norm. This is the situational shame which arises from a good person doing a bad thing, and feeling that they have failed to live up to their ideals. The feeling of shame in this case is associated with embarrassment and humiliation. It is likely to lead either to an acceptance of lower status, in recognition of the transgression; or to an attempt at restitution, in order to regain status. Each of these strategies is indicative of shame functioning in the maintenance of social conformity.

It is also possible that the self is an agent of excess status, as a consequence of the social actor's unsubstantiated conception of self. This type of shame is represented in the lower-left cell of the table. In this case an excessive claim to status is taken on the basis of an actor's overestimation of their competence or achievement. This is not the shame of a good person doing a bad thing, but shame caused by a failure to experience oneself as good enough. The feeling of this type of shame will include a component of fear. This introjected shame based on unrealistic conceptions of one's own self can be characterized as narcissistic shame: it is associated with a disarticulated self-concept. In general terms, narcissistic shame leads to social withdrawal, so that the reflexive project of self-making may continue or remain unimpeded by unwanted external influence. Because this type of shame sheds doubt on an inadequate self-concept, it is experienced as extremely painful, even toxic.

The right-hand column of the table indicates two additional types of shame experience. The instrumentality of the other in an experience of shame can be implicated in self's excess of status both through external and internal default, that is, through a failure of norms or rules, on the one hand, and through failures of competence or performance, on the other.

When an actor receives an excess of status because another entertains exaggerated expectations of their abilities, the resulting shame is associated with a feeling of hostility and possibly also a feeling of guilt. This type of shame is represented in the lower-right cell of the table. Kemper's account of extrojected shame, described earlier, covers much of this form of shame. The other's exaggerated appreciation of self's capacities can lead to self's hostility toward the other, as we have seen. Additionally, acceptance of undeserved status gives self excess power over others, which generates guilt. At the same time, the tension between what self is and what self receives credit for can be resolved by attempting to perform to (unrealistic) expectations. Thus the typical response of this type of shame is deference and rigid conformity. It can be called deferential shame.

Inadequate and disarticulated norms or rules can also lead to excess status, as in the upper-right cell. A regulatory system which both overvalues socially trivial or societally irrelevant capacities and achievements, such as sporting prowess, and rewards relative incompetence and underachievement, by social selection on grounds of ascriptive qualities for instance, is likely to produce shame in those it advantages. Shame arising in this way from the prevailing system of norms is likely to be associated with feelings of hostility, for the same reason that it does in Kemperian extrojected shame. In the case of shame arising from inadequate norm formation, however, rage is also possible if the source or agent of excess status cannot be moved or otherwise affected by the hostility of the shamed actor. The impersonal nature of the agent of shame exacerbates the subject's hostility, possibly leading to rage. The external source of shame in this case leads to the blaming of others, and aggressive behavior toward them. This can be called aggressive shame.

## Conclusion

The schematically presented types of shame described in the foregoing seldom present themselves in reality with the same clear-cut definition with which they appear here. Yet the purpose of the discussion here would be lost if real cases of shame experience were not recognizable in the four distinct forms of shame identified in Table 5.1 and the four sets of corresponding causes.

In addition to the verisimilitude of the model of shame outlined here, the general account of the different expressions and forms of shame, in terms of causal bases of excess status, is thoroughly sociological. In this regard it demonstrates that social factors can not only identify but explain emotional experiences.

Each of the four types of shame identified here does not equally lead to social conformity. In particular, narcissistic shame and aggressive shame bear a problematic relationship to social order. The types of conformity these forms of shame induce are as potentially disruptive of a larger harmony as they are of supporting it. Having said that, however, we can see that the predominant forms of shame unequivocally do contribute to social conformity. By knowing what are the social bases of shame, we can be informed on the likely incidence of its distinct types.

Having shown that shame is not only a social emotion, but an emotion with identifiable social bases, we can say that changes in the structure of norms and in self-formation will inevitably lead to changes in the expression and the experience of shame. This proposition was given implicit support at the beginning of this chapter, when Adam Smith's account of the relationship between envy, sympathy, and shame was reported.

The association of shame and conformity has a long history in social commentary and analysis. Not only is shame an essentially social emotion, as all who have written on the subject have indicated, but it is the emotion most implicated in processes of social conformity.

# 6  Rights, resentment, and vengefulness

This chapter addresses the questions of human or basic rights, how such rights might be sociologically understood, and how they may be explained in terms of emotions categories. Sympathy is an emotion most frequently associated with the achievement of basic rights. It is argued here, though, that sympathy bears a problematic relationship with rights. Indeed, through a consideration of the case of lynching, it is shown that, rather than find their rights in the sympathy of others, persons who have lost their rights are likely to restore them through an active expression of resentment.

The chapter goes on to explicate and distinguish between the emotions of resentment and vengefulness, and to show how each contributes to the realization of basic rights. There is, it is true, a widely held supposition that these emotions drive not rights but bloody feud: well may they do so. But when the primary focus of analysis is on rights, then the more limited role and scope of the distasteful emotions of vengefulness and resentment emerges. To discuss them in this context, then, is to pick up what is most frequently not broached. The account of these emotions concludes with a discussion of the basis on which the social perception of their acceptable forms, as variants of justifiable anger, emerge.

Vengefulness and resentment are the emotional apprehension of a social violation of the satisfaction of a need. A discussion of basic needs is also provided in this chapter, in which three types of need are distinguished. A demonstration of the fundamental nature of the need for cooperative interaction, and of a provocation of emotion claiming a basic right through its contravention, is provided through a discussion of Harold Garfinkel's breaching experiments.

Finally, the changing nature of the form of cooperative interaction is considered in discussion of the historical variation of conditions in which rights are claimed.

## Introduction

As a topic of sociological inquiry, rights have attracted little attention. There have been notable sociological discussions of rights (Ginsberg

1965; Runciman 1972), certainly, but these are isolated explorations, with no cumulative production of a sociology of rights. The reason for the pervasive sociological indifference to rights is largely in the nature of rights themselves. Rights that are most secure, for instance, are given legal expression, and disputes over rights are most frequently conducted politically. Thus in the division of labor between academic disciplines, the treatment of rights has been generally confined to law and political theory.

There is a further good reason why sociological indifference to rights is widespread: whatever else they might be, rights are not determinants of action, social or otherwise. Even though social action might be taken in defence or expression of rights, rights themselves do not constitute structures which dispose persons to particular courses of action. From these perspectives, then, rights contribute little to social processes in any direct way. Yet to go only this far fails to appreciate that rights are integral to social organization, and therefore that sociology can not properly ignore rights.

The possession of a right is the realization of a claim made on others and accepted by them. Here is the inherently social nature of all rights: that rights are substantiated in particular capacities and entitlements of persons. Property rights, for instance, include the capacity to exclude others from access to the trees, say, a person owns, and also their entitlement to the fruit of the trees, even though others (whom they pay to do so) may pick the fruit. Because rights are claims made on others which have to be accepted by them to be effective, the involvement of law in consolidating rights, and political contestation over them, is not surprising. Yet the social aspect of rights is central. Rights, as capacities and entitlements, that is, as social resources or powers, are associated with the facilitation of social actions in various ways.

Perhaps another reason why rights, even when their social nature is understood, have tended to be ignored in sociology is that they are relatively uninteresting, because sociologically unproblematic, when they are claimed between equals or between persons who have more or less equal access to the means of securing rights. This is because trust, required in the processes of enforcing an acceptance of another's claim to capacities or entitlements, is not at issue in such circumstances. Rights of contract, for instance, and civil and other citizenship rights are generally of this type. These rights function in terms of what James Coleman (1990, pp. 52–3) calls a power-weighted consensus.

But there is a class of rights which are claimed precisely in the absence of trust, which by their nature can have no necessary support in law. These are human, or what I would prefer to call basic, rights. These are rights which are claimed when taken for granted and basic necessities of human existence are denied. Basic rights pose particular sociological problems. Whereas rights in general are realized through the acceptance by others of an actor's claim to capacities and entitlements, the notion of human or basic rights holds that individuals, by virtue of their humanity, possess fundamental rights beyond those prescribed in law.

Although sociological interest in the question of rights has been low, there is nothing sociologically opaque about rights as integral to a social fabric of expectations of an actor's due to exercise discursively and consensually defined powers. Human rights, however, seem to be based on something beyond the social fabric of which rights in general partake. They therefore pose the problem of how they might be sociologically grounded. In its own terms, human-rights doctrine assumes that these rights are integral to an aspect of human nature, as opposed to human society. Recent sociological endeavors to explicate human rights have not gone very far beyond this starting point.

Ted Vaughan and Gideon Sjoberg (1986, pp. 138–9), for instance, argue that human rights derive from a universal right to the social conditions of reflexivity, as reflexivity is an "essential characteristic of humankind." Here, the social dimension of the thing is only in the condition required to sustain the right; the right itself is in or derived from an aspect of human nature. This form of argument persists in Bryan Turner's (1993) theory of human rights.

The ontological basis of human rights, according to Turner (1993, p. 501), is in the frailty of the human body and the precariousness of social institutions. The relevance of institutional precariousness to the argument is necessarily secondary, as human frailty includes physical ageing and mortality, factors beyond the reach of even the most caring institution. We will see that Turner's distinction between human nature and social institutions is unsatisfactory for additional reasons. While human rights are founded in the nature of the human body, they are realized, according to Turner (pp. 506–7), in the social facility of sympathy, a collective compassion linking human frailty with human rights.

Turner's reference to the emotional force of sympathy in the realization of human rights is important. This is because it raises the larger question of the place which might be given to emotion in an account of rights. It will be argued in the following, that social emotions other than sympathy, in particular vengefulness and resentment, are more fully implicated in claims to basic rights. The latter emotions are widely regarded as negative forces, and are therefore intuitively unsuitable sources of such positive phenomena as rights. But, as intentionality is a feature of emotion, it is pointless to describe an emotion as negative before knowing to what it is directed. To resent injustice is not negative.

The distinction between the natural and the social, a pervasive if no longer entirely fashionable artifact of Western or modern thought, continues to inform the idea of human rights. Even in its sociological guise, human-rights theory has found it difficult to remove itself wholly from its origins in natural-rights doctrine. The ontology of human rights therefore gravitates to what is natural in humankind rather than to what is social, whether it be psychic reflexivity or physical frailty. The argument of the present chapter, on the other hand, is that humankind is naturally social, and that social transgressions of particular types lead to emotional reactions which form the bases of claims to rights. Here, the ontology of basic rights is in the social (and emotional) reaction to transgressions against established social boundaries which maintain social being.

## Sympathy

Sympathy, Turner says, "is crucial in deciding to whom our moral concern might be directed" (1993, p. 506). Additionally, persons will desire recognition for their rights "because they see in the plight of others their own (possible) misery" (p. 506). The relevance of sympathy to basic rights is thus clear in the fact, as the German philosopher and social theorist Max Scheler put it, that sympathy provides a sense of the reality of others equal to our own reality. It follows, therefore, that sympathy or fellow-feeling entails "acceptance of a common status" (Scheler [1913] 1954, p. 98). In sympathy, then, can be located the emotional realization of the unity of humankind. As sympathy reveals a universality of human need, so it must be regarded as an attribute of human nature. Indeed, the eighteenth-century philosopher David Hume ([1740] 1911, p. 287) describes sympathy as the first principle of human nature.

Some problems with the concept of sympathy in Adam Smith's writing and in liberal theory in general were noted in the previous chapter. The realization of the moral unity of humankind through the emotion of sympathy is indeed a poor foundation for basic rights. There are three reasons for this. First, sympathy is necessarily at one remove from the actual claim to rights. Sympathy is the emotion of the observer, not the violated; in Scheler's terms, sympathy is the ethic of the spectator rather than of the person as such (1913, p. 5). As we shall see in the following, successful claims to basic rights are generally made by the claimants on their own behalf.

Second, sympathy is notoriously unreliable in ensuring the rights of others. Indeed, the violation of rights can be taken to indicate the probable absence of sympathy. The requirement of sympathy is that it is "impossible . . . to be totally indifferent to the well or ill-being" of another, as Hume ([1751] 1962, p. 230) says. While the eighteenth-century moral-sentiment theorists, especially David Hume and Adam Smith ([1759] 1982), held that the moral and social orders were supported principally by sympathy, they were aware that the fragility of sympathy was most apparent when confronted with self-interest.

Hume ([1740] 1911, p. 281), for instance, said that while sympathy might lead one to experience pain when observing another's uneasiness, it would not lead one to sacrifice one's own interest for another's satisfaction. In a later work, in which the significance of sympathy is more consistently and forcefully defended, Hume ([1751] 1962, p. 229) continued to make the point that sympathy "is much fainter than our concern for ourselves, and sympathy with persons remote from us much fainter than with persons near and contiguous."

Hume's point has enormous implications for the role of sympathy in basic rights, for it indicates the fact that particular interests cut across the recognition of universal rights. Communities of interest based on common human needs are consolidated through sympathy, certainly: but this is also to say that it is difficult for sympathy to go beyond the community of interest. This suggests a third limitation of sympathy as a foundation for basic rights, namely that sympathy can be part of the process of the denial of basic rights. This and the other two difficulties with sympathy as a source of basic rights can be demonstrated through a consideration of the case of lynching.

In the Southern states of the United States of America lynching was a non-legal but socially accepted means of preventing improvement in the conditions of the Black population (Cox [1948] 1970, pp. 548–64). Lynching continued to be an aspect of the Southern social system until the early 1960s. In the situation in which lynching was a routinely exercised means of social control there were nevertheless sections of the White population sympathetic to Blacks and their basic rights, that is, opposed to lynching. It was part of the social system in which lynching functioned that the claim to the right not to be lynched was not typically made by Blacks themselves. Massive oppression tended to prevent Blacks from acting on their own behalf. In any event, the stock of White sympathy for Black rights was in short supply: most Whites did not experience a fellow-feeling with Blacks. And, even more telling, the White sympathy which did exist was part of the cycle of lynching which denied Blacks basic rights.

Cox ([1948] 1970, p. 563) explains that individual options within Black communities which faced White lynch-mobs were limited in the extreme. In particular, recourse to legal protection, including the sanctuary of a police station, would symbolize to the mob a Black assertion of rights antithetical to the mob's objectives, and was therefore likely to escalate lynch violence. The only recourse open to Blacks during lynching episodes, therefore, was to seek the protection of sympathetic "White friends" (pp. 550, 563). Yet this practice was a part of the cycle of lynching itself, and served to maintain lynching in the system of social control.

Black reliance on White sympathy for primary security reinforced both White supremacy and Black subservience (Cox [1948] 1970, p. 564). In seeking the protection of sympathetic "White friends," Blacks demonstrated to the White population and acknowledged to themselves that the guarantee of any rights which they might possess derived from their acceptance of the personal authority and guardianship of Whites. In addition, Black indebtedness to White sympathy was repaid with the curtailment within the Black community of any movement of revolt against lynching in particular and White dominance in general.

The social system in which lynching played a pivotal role of control was finally overturned when Black claims to rights were asserted on their own behalf. This could only occur when White sympathy was displaced by open Black resentment in claims for basic rights. In a document contemporary with the cessation of lynching as a means of social control in the South, Louis Lomax notes that the changes which began with reaction to the lynching of Emmett Till, and gained pace through school-integration violence in Little Rock, Arkansas, was achieved with Black acknowledgment of resentment against White injustice (Lomax 1963, p. 87).

The role of resentment cannot be overemphasized in this process; not only is its expression signal in claims to rights, but its suppression is central to the denial of rights. The point is well made by Cox's ([1948] 1970, p. 551, note 9) observation that: "'Law and order' in the South implicitly but resolutely insist that the family, or worse still, Negroes of the community upon whom this appalling atrocity has been committed do nothing to show that they harbor resentment." It was impossible to contain Black resentment against the lynching in Money, Mississippi, in 1955 of Emmett Till, a fourteen-year-old vacationing from Chicago. This was because the Black community involved was for the first time not local but national. The Southern sanctions of White supremacy could not limit the resentment of Blacks outside the South (see Williams 1987, pp. 39–57).

This focus on resentment in providing a foundation for basic rights offers a rather different perspective on rights than that drawn from the argument concerning the role of sympathy in basic rights. Yet it is not entirely unfamiliar. The practice of setting things right draws less on sympathy and more on what William James calls "the hating and fighting impulses." He says that:

where the loving and admiring impulses are dead, the hating and fighting impulses will still respond to fit appeals. This evil which we feel so deeply is something that we can also help to overthrow . . . Life is worth living, no matter what it brings, if only such combats can be carried to successful termination and one's heel set on the tyrant's throat. (James [1897d] 1956, pp. 47, 49)

This statement shifts the focus from sympathy to interest, from other to self. Sympathy implies an interest in others; that an actor cares about others. But attaching the category of care to interest suggests that an actor's caring might support emotions other than sympathy. Hating another indicates an actor's caring about another's transgressions, and about their own interests, and their own rights.

None of this is to say that sympathy has no role in the realization of basic rights, but rather that rights cannot be based primarily on sympathy alone. Max Scheler observed that: "There can be no full development of the higher, though necessarily rarer, emotional powers in man, where the lower but more common ones have not been fully cultivated" ([1913] 1954, pp. 103–4). Without referring to any particular emotional formations, Scheler goes on to say that the failure to acknowledge the lower emotional powers "is to cut away the ultimate roots upon which all the 'higher' forms of sympathetic and emotional life depend for their subsistence" (p. 104). In the context, Scheler is suggesting that, in order to cultivate love, lust must be experienced, felt, and understood. If sympathy is to support basic rights, resentment must be given its due.

It was mentioned earlier that the possession of a right is the realization of a claim made on others and accepted by them. This is the source of the essentially rhetorical nature of rights. It is also the basis of the possibility that claims to rights may be made on behalf of others, as well as by actors on their own behalf. It has been argued that sympathy, as compassion or benevolence, is an inadequate basis for claims to rights. This is only partly because such claims are necessarily made on behalf of others. The conclusion of the discussion so far, however, that the effective claim to rights is based on the resentment of the violated rather than the sympathy of the observer, requires two qualifications.

The preceding argument is not to dismiss sympathy from a consideration of rights. Claims to rights only fully succeed when they are accepted by others, and sympathy must play a role in this. But the idea that sympathy means only compassion or benevolence, as in Hume and also Turner, for instance, is not sufficient. Clearly, compassion for others is important when it arises, but it does not arise reliably in human affairs. Hume's contemporary, Adam Smith ([1759] 1982, p. 10), saw sympathy not as "pity" for another's "sorrow" but as shared feelings in a wider sense, including feelings of resentment, as we shall see.

Sympathy in the Smithian sense continues to provide a place for the observer in claims to rights, but it means that the primary claimant has a role larger than merely to suffer. It has been shown that an active claim to basic rights arises in expressions of resentment against injustice by those so violated. This leads to the second qualification of the preceding discussion. The basis of a claim to basic rights through moral anger against injury includes not merely expressions of resentment but also vengefulness. This qualification will be elaborated in what follows.

### Vengefulness and resentment

There should be nothing exceptional in the proposition that emotion is implicated in basic rights, or, for that matter, in any other aspect of the social process. To summarize relevant aspects of preceding discussion: emotions are generally thought of as feelings and sensations. Emotion includes these, certainly. But, unlike mere feeling and sensation, an emotion has direction and therefore an object. Although their emotions do not automatically set a person on a course of action, they do leave a clear stamp on an actor's disposition and intentions. Emotions situate actors in their relations with others. Actors are moved in their interactions with others by their emotions, and their emotions lead them to evaluate and change the course of their conduct in the relationships and situations they face. It is through their emotions that actors are engaged by others, and through their emotions that they alter their relations with them.

Subjection to arbitrary power, punishment when there should be reward, frustrated attempts to satisfy needs: these are sets of relationships which are likely to be experienced through strong emotions, including depression, fear, and anger. In any event, it is difficult to conceive of an actor's engagement in such circumstances except through their emotional assessment of where they stand and their emotional appraisal of a desirable direction in which the situation might be taken.

A likely reaction to subordination, unfair treatment, or denial of satisfaction of need may be avoidance or flight, what Barrington Moore has called "one of the common man's most frequent and effective responses to oppression" (1978, p. 125). Another possibility mentioned by Moore is vengeance:

Vengeance means retaliation. It also means a reassertion of human dignity or worth, after injury or damage. Both are basic sentiments behind moral anger and the sense of injustice. Vengeance is a way of evening things out, and of course one that never works completely. There is no such thing as a complete restoration of injuries once inflicted. Vengeance may be the most primitive form of moral outrage. But if primitive, it is also highly contemporary. (p. 17)

Vengeance, then, is the active apprehension of both injury and a desire for retribution; it is a sentiment or emotion directed to setting things right.

Vengefulness and resentment are frequently treated together as forms or expressions of moral anger associated with claims to basic rights. The details of their association, however, and therefore of their particular contributions to claims to rights, are not always clearly indicated. But, before treating the distinctions between them, it is important to acknowledge the agreement in discussions of these emotions, with one exception, that they are the source of rights or justice. For instance, Adam Smith describes resentment and revenge as "the guardians of justice, and of the equality of its administration" ([1759] 1982, p. 35); William McDougall similarly says that vengefulness "has been one of the principal sources of the institution of public justice" ([1908] 1948, p. 120). Robert Solomon (1991) makes a similar case for both vengefulness and resentment.

Against this current Friedrich Nietzsche acknowledged that resentment "[attempts] to sanctify revenge under the name of justice," but he believed that the acceptance of such a view was the result of false consciousness or self-deception ([1887] 1992, pp. 509–10). Nietzsche did accept that resentment, or what he called *ressentiment*, had moral force. In his critique of the Judeo-Christian tradition, however, he regarded resentment as historically the basis of "slave" morality and priestly power, forces to which he was opposed; and in his own day he saw resentment most frequently given expression by "anarchists and anti-semites," types he thought despicable (p. 509). The institution of law, for Nietzsche, is not so much the result of resentment as a means of displacing it; law takes "the object of *ressentiment* out of the hands of revenge" and establishes independent norms for the restitution of injury (p. 511).

Nietzsche's rejection of resentment's contribution to claims to rights – he acknowledges that it represents only an illusion of such a claim – derives in part from his conceptualization of resentment as significantly passive. When discussing what he calls the "actual physiological cause" of resentment, Nietzsche says it is not to "prevent any further injury" but rather to "deaden pain by means of affects" ([1887] 1992, p. 563). It performs this latter function by spitefully blaming others for one's own suffering. Nietzsche's strong individualism requires that one is responsible for one's own suffering. The connections and imputations implicit in resentment, therefore, are disallowed by him. The idea that resentment is not active in preventing further injury but anesthetic in deadening the pain of past injury is continuous with the idea that resentment arises in those denied action or "deeds, and [who] compensate themselves with an *imaginary* revenge" (p. 472, emphasis added).

It will be shown here that Nietzsche's view of the essential passivity of resentment is not readily supported by evidence or argument. It has already been shown to be so in the case of lynching, in which Black passivity was reversed with an acknowledgment of resentment, which was in turn associated with a rise of Black activism. Thus an implicit distinction between resentment and vengefulness, which supposes that the former arises in inaction and the latter in manifest deeds, does not meaningfully distinguish between them. Neither does the distinction proposed by William McDougall, that resentment is the emotion associated with action taken immediately to avenge insult, whereas "vengeful emotion" arises in an unsatisfied desire to settle a score ([1908] 1948, p. 120). A third possibility, suggested by Adam Smith, that resentment is the passion attached to revenge, which is the action ([1759] 1982, pp. 34–5), is also rejected here. A firmer basis of distinction between resentment and vengefulness is required, which indicates the contribution of each to basic rights.

In the quotation from Barrington Moore, given earlier, vengeance was described as an emotion associated with a reassertion of dignity after injury. In an even more pointed description of its qualities, Robert Solomon highlights the personal involvement in action to get even, which he says is implicit in vengefulness, and which distinguishes it from mere anger and also from resentment (1991, pp. 256–7). A residual Nietzschism gives more emphasis to action and less to personal involvement, but it is the latter which is primary in the characterization of vengefulness and in distinguishing it from resentment. In his excellent but neglected discussion of what he calls "vengeful emotion" McDougall ([1908] 1948, pp. 120–4) reinforces just this point when he describes vengefulness as anger developed in connection with the self-regarding sentiment (pp. 120, 123).

McDougall offers a relational account of the cause of vengefulness: "The act that, more certainly than any other, provokes vengeful emotion is the public insult, which . . . lowers one in the eyes of one's fellows. Such an insult calls out one's positive self-feeling, with its impulse to assert oneself and to make good one's value and power in the public eye" ([1908] 1948, p. 120). According to this account, vengefulness arises in relations in which the subject's regard for themselves is injured. On one level it could be said that the subject is shamed, not by what they have done but by what is done to them by coercive force or power. The second phase in the development of vengefulness is the subject's anger directed toward the infliction of reciprocal injury in order to reassert the subject's own power in the relationship and thereby restore their own self-regard or standing.

The injury inflicted by power in the first stage of the formation of vengefulness may take a number of possible forms. Personal physical injury, financial disadvantage or being cheated, political out-maneuvering, social neglect, and so on, are all consequences of an exercise of power in which the subject may lose an aspect of what they regard, in the context of their social interactions, as a self-defining attribute. The second stage of the formation of vengefulness is the subject's emotional disposition to restore their previous position substantively and also in the structure of power relationships. This is not only to undo the injury itself but to inflict an analogous injury or punishment on those who wielded power against them.

Vengefulness in claims to rights operates at both the collective and the individual levels. A neglected aspect of social movements, for instance, is vengefulness against the agents of subordination, indeed, humiliation, which movements oppose in asserting the dignity and standing, the rights, of their members. Impolite as it might be, getting even with patriarchs, White supremacists, foreign corporations, and so on is an important, even unavoidable aspect of social-movement claims for rights. Treatments which neglect this aspect of the process and instead focus on cultural expressivity or resource mobilization define social movements teleologically and ignore their basic animus.

At the individual level, what Erving Goffman (1952) describes as the need to "cool the mark out," demonstrates the likelihood of vengeful anger if a social injury is not made by its perpetrators to seem inevitable. The corollary is that, without such manipulations of the situation, social injury typically promotes vengefulness in the victim's attempts to set things right.

Vengefulness is an emotion of power relations. It functions to correct imbalanced or disjointed power relationships. Vengefulness is concerned with restoring social actors to their rightful place in relationships. It is therefore both an appeal against an abrogation of rights and an assertion of an actor's rights both to their accepted position and to punish those who would dispossess them of their rightful place.

While some writers, including McDougall, treat resentment as continuous with vengefulness, it should in fact be regarded as a quite different emotion. Resentment converges with vengefulness in being concerned with basic rights, but it differs from it in being implicated in non-coercive relations rather than only in power relations, and by not requiring such a directly personal involvement in subordination and retaliation.

One problem for an understanding of resentment is that certain of its secondary and contingent features are frequently regarded as its defining characteristics. For instance, the object of resentment, following Nietzsche, is often understood to be power (Solomon 1991, p. 264), but, as we shall see, the connection between resentment and power is indirect. The object of resentment, in fact, is not power but normative elements of social order. The interactional basis of resentment is a third party's gain in status which a social actor evaluates as undeserved (Kemper 1978, p. 111; Ortony, Clore, and Collins [1988] 1990, p. 100; Solomon 1991, p. 248). Resentment, then, is the emotional apprehension of advantage gained at the expense of what is desirable or acceptable from the perspective of established rights.

A particular case which brings out the nuanced complexion of resentment is provided by James Scott's (1985) discussion of peasant politics in Malaysia. In emerging tenancy arrangements, consequent upon the mechanization of agriculture, landlords increasingly lease land to rich rather than poor tenants, thus marginalizing erstwhile modest producers into unproductive destitution. Poor agriculturalists are predominantly ethnic Malay, while many of the usurpatory tenants are ethnic Chinese. Nevertheless, "the bitterest resentment," Scott (p. 168) says, "is reserved for the Malay landlords." This is because poor Malays, even though outbid and displaced by richer Chinese tenants, have no expectation that Chinese practices be other than utilitarian and profit directed. But in making land available to Chinese rather than Malay tenants, Malay landlords betray their obligations to friends, neighbors, and relatives (pp. 168–9).

Whereas vengefulness is driven by self-regard, resentment is driven by regard for an externally accepted set of standards, values, or norms, which in the preceding case were contravened by the Malay landlords. Whereas vengefulness serves to repair an injury suffered by the actor, there is no necessity in resentment that the other's advantage be gained at the particular actor's expense. That the Chinese tenants are advantaged over Malay tenants is resented by Malays who do not necessarily aspire to tenancy. Resentment, then, is based not on personal involvement so much as personal insight in the disjuncture between social rights and social outcomes.

Having insisted that resentment does not require a personal loss, we should notice that the intensity of resentment increases when another's unjust gain is at the actor's own expense (Ortony, Clore, and Collins [1988] 1990, pp. 100–1). The strongest resentment was felt by usurped

Malay tenants. It is not erroneous, therefore, to treat an actor's resentment in terms of their own loss (as Smith, Nietzsche, and McDougall do), but it is misleading to treat that contingency as necessary, because it would suggest an unwarranted integration of resentment and vengefulness.

While resentment is primarily focussed on advantage gained through some contravention of social norms or rights, associated with outcome or procedure, the agent of such improper advantage may also be the subject of an actor's resentment. This is especially likely when the other is responsible for their own undesirable advantage. It is at this point that power and also blame may come into the account of resentment, but again as contingent rather than defining characteristics. Another's undeserved advantage may arise from their own power or that of a third person. If the power is that of a third person (the boss who gives the salary rise to an undeserving colleague) then the emotional apprehension of the situation is contempt for the powerful actor, not resentment (Ortony, Clore, and Collins [1988] 1990, p. 103). And if the other's advantage raised by a third person's power is to the actor's own disadvantage, then vengefulness rather than contempt joins resentment.

These last remarks indicate how resentment readily reinforces vengefulness, and also suggests how vengefulness may almost always be experienced together with resentment, even though situations in which resentment arises do not necessarily attract vengefulness in the same way. Resentment is not necessarily an emotion of subordination, nor attached to a desire for retaliation, as vengefulness is; rather, it is an emotional apprehension of departure from acceptable, desirable, proper, and rightful outcomes and procedures. It is more directly focussed on rights than is vengefulness, which is instead focussed on injury, and it therefore orientates vengefulness to the dislocation of rights in which the injury occurs. Where vengefulness punishes transgressions of power, resentment, when it addresses power at all, exposes its hypocrisy. Vengefulness is necessarily concerned with an actor's own particular rights, injured through subordination to power. Resentment is more disinterestedly concerned with patterns of rights, and engaged by undeserved advantages arising from the disregard or disruption of those rights.

All this seems to paint vengefulness and resentment in rosy hues. But it has to be acknowledged that they are in fact unavoidably emotions of ill-will, and as readily associated with malevolence as with rights. They have variously been called "vindictive emotions" (Solomon 1991, p. 256), "distasteful" emotions (Ortony, Clore, and Collins [1988] 1990, p. 100), and the "disagreeable passion[s]" (Smith [1759] 1982, p. 15).

The pathological forms of vengeance and resentment, measured by their departure from the constructive realm of basic rights, places them in the destructive world of feud and vendetta. This latter, which is removed from our theme of rights, is the one most usually treated in accounts of vengefulness and retaliation. Indeed, a sizeable literature which discusses "societies of honor and shame," especially in the Mediterranean region (Peristiany 1965), but not exclusively, understands the feud in terms of what have been called "character contests" (Goffman 1967, pp. 239–58). It has been necessary, however, to paint these distasteful emotions into a different picture from the ones in which they are usually shown. This is because while vengefulness may be central to bloody feud, it also plays a crucial but neglected role in justifiable anger and claims to basic rights.

The balance in such claims between the fact that vengefulness and resentment are disagreeable in their "immediate effects" as "mischief to the person against whom they are directed," and agreeable only in their "remote effects," as Adam Smith ([1759] 1982, p. 35) puts it, is struck by the particular circumstances and objects in which these emotions are expressed.

In Smith's discussion, the issue is the structure of sympathy. The question is whether an observer's sympathy will be with the resenter or the resented ([1759] 1982, pp. 34–8). The "gratification of resentment [is] completely agreeable," says Smith, when the "spectator thoroughly sympathize[s] with our revenge" (p. 38). He goes on to say that the "only motive which can ennoble the expressions of this disagreeable passion" is "a regard to maintain our own rank and dignity in society" (p. 38). It is in the defence of publicly understood and accepted social standing that vengefulness and resentment can find sympathetic support. Otherwise, those subject to the vengefulness and resentment of others will draw sympathy. A further possibility is the withholding of sympathy from either party. This became Mercutio's response to the feud between the Montagues and the Capulets: "A plague o' both your houses."

In effect, Smith argues that persons do have a right to maintain their own rank and dignity in society. The connection between such a right and the disagreeable passions is suggested by Robert Solomon's statement that: "the notion of rights requires an almost visceral sense of inviolability, absolute unacceptability of certain intrusions, interferences, offenses. But it isn't the right which explains the inviolability; it is the sense of inviolability that accounts for the ascription of rights" (1991, p. 244). The active recognition that a person has been subject to intrusion, interference, and offense is precisely in their acting with moral anger, and in circumscribed manifestations of vengefulness and resentment.

## Basic needs in society

The inviolability which accounts for the ascription of rights is the inviolability of need. The satisfaction of needs is the constituting requirement of being. Thus violation of the satisfaction of needs produces a passion which claims a right. Basic rights therefore require basic needs. The problem with human needs, however, is the unavoidable irony of cultural variation, in which the acquired is held to be the constitutional need. In society, therefore, the distinction between need and want or desire tends to be arbitrary if not contingent.

One possible solution to the vagary of need in culture is to ground it in nature, and in particular in the physical nature of the human body. Human subsistence is taken to provide a baseline from which human frailty can be deduced, and either one of these might be taken as a standard against which basic rights can be measured (Solomon 1991, p. 187; Turner 1993, p. 180). Yet the limitations of this approach have not gone unnoticed (Sen 1982, pp. 12–14). "To say that 'our only initial datum is the body'," as Max Scheler puts it, "is completely erroneous." This is because, as he went on to indicate, the "relation . . . is a *symbolic* not a causal one" ([1913] 1954, p. 10, emphasis in original). That the relation is not causal means that human nature is not so readily separated from society, and that human frailty is not merely a condition of the body, so much as a symbolic reflection of the social condition.

At the most rudimentary level, natural or physical needs include the need for clean air and water, adequate nourishment, and freedom from pain. Yet the failure to have even these needs satisfied could not in itself lead to a claim to basic rights. This is because the satisfaction of physical need is socially mediated. Not even physical pain is a merely natural or basic phenomenon. Tolerance for the most extreme pain can be socially learned (Moore 1978, p. 79). All that is required is that pain be perceived as inevitable (Lockwood 1982; Moore 1978, pp. 438, 458). Under circumstances in which pain is regarded as inevitable and without apparent social or, more properly, political cause, pain may be accorded legitimacy; and resignation toward such pain can become a source of pride (Moore 1978, pp. 61, 458–9). These things make of suffering a strong conservative force undermining any claim to basic rights against pain.

A discussion of needs, led by a concern for rights, can easily ignore a category of human needs in addition to the physical. These are nurturing needs, the need for love and respect. Like the physical needs, the nurturing needs relate to individual satisfactions, but unlike physical needs they point in the direction of a need for social and not only physical exchanges. Nurturing needs are the needs an actor feels for others. Yet even this formulation inadequately appreciates the significance of nurturing needs, for in the human condition the nurturing needs link the physical and the social and indicate the social form of human nature, as we shall see.

A third category of need, then, can be identified, in addition to the physical and nurturing needs. This is the need for society, the need for collective and cooperative activity. This category of need is often overlooked because of the unfounded but continuing separation in thought of nature and society. According to this mistaken view, needs are with nature, wants with society. Barrington Moore's (1978, p. 8) statement that the "need to cooperate with other human beings produces a new and distinct system of causation for human behavior" captures the significance of social need but unnecessarily reconfirms the ontological separation of nature and society by referring to it as a "*new . . .* system of causation" (emphasis added). This is not a new phenomenon which arises in the course of human history but is original to the human condition, original to humankind. The need for society explains the special quality of physical and nurturing needs in humans, which have just been mentioned.

Moore's discussion of the human need for cooperation is strikingly reminiscent of David Hume's argument in *A Treatise of Human Nature*, concerning the origins of justice ([1740] 1911, Book III, Part II, Section 2). Like Moore, Hume begins with the observation that, in Moore's words, as "a biological specimen man's individual capacities to cope with the environment are quite unimpressive" (1978, p. 8), but "all his infirmities are compensated," says Hume, "by society" ([1740] 1911, p. 191). Thus a new and unnatural "artifice" is created by a "convention" in order to supplement the natural deficiencies of humankind (pp. 194–5). Society, according to this view, is an artificial adjunct to natural propensities. Hume argues that an awareness of the advantages of society occur to natural man and woman in the "natural appetite betwixt the sexes . . . [and] in their concern for their common offspring" (p. 192). For Hume, the natural family as a region of cooperation and care is a microscopic anticipation of artificial society.

But this historical fiction and the distinction it insists upon are unfounded and unnecessary. As, for instance, Ian Suttie (1935) and John Bowlby (1969, 1973, 1980) have shown in the development of Attachment Theory, sociality is not merely suggested by child–parent relations but is innate in them, and in that sense the human capacity for social relations is derived from biologically based needs. The Darwinian understanding, that humans are animals, is in this context used to show that the divide between nature and society is intellectually untenable, by demonstrating that humankind is naturally social. The view that humankind is naturally social was in fact expressed in a pre-Darwinian form by Hume's contemporaries, Adam Ferguson ([1767] 1966, pp. 16–19) and Adam Smith ([1759] 1982, p. 85). The need for social cooperation is a human need on the same level as the needs for nourishment and nurture.

The need for society, then, is a natural human need, which does not simply and contingently coexist with innate physical needs of human beings. Not only are the means of satisfying biological needs almost entirely subject to social variability, but expressions of the consequences of contraventions of physical need are also socially variable. It was shown earlier that pain and suffering cannot be reliable guides to unattended physical needs because social learning not only diminishes pain, but may produce it. Basic rights, therefore, are more likely to be commensurate with the need for society than with physical needs born of the frailty of the human body. The meaning which frailty may possess is given to it socially.

The violations which provoke emotions claiming a basic right can therefore be seen as violations of the satisfaction of the need to cooperate with other human beings. Claims to basic rights arise out of the anger provoked by breaches of established practices or rules of social cooperation, which include breaches of status. It is not the mere fact of a death, the loss of crops, or the destruction of a dwelling which leads to a claim for basic rights. It is the understanding that such events arise through violations of conditions of social being. Every human being, except those disqualified by immaturity, infirmity, or insanity, inevitably occupies a status position through being located in various socially cooperative activities. It is these that are basic to social – it should be said, human – existence. The concept of status is used here for purposes which will be elaborated in the following. The important point at this stage of the argument is conveyed by the term breaches of status, and its association with Harold Garfinkel's breaching experiments (Garfinkel 1967).

The significance of the breaching experiments have never been properly explored, because the cognitive focus of ethnomethodology ignores the emotional dimension of the experiments, and what it offers for interpretation. The suggestion here is not that Garfinkel was unaware of emotion. Indeed, he says that his procedure was "to produce and sustain bewilderment, consternation, and confusion; to produce the socially structured affects of anxiety, shame, guilt, and indignation; and to produce disorganized interaction [which] should tell us something about how the structure of everyday activities are ordinarily and routinely produced and maintained" (Garfinkel 1967, p. 38). But the emotional component of the breaching experiments was simply part of a device to provoke challenges to cognitive understandings. It was the structure and reproduction of these cognitive understandings which were the real focus of Garfinkel's concern.

The experiments which Garfinkel's students performed were to investigate the texture of taken-for-granted and common-sense knowledge which underlies mundane conduct. Mundane conduct is based on practically established and publicly accepted patterns of expectation (Garfinkel 1967, pp. 53–4). By breaching these patterns of expectation in various ways, the experiments demonstrated the propensity of social actors faced with discrepant behaviors to attempt to normalize the situation and return to the form of social exchanges reliant upon established cognitive expectations (p. 42). The expression of hostility to breaches in expected conduct are therefore to re-establish meaning in perceived environments, and to refuse the apparent senselessness of breached expectations of understanding.

Garfinkel was aware that breaches of expectation or abrogations of trust typically produced anger in social actors, and he commented on the "strong relationship between common understandings and social affects" (Garfinkel 1967, p. 50). But, because he was committed to the view that actors are engaged by the meaningfulness of everyday activities, Garfinkel entertained only the notion that common-sense knowledge and understandings were implicated in mundane conduct and order. This is a purely cognitive universe in which the epistemological consequences and potential purpose of emotion must be disruptive. But the evidence of the breaching experiments demonstrates that violations of publicly accepted patterns of expectation, which might technically be called roles, typically generate a sense of outrage, and a feeling of moral anger.

The situations the breaching experiments address include the meanings social actors assume in their practical understandings of appropriate behavior in given interactions or social exchanges. In a different terminology, then, the breaching experiments denied social actors' role expectations. The concept role refers to the repertoire of possible behaviors associated with social position in the cooperative relations constitutive of society, that is, associated with social standing or status. The terms role and status have an unfortunately *passé* ring about them, and in sociology they have more or less fallen into disuse. They are resurrected here because in considering a social-emotions approach to basic rights, it is necessary to distinguish between the principles and rules of social relations, of cooperative or reciprocal activities, on the one hand, and the positions social actors occupy within them, on the other.

The category status has been diminished in two ways over the last fifty years or so. First, it has come to mean almost exclusively stratificatory status. The Weberian version of this, in referring to prestige and deference, retains something of the conventional character of status, but loses the connection between status and social capacities or rights which are necessary to the category. Second, the vernacular focus on role has been at the expense of any analytic value in the category of status. Status is the social-relational location or place in social structure which anchors role. But in a society in which voluntaristic scripts play a predominant ideological function, the category status has atrophied.

Role refers to possibilities of individual action. In a climate of supposed individual autonomy the concept of role has come to suggest a much higher degree of plasticity than the notion of status itself could permit. In late-capitalist societies, roles appear to be freely chosen, and their performance determined by the personal interpretations their incumbents invent. The social character of status is almost totally lost through the highly ideological associations which have come to the category of role.

But, as the breaching experiments indicate, there are quite clear and distinct boundaries to statuses, which, when breached, provoke strong expressions of grievance and moral anger. This conclusion deserves to be generalized from the level of face-to-face interaction to that of the social division of labor, for the same principles operate. The fabric of society is made up of sets of expectations about the capacities or powers of and the entitlements associated with different social positions. The boundaries between different statuses are never final, and they can only be known at any given time by social actors seeing just how far they can go. But, at the end of the day, it is clear that the particular capacities and entitlements associated with a particular status are bounded by convention and practice, and that if such boundaries are breached, then the social existence of the incumbent is felt to be threatened.

When the boundaries of social actors' statuses are breached and the capabilities associated with them disrupted, then a moral outrage and anger prefigures and energizes their claims to rights which are to restore the means of their social existence (Smith [1759] 1982, pp. 79–80). The assertion of right in breaches of status typically takes the form of vengefulness, as was demonstrated earlier. But changes in the principles and rules of socially cooperative and reciprocal action, of social relationships, occur in which an actor's own status need not be directly at risk. These too are likely to provoke moral anger and a sense of injustice in social actors (Moore 1978, pp. 5, 20, 23, 34, 43, 455), which will typically take the form of resentment. As we have seen, resentment is also associated with claims to basic rights. The social emotions of vengefulness and resentment direct and energize claims to basic rights, which are to restore the fragile balance on which social life is always suspended.

## Historical origins and end of basic rights

As social forms change through time, so the category of basic rights, the context in which claims to such rights arise, and the ways in which vengefulness and resentment are efficacious in promoting claims to rights, will also be subject to historical variation. The question of the institutionalization of basic rights has been avoided in the discussion up to this point. In concluding this account of the bases of claims to rights it is necessary to turn to the historical origins and current state of the social organization of basic rights.

The historical institutionalization of basic rights was coterminous with the collapse of the *ancien régime*. The Declaration of Independence of what became the fourteen United States of America in 1776, was the first national document formally to incorporate the idea of human rights, in its claim, as a self-evident truth, that there are "certain unalienable rights." In 1789, a Declaration of the Rights of Man and of Citizens was adopted by the National Assembly of France. It held that "ignorance, neglect, or contempt of human rights, are the sole causes of public misfortunes and corruptions of Government" and that these rights are "natural, impre-scriptible, and unalienable."

In a contemporary explication of these early developments Thomas Paine explained that persons "in right of [their] existence" naturally possess "all those rights of acting as an individual for [their] own comfort and happiness" ([1791] 1992, p. 39). In society, and by contract, those natural rights which individuals possess but are unable to secure for themselves, become converted into civil rights. Paine draws three conclusions concerning the relations between natural and civil rights. First, civil rights are dependent upon natural rights; second, civil rights serve "the purpose of every one"; and, third, individuals do not lose their natural rights by virtue of living in civil society, and civil rights, therefore, "cannot be applied to invade . . . natural rights" (p. 40).

Paine's conclusion, that individuals, by virtue of their humanity, possess fundamental rights beyond those prescribed by law, is embodied today in documents of international organizations. In particular, the Universal Declaration of Human Rights, adopted by the General Assembly of the United Nations in 1948, through its various covenants and protocols, has now acquired the status of an international treaty. In addition, the European Court of Human Rights, established within the framework of the European Convention for the Protection of Human Rights and Fundamental Freedoms, promulgated in 1953, has binding powers over national states (Weissbrodt 1988).

While Paine and the eighteenth-century revolutionary constitutions of the US and France may be seen as precursors of present-day institutionalizations of basic rights, it should not be forgotten that Paine's *Rights of Man* was the culmination of a doctrinal development which occupied two hundred years of philosophical and political debate. The work of Grotius, Locke, Rousseau, and others reflected economic and political changes which were given expression in reconceptualizations of law and of nature. The historian R. H. Tawney summarizes these developments in this way:

The law of nature had been invoked by medieval writers as a moral restraint upon economic self-interest. By the seventeenth century a significant revolution had taken place. "Nature" had come to connote, not divine ordinance, but human appetites, and natural rights were invoked by the individualism of the age as a reason why self-interest should be given free play. ([1926] 1948, p. 183)

The modern understanding of human rights, in Tawney's account, has its origins in the market economy which replaced the customary and local economy of feudal society.

In the simplifying terminology of Henry Maine, the advent of human rights therefore corresponds with the predominance of contract over status ([1884] 1905, p. 151). By status is meant here not merely the position of a person in relations of social cooperation, but rather their dependence upon and extrinsic control by familial and traditional superordination (pp. 147–51). Under these circumstances a larger network of support than the restitutive actions of individual initiative maintain the standing of persons in the social relations in which they are located.

Indeed, the constitution of persons in these conditions, and the restraints upon them, preclude the possibility of self-interested action which might violate or defend a person's standing in relation to others. It is not that social harm could not occur, but that if it did two possibilities arose, neither of which could invoke a response similar to a claim to modern basic rights. First, the social institutions themselves would be the locus of a corrective assertion of right, and the injury would not be experienced as personal. Second, the events would be regarded as beyond the control of the persons involved in them, and therefore moral anger would fail to arise for want of direction. In neither case could a modern natural right be claimed.

With the dual processes of political centralization and market expansion, including the creation of labor markets, the structure of social standing or status underwent fundamental change, and self-interested action was now not only possible but necessary if individuals were to maintain their particular standing relative to others. Under these circumstances, persons would experience violations to their status as threats to their social being, and were thereby moved by vengefulness and resentment against the social agents of the challenges to their standing and the violation of their means to social existence.

The social fabric is now experienced as a weave of individual propensities and capacities, each set of which constitutes the arena of the person's universe of social existence. These propensities and capacities are limited in various ways, and the furthest reach of their extent is the boundary of the social actor's competency. Any breach of this boundary and any interference in the actor's legitimate practices within it would be experienced as a violation of their social existence. Such interferences promote in the actor a response which in its affective or emotional expression is given in the form of vengefulness against the violator and resentment against the violation, and in its political expression would be a claim to basic rights.

In the large historical changes which have intensified the processes begun with political centralization and market extension, the parameters of individual social existence have expanded by becoming more abstract, but also contracted through fragmentation. There is increasing impersonality of social existence, a process associated with an increase in the numbers of social encounters and their frequency. At the same time, an intensification of the social and technical divisions of labor means that these more generalized relations are made of smaller pieces. An adequate short-hand for these developments, described by Ferdinand Tönnies, is the movement from *Gemeinschaft* to *Gesellschaft*. These continuing changes make the boundaries of social being narrower in their scope because more specialized and numerous, and also more fragile because more abstract and thin.

One consequence of these developments is that the possibilities of encroachment on and violation of the limits of social existence of individuals is necessarily increased. This increase arises from changes in the structure and pattern of social boundaries themselves, and not from an increase in grievous activity. This development is sufficient to account for a rise in vengefulness and resentment among individuals through an increased fragmentation of status, experienced as role proliferation and apparent role choice. It also accounts, therefore, for the increased propensity of persons to claim basic rights over what in the past might have been regarded as trivial transgressions.

The major consequence of this is to render less effective the vocabulary of rights in political practices. The proliferation and trivialization of claims to rights which is commonplace today is not an "abuse" of the rights vocabulary, as some writers claim (Solomon 1991, p. 191). Rather, it is a consequence of the necessary connection between particular emotional reactions to violations of social standing under conditions of societal fragmentation of status.

## Conclusion

The argument developed in the preceding elaborates four basic propositions. First, social action is best understood as an emotional process. Emotions are emergent in social relationships and constitute a source of change within them. Second, a basic human need is for social existence. The boundaries of individual social being are the extent of a social actor's propensities and capacities. For social being to be secure, the boundaries of and standing within collective and cooperative activity are experienced as inviolable.

These two propositions combine to produce a third, namely that violations of the conditions of social being generate emotional patterns which direct the action of the injured actor to restore their social standing. The emotions implicated in this are typically vengefulness and resentment, which relate to power and normative aspects of the situation, respectively. Finally, the principles of collective and social cooperation, and the structure of standing within them, are historically variable. Thus the precipitants of vengefulness and resentment, and of claims to basic rights, will differ under different social conditions.

# 7   Fear and change

Fear is an incapacitating emotion. But that it is necessarily so is questioned in this chapter. Indeed, the idea that fear leads to an actor's realization of where their interests lie, and points in the direction of what might be done to achieve them, is not forced or artificial. These are the aspects of fear emphasized in the discussion to follow.

The conventional view of fear, that it does inhibit action and prevents rather than directs change, is given expression in Darwin's classic characterization of it. Darwin's account of fear is examined in the following. Certain of its assumptions, and especially the claim that fear is a reaction to danger, are then considered. The difference between the cause of fear and its object is noted in order to specify that to which in general fear is a reaction. In this vein the substance of the concept of threat is clarified and the temporal object of fear indicated.

The nature of social fear is next discussed. This topic relates to not only what is feared, but also by whom. The formal constitution of groups is considered in order to develop the notion of an emotional climate, and especially a climate of fear. Fear is caused by an incapacity to deal with danger or threat. But it is not only powerless social actors who experience fear. Elites may fear that their privileged position is threatened when the system they dominate undergoes a relative shift in power relations. Indeed, it is likely that elites will frequently experience fear.

The conventional understanding is that a power deficit will lead to fear, which is experienced either as withdrawal or counter-challenge, as flight or fight. Elite fear raises another possibility, however. Elites may attempt to contain the threat they fear. Such containment activity produces organizational innovation and development. This is to say that elite fear typically provokes containment behavior, which in turn produces change.

After exploring containment as a form of fear behavior, and its implications for social and organizational change, this chapter provides an empirical demonstration of the argument. It does this through a discussion of the British elite's fear of the labor movement during the period of the First World War and its immediate aftermath. In its endeavors to contain the threat it feared, the British political elite initiated a number of key social and political changes. These not only reorganized the labor movement, but also the structure of the state itself. By doing these things the British elite was able to allay its fear of labor.

## Introduction

The importance of fear to both the constitution of interest and the direction of action is practically axiomatic for an understanding of social behavior. Max Weber's point, that action in a political community is "determined by highly robust motives of fear and hope" (Weber [1921b] 1970, p. 79), succinctly indicates the manner in which an actor's operational assessment of present circumstances can be influenced by expectations of either painful disadvantage or pleasurable advantage.

The primary significance of fear is not diminished by Weber's reference to both fear and hope. It is true, as the philosopher Baruch Spinoza ([1677] 1970, p. 131) argued long ago, that fear and hope each implicates the other, as negative expectations are structured by positive possibilities, and vice versa (see also Ortony, Clore, and Collins [1988] 1990, pp. 112–18). Yet, as their fears express a subject's vulnerability in a relationship, they therefore constitute an imperative for the subject to consider their options and an incentive for them to effect those changes which will more adequately serve their interests.

Such realizations, of where a subject's interests lie and what changes in their present circumstances are desirable in order to achieve them, seldom occur when the predominant emotions are infused with satisfaction concerning the status quo (for a discussion of Weber's awareness of such a point in a different context, see Barbalet 1980, pp. 415–16). It is for these reasons that fear has special relevance to an understanding of interested action.

Although it is seldom acknowledged, an explanation of socio-political change as a consequence of action stimulated by fear can be located at the very center of the Western tradition of political analysis. Thomas Hobbes, in *Leviathan*, did not only develop an argument about the origins of a sovereign commonwealth ([1651] 1962, pp. 87–90), but also discussed the nature and significance of the passions (pp. 23–30). These concerns are not unconnected in his account. Fear, born of a life which is "nasty, brutish and short," is served by reason, according to Hobbes, in the institutional innovation of the original building of the political state. One does not have to eat the whole Hobbesian pie to savor one of its cherries.

While the concept of fear, it will be shown, has an obvious place in accounts of social and political change, there is in fact an absence of such a discussion of fear and of its significance for change. Indeed, the way in which fear is discussed in the literatures which treat it points in the opposite direction. The relevance of fear to constructive aspects of social processes is almost wholly ignored. Instead, its contribution to individual motivation and behavior is typically depicted as leading to withdrawal if not inertia or paralysis on the one hand, and displacement-anger or even rage on the other.

The conceptualization of the consequences of fear as flight and fight is inadequate, however. It will be shown that a third possibility, containment, is typically implicated in responses to fear which have both a social object and are experienced inter-subjectively as an aspect of collective processes. The discussion to follow will also show that these processes may relate to both subordinate and elite groups. Relative power disparities frequently lead to elite fear. It will be shown that subsequent containment behaviors produce organizational change.

In order to indicate its significance for social and political change, it is first necessary to consider the conventional conceptualization and understanding of fear. As currently formulated, these have nothing to offer an argument about the social capacity of fear to realize organizational change, even though the good sense of such an argument is readily demonstrated.

### Fear as a basic emotion

While fear can be a positive and dynamic force in social relationships for organizational innovation and change, the most frequent representation of it indicates the opposite. Indeed, the classic description of fear emphasizes the debilitating or incapacitating qualities of the emotion. The representation of fear as involving rapid heart beat, pallid skin, cold sweat, bristled hair, muscular tremors, rapid breathing, dryness of the mouth, trembling lips, and a husky voice has been restated many times since Charles Darwin ([1872] 1965, p. 290) first presented it as a characteristic descriptive account. Because his statement is so authoritative, but also so unsuitable for the purposes of indicating the social salience of fear, it is appropriate briefly to consider it here.

Darwin claimed that the etymological source of the term indicates the precipitous basis of fear in sudden and dangerous events ([1872] 1965, p. 289). The extreme manifestation of fear Darwin described is certainly consistent with fear born of surprise and shock; but these are not required for the experience of fear in any general sense. Darwin's suggestion that they are so required derives less from an etymological justification and more from his principal interest in the expression of emotions.

Darwin's discussion of fear, and, as we saw in a previous chapter, of emotion in general, is almost wholly in terms of its expressive features. These are most obvious in their most extreme and visceral emotional presentations. Darwin acknowledges this fact when he closed his discussion by saying that he had "describe[d] diversified expressions of fear" from "surprise into extreme terror and horror" ([1872] 1965, p. 306), a series which hardly covers the full range of possibilities. When referring to what he called "slight fear," however, Darwin (p. 290) acknowledged that its expressive qualities are different from those upon which he had concentrated. In fact, what he called slight fear, in which the extreme expressions are not evident, is the more typical form.

The limitations of Darwin's account of fear are at the same time the elements of the conventional understanding which can be readily located in other writers. The context of Darwin's discussion of emotion, including fear, is its evolutionary nature. Second, he held that fear is precipitated by danger, and finally, that it is behaviorally manifest in flight (Darwin [1872] 1965, pp. 289, 307).

An acceptance of the evolutionary significance of fear has led some writers to regard it as a primary or basic emotion. Not all writers on emotion accept the notion of basic emotions, but those who do hold that such emotions are rudimentary in the sense that the capacity for fear, for example, is "hardwired" and also that fear, in combination with other basic emotions (such as anger or joy) form more complex emotions. Although the number of basic emotions differs between distinct theories of them, with very few exceptions writers who employ the notion include fear as a basic emotion. Of the fourteen theorists of basic emotions indicated by Ortony, Clore, and Collins ([1988] 1990, p. 27), only two failed to mention fear as a basic emotion.

Basic emotions assume significance in evolutionary processes. The capacity for feeling fear, according to this perspective, is universal in primates and other mammals, and is associated with species survival through its role in motivating the escape of individuals from (anticipated) danger or the threat of danger. Rather than disagree with this perspective, it is sufficient to point to its narrowness when applied to human populations.

In human populations fear frequently arises in social contexts in which the source of fear simply cannot be fled from, and which threatens not individual well-being (the integrity of being as a bounded organism) but social well-being (the integrity of being relative to the standing of others). In addition, fear may be experienced socially in the sense that the fear is not simply an individual reaction to threat but an inter-subjective experience in which each individual necessarily contributes to the social experience of the fear others also feel.

Thus the conception of fear as an individual reaction to physical threat offers very little for an understanding of social behavior and action. And yet, this is the way in which the term is frequently used in the scholarly as well as the lay literatures. Before the social dimensions of fear can be discussed, it is necessary to consider the association of fear with danger or threat.

## Danger and fear

The danger–flight, threat–withdrawal couple, which characterizes commonplace accounts of fear, makes sense when the source of fear is a direct and physical challenge. But physical threat as a source of fear is an inadequate basis for a conceptualization of the generalized object of fear. Indeed, the treatment of fear as an emotional reaction to threat or danger has led to a conflation of the cause and the object of fear, which have to be treated separately.

The cause of fear, that is, the generalized conditions under which the emotion is experienced, has to be understood in terms of the structure of the relations in which fear arises. The object of fear, on the other hand, is what the emoting subject is orientated to in their fear. On the basis of this distinction, withdrawal from danger refers to a type of behavior, withdrawal, which is orientated to the object of fear, characterized as danger. The cause of fear, in this context, could preliminarily be described as an incapacity to deal with danger.

Fear behavior typically includes not just flight but also fight. That these are apparently opposite types of behavior attached to a single orientation requires explanation. In one of the few accounts which clearly distinguishes the cause from the object of fear, Theodore Kemper (1978) was able to explain these dual fear behaviors on the basis of a causal account of fear.

According to Kemper, it is the "structural conditions of insufficient power . . . or . . . the excess of the other's power" which causally give rise to fear (1978, pp. 55–6). From this point of view it is possible to determine whether flight or fight behavior will be engaged by reference to what Kemper called the "attribution of agency," that is, the attribution of responsibility for the subject's insufficient power as residing with the subjects themselves, or with the other.

The belief that the subject's lack of power results from their own incapacities is concomitant with a feeling of helplessness (Kemper 1978, pp. 56–7), with which is associated flight as fear behavior. When the other is the agent of the subject's insufficiency of structural power, then the subject's behavior toward the other will be hostile (pp. 57–8) and fight rather than flight is probable. On this basis, Kemper distinguishes between introjected fear as "subjugation" and extrojected fear as "rebellion" ( pp. 57–8).

Fear behavior as flight or fight is generally taken to imply a physical object or foe from which the subject flees or with which they fight. It has already been shown that the object of fear should not be conceived of as being the same as the cause of fear. Following Kemper, the cause of fear is treated as insufficient power. The object of fear, on the other hand, is what the emoting subject is orientated to in their fear. Up to this point, the object of fear has been regarded as threat or danger.

If fear is construed as an emotional reaction to threat, then it is appropriate to ask what constitutes a threat in the formation of fear. Given the consensus, from Spinoza ([1677] 1970, p. 117) to Robert Solomon (1976, p. 313), that anything may precipitate fear, then the nature of "threat" requires closer consideration than it frequently receives. In his classic study of the nature of fear, the psychologist D. O. Hebb (1946) used models of mutilated and also real but unresponsive bodies to generate fear in his chimpanzee subjects. In human populations fear may similarly arise from situations which do not threaten in any directly meaningful way those who fear them. While often taken for granted, the relationship between threat and fear is not entirely obvious. Hebb's discussion offers some highly stimulating suggestions, which can contribute to a conceptualization of the object of fear.

While Hebb's argument is neurological, it is not without relevance to a sociology of fear. He showed that it is not a property of a subject's perception of "a strange person" which would determine fear of the stranger. Rather than a result of "sensory excitation," Hebb held that fear is experienced when there is "some discrepancy of the pattern from those which have been frequently experienced by the subject – by a complex relationship, that is, of the sensory event to pre-existent cerebral processes" (1946, p. 267). Hebb went on to say that this point of view leads to the proposal "that fear occurs when an object is seen which is like familiar objects in enough respects to arouse habitual processes of perception, but in other respects arouses incompatible processes" (p. 268). This is what Hebb aptly called a "disruptive stimulation" (p. 270). It is this which he proposed as the neurological basis of fear, and it is fear which characterizes the object of the disruptive stimulation as a threat. As Thomas Scheff (1984, p. 165) said of laughing: we do not laugh because we feel joy, we feel joy because we laugh; so we do not fear because we are threatened, we feel threatened because we fear.

The relevance of Hebb's argument for our purposes is in the suggestion that change itself is a potential source of fear. Social experience, even within a brief time-frame, is typically replete with "objects" sufficiently familiar to arouse habitual processes of perception but at the same time unfamiliar enough to arouse incompatible processes. Not all change leads to fear, of course: but under conditions of the social actor's perceptions of insufficient power, the experience of change is likely to lead to fear. This notion matches the intuitive supposition that change is to be feared, which raises the possibility of deteriorating prospects for subjects whose power is insufficient to provide compensating or mollifying adjustments.

The object of fear, then, is not adequately conceptualized as a threatening agent who or which should be avoided. Rather the object of fear is an expectation of negative outcome. This is implicit in the idea that fear is the emotional response to danger, for the concept of danger refers not to an event or agent, but to a liability or prospect of injury. The object of fear, then, is a prospect, the prospect of harm or injury.

If an agent is implicated in another's fear, it is not because of what they have done or failed to do, as it is with anger, for instance. Rather, an agent is implicated in another's fear because of what they are likely to do. The past behavior of an agent may lead to another's fear of them, certainly. But this is not directly because of what the agent had done, but because what they had done leads to an anticipation of what they might do. It is important to add here that it is not necessary that an agent in any meaningful sense be the cause of another's fear. One may fear the dark, or water, or change. It is because of what might happen in the dark, what might happen in the water, what might happen in the future, that these things are fearful.

The argument here agrees with the proposal by Andrew Ortony and his colleagues (Ortony, Clore, and Collins [1988] 1990, pp. 109–14) that fear is a prospect-based emotion, that fear is displeasure about the prospect of an undesirable event. Ortony, Clore, and Collins distinguish emotions in terms of whether they are reactions to events, agents, or objects. Fear, as a prospect-based emotion, is regarded as a reaction-to-events type emotion. But there is a confusion here: fear is not a reaction to an event, but to a prospect of an event. The prospective aspect of fear means that its generic object might best be specified in temporal terms. The objects of many emotions are discrete others, but the objects of some emotions, including fear, are temporal phases or states, as we saw in chapter 4 earlier.

Discussions of fear frequently touch on the question of temporality, with some emphasis on future orientations. Adam Smith, for example, in *The Theory of Moral Sentiments*, said that fear "is a passion derived altogether from the imagination, which represents . . . not what we really feel, but what we may hereafter possibly suffer" (Smith [1759] 1982, p. 30). Similarly, Kemper argued that power insufficiency "makes the future both uncertain and uninviting, [which are] suitable conditions for fear-anxiety" (Kemper 1978, p. 56).

As fear is an emotional apprehension of a negative prospect it is anticipatory and in that sense future orientated. But it is necessary to qualify and more carefully state what is the temporal plane of fear. Anxiety is certainly a negative apprehension of the future, but fear, it will be argued, is an anticipation of a present threat or danger. This is to say that fear is an emotional apprehension of the present as a temporal plane or site. Indeed, fear is implicated in the very constitution of an experienced present, that of a particular negative type.

The horizons of the past and the future are in principle wide and expansive. The present, on the other hand, which is distinct from both the past and the future, is the moment which divides one from the other. In this logical sense, then, the present is without duration. This understanding led William James to say that, while the present "*must* exist, . . . that it *does* exist can never be a fact of our immediate experience" (James [1890a] 1931, p. 609, emphasis in original). Experientially, however, there is a present, which takes on an entirely different form than a durationless moment: in James's terms, "the practically cognized present is no knife edge, but a saddle-back, with a certain breadth of its own on which we sit perched, and from which we look in two directions into time" (p. 609).

The explanation offered by James of the practically cognized present, which he comes to call in the course of his discussion "the specious present," is that it is a cumulation of overlapping sensational brain processes, with the extent of overlap determining the feeling of the duration occupied ([1890a] 1931, pp. 635–6). But it is not sensation which engenders a feeling of duration, but being moved by sensation, or reflection, or something else. Perhaps the philosopher Alfred North Whitehead captured it better when he said that "what we perceive as present is the vivid fringe of memory tinged with anticipation" (quoted in Whitrow 1961, p. 83). Emotion is implicated in both memory (Bolles 1988, pp. 29–41) and anticipation.

One source of the feeling of duration constitutive of the specious present, then, might be fear: the anticipation of a threat or danger which is not in the future (as with anxiety) but imminent in the present. Indeed, the anticipation of a present danger in fear extends the saddle back of the specious present, which, in having to be endured, now has duration. The conventional association of fear and paralysis or inaction can also be understood and reinterpreted in terms of the manner in which emotion, and fear in particular, constitutes the specious present. In his discussion of the unit act, Talcott Parsons said that the future is a state "which would not come into existence if something were not done about it by the actor" (Parsons 1937 [1968], p. 44). If the agency of the actor makes the future, then the absence of agency – inactivity – extends the present. The suggestion is not that fear necessarily immobilizes, but that even "rebellion," in Kemper's sense given earlier, addresses the actor's present circumstances. These will include the actor's power deficit, which has to be dealt with before they are able to go on with the business of creating a future. That is, before engaging in agency.

These different elements of the argument, that the cause of fear is insufficiency of power, that the object of fear is the subject's understanding of their prospects, and therefore that threat has first a phenomenological nature before, if at all, a physical one, have to be untangled. The preceding discussion has shown how this can be done.

## Social fear and emotional climates

It has been noted that the dispositional aspects of fear are widely conceived of in terms of the avoidance of physical threat or danger. This conceptualization features even in the findings of social psychological research, for instance, in which the antecedents of fear have been identified as traffic, interaction with strangers, and novel situations (Scherer, Wallbott, and Summerfield 1986, p. 80). But in human populations the source or specific object of fear is typically social rather than physical.

This crucial but infrequently acknowledged fact was noted by the early American sociologist, Charles Horton Cooley:

if we take fear, for instance, and try to recall our experience of it from early childhood on, it seems clear that, while the emotion itself may change but little, the ideas, occasions, suggestions that excite it depend upon the state of our intellectual and social development, and so undergo great alteration. The feeling does not tend to disappear, but it becomes less violent and spasmodic, more and more social as regards the objects that excite it, and more and more subject, in the best minds, to the discipline of reason. (Cooley [1922] 1964, pp. 289–90)

Key elements of this perspective have been confirmed by more recent research. The psychologist Robert Lazarus (1984, p. 254), for instance, has reported that even though fear emerges earlier in ontogenesis than the more complex and symbolically based emotional reactions such as indignation and guilt, it can nevertheless "have highly complex and symbolic social and psychological determinants."

Continuing his argument concerning the social nature of fear, Cooley goes on to say that:

Yet these [social] fears – fear of standing alone, of losing one's place in the flow of human action and sympathy, fear for the character and success of those near to us – have often the very quality of childish fear. A man cast out of his regular occupation and secure place in the system of the world feels like that of the child in the dark; just as impulsive, perhaps just as purposeless and paralyzing. (Cooley [1922] 1964, p. 290)

The claim that these fears are like those "of the child" can be taken as an indication of their authenticity as fear. But there is an aspect of social fear which sets it apart from the isolating and essentially individual fear of "the child in the dark."

Cooley's reference to unemployment – a "man cast out of his regular occupation" – as a pervasive social fear is highly appropriate. C. Wright Mills, for instance, noted that "the facts of unemployment *are* felt as fears, hanging over the white collar world" ([1951] 1956, p. xv, emphasis in original). In a more general and comprehensive statement, the British sociologists Robert Blackburn and Michael Mann have noted that both US and British research indicates that unemployment is a real possibility for most people during their working lives. And while unemployment tends to be concentrated in particular social groups (defined by ethnicity, region, and skill-level) and at certain life-cycle phases (the first and last five years of work), "the threat is sufficiently real yet unpredictable to worry most workers" (Blackburn and Mann 1979, p. 34). Which is to say that most workers fear unemployment.

The fear of unemployment is not a social fear simply in the sense that its object is social. More to the point in the present context, it is a social fear also in the sense that it is a fear experienced and shared by members of a social collectivity, namely employed persons as a group. The term group can be used in two senses. In one sense a fear of unemployment is a social fear by virtue of the fact that a number of individuals have a similar fear and can therefore be seen as an aggregate identified by a common fear of unemployment. But a social aggregate is not the only kind of group, and an aggregate emotion is therefore not the only kind of social or group emotion.

It is necessary to distinguish between what are conventionally called distributive aspects and relational or structural aspects of social formations (the classic statement is Dahrendorf 1959, p. ix; see also Béteille 1969, p. 13). The term "social group" may be understood as a descriptive category applied to an aggregation of members who are similar in the social facilities, including emotions, they possess. A quite different type of group is one in which membership is not ascribed on the basis of the distribution of social resources or attributes, but which forms through the relationships between its members. These groups emerge in shared structural conditions.

It is not required of a group in this second sense which fears unemployment that every one of its members experience a similar fear, as with the first type of group. A group formed through the relationships between its members rather than on the basis of their common attributes will be composed of individuals who occupy different positions in relation to each other. Their individual feelings, therefore, are also likely to differ from each other. Yet in their relationships they will each contribute to the feelings of the group *qua* group, to its emotional formation or climate.

The emotional experiences referred to here are necessarily collective, and the concept of emotional climate, with some qualification, is appropriate to them. Serge Moscovici (1987, p. 51), for instance, distinguished crowds by their emotional climates; E. V. Walter (1969, p. 11), on the other hand, suggested international emotional climates; and the level of nation-state was the focus of Joseph de Rivera's (1992) discussion of distinct emotional climates. Emotional climates are sets of emotions or feelings which are not only shared by groups of individuals implicated in common social structures and processes, but which are also significant in the formation and maintenance of political and social identities and collective behavior. Emotional climate therefore includes emotional tones and patterns which differentiate social groups or categories by virtue of the fact that they are shared by their members and unlikely to be shared with non-members.

By functioning as a locus or point of reference for feelings and sentiments about social and political conditions, and opportunities and limitations, shared with others, emotional climates are both social influences on individual behavior and constitute a source of collective action. Indeed, the contents of emotional climates not only identify a subject's socio-emotional milieu, but will also point or orientate the subject against, or toward, those outside that milieu to whom these emotions may be directed.

A final consideration concerning emotional climates, overlooked by others who have written on them, and which must be stressed, is that although climates are shared, individual participation in them will be patterned and therefore unequal. Emotional climates are group phenomena. Groups are structured by differences in role, capacity, power, and so on. It follows that the emotional experience of each member of the group which will contribute to the overall climate will be not only complementary but also distinct in terms of such things as differences in role and asymmetries of authority. An emotional climate is not a blanket which equally covers each member of the group associated with it. Each group member will contribute differently to the formation of the climate and will experience it in terms of their particular place in the group.

A treatment of group emotion of this kind was raised in a reassessment of the logic of accounts of social historical change. William Reddy (1987) argued that within the structural parameters of the industrial-employment relation workers are bound together in honor. But the honor implicated in employment is not the individual honor of each worker, but an honor pertaining to the group in which each individual partakes. In these circumstances each worker is bound in honor, "not to defend his or her honor as such, but to struggle for collective marketplace goods" (p. 164). In this account, the significant structural factors of group formation are emotions, arguably emotional climates.

Fear of unemployment experienced as a group emotion is not only manifest collectively but is social, indeed institutional and organizational, in its consequences. Fear of unemployment has always maintained the authority of employer over employee, and therefore functions as an instrument of industrial discipline (Beveridge 1944, pp. 194–5). Relatedly, this fear of unemployment has served to prevent the unionization of workers. Donald Roy (1980), for instance, has shown that fear of discharge, of plant closure or relocation, and of layoffs through reduction of level of plant operation, have successfully been promoted by employers to counter unionization campaigns and membership drives.

Thus there is evidence that the conventional understanding of the impact of fear on individual behavior applies also to its group or collective manifestation. As de Rivera (1992, p. 201) stated in his descriptions of different emotional climates, "a climate of fear isolates people from one another." Yet the evidence presented earlier is incomplete, and what de Rivera says of fear applies more properly to terror. A climate of fear may lead to organization as much as to disorganization, and a climate of fear of unemployment has not only curtailed particular unionization drives, it has also been the emotional context of the historical formation and development of the trade-union movement.

Nineteenth-century English trade-union rules and statements frequently referred to the fact that "there is always a fear prominent in the mind of [every worker] . . . that to-morrow may see him out of employment" (as quoted in S. and B. Webb 1920, p. 430). The Webbs showed that fear of unemployment was central to an understanding of the trade-union principles of the Normal Day, opposition to overtime, and to campaigns for reduction of the hours of labor (pp. 440–1). Indeed, the fear of unemployment was central to the emotional patterns which led to the foundation and formation of the trade-union movement itself (see also Goodrich 1921, pp. 72–91).

Cooley's suggestion, noted earlier, that fear may be subject to "the discipline of reason" can be taken to mean not only that reason suppresses fear, but also that fear leads to action, executed with reason, to offset its cause. In this way, the fear of unemployment and the organizational innovation of trade unionism are connected. Thus Cooley's claim that social fear is like the fear of the child in that it is "just as purposeless and paralyzing" has to be rejected as an invalid generalization.

### Elite climates of fear and social change

Although the claim is seldom made explicit, it is frequently assumed that fear is exclusively an emotion of those in subordinate or weak positions or roles. This is only apparently implied in the explanation that fear is a consequence of power disparity. A relative rather than an absolute power imbalance can be responsible for fear in those who occupy strong and superordinate positions. It is not contradictory to say that a political or social elite might experience fear.

An incremental shift of power relations, for instance, in which there is a relative decline in the power of an elite or a relative increase in the power of a subordinate or dependent group, is likely to lead an elite to fear that its privileged position may be in jeopardy. As in other cases, so too here, fear functions as a signal indicating that interests are threatened by the prospects arising from the relations of power in which the subject is implicated. But it is unlikely that elite fear will lead to subjugation, even if the relative power deficit is located in the elite structure itself. Similarly, rebellion is an inappropriate conceptualization of more strident elite fearbehavior. It is therefore necessary to develop the schema proposed by Kemper (1978, pp. 56–8), mentioned earlier.

Kemper hypothesized that the attribution of agency for structural power deficit, with self or other, determines whether fear is experienced as introjected or extrojected, corresponding respectively to behaviors of flight or fight, withdrawal or counter-challenge, subjugation or rebellion. There is a third generic possibility which might be hypothesized, however, which is neither merely retreat nor defiance, but containment. In this context, containment is not simply reactive, as are flight and fight, but constructive: containment may operate by putting in place what was previously absent. In this way, a power deficit may be corrected by structurally channeling the direction of the other's power, away from self, or enhancing the effectiveness of self's power. In the social arena, this is to say that fear may lead to organizational innovation and development.

The notion of containment outlined here requires an understanding of the role of resources in addition to orientation in the determination of fear-behavior. Other things being equal, the resources required for containment are greater than those required for rebellion, and those required for rebellion are greater than those required for subjugation. It should not be forgotten, however, that the organization of numbers is a resource in power relations available to subordinates. An emotional climate of fear of unemployment, it was mentioned earlier, led to the containment of employers' power through the organizational innovation, by members of the working class, of trade unions.

As elites have ready access to resources it is likely that elite fear will not lead to subjugation or rebellion, but principally to containment. It can be hypothesized, therefore, that elite fear will lead to organizational change. It is not being claimed that all experiences of fear lead in this direction, nor that all organizational innovation results from fear. It is being proposed, however, that organizational innovation is one consequence of fear. Indeed, the basis in fear, and especially in elite fear, of organizational development and change is highly significant, and largely overlooked.

The source of organizational change in elite fear and the role of fear in organizational change has great importance for sociological inquiry. Yet the point is hardly noted in the sociological literature, and where it is discussed, frequently denied.

In a recent paper, Helena Flam (1993, p. 59) argued that fear is a "subjectively felt product of power relations" and the "emotional foundation" of interest. She went on to say that "fear is a reality check" in the sense that it "signals the . . . threat to one's self stemming from a violation of the power relations," and also in the sense that "in signalling that a pursuit of a specific preference invites danger, it begs the question whether it should remain a preference" (p. 60). All these statements more or less agree with the position developed in the present chapter. But Flam went on to show that the consequences of fear in the organizational setting are to maintain or conserve and not to change or develop the existing pattern of organization.

Fear prevented Polish Communist Party members, for instance, from leaving the organization they no longer regarded as a just authority (Flam 1993, pp. 63–4). Fear leads organizational managers to conformity and conservatism (pp. 70–1). Fear, then, for Flam, is the basis of organizational inertia if not stability. While her conceptualization of fear, as already noted, is similar to the one presented here, her argument differs from the present one in that her conclusions reinforce the perception of fear as necessarily associated only with subjugation.

As well as focussing on fear at the individual rather than the group level, Flam's account fails to consider the question of the resources available to actors in their fear-behavior. Neither does Flam's account entertain the possibility of types of fear-behavior in addition to subjugation. The case she discusses cannot, therefore, lead to general conclusions about the organizational consequences of fear.

In what is possibly the only discussion of elite fear in the sociological literature, Floyd Hunter ([1953] 1963) argued that fear, in generating caution, interferes with the organized structure of the community (p. 223). Hunter stratified the community of Regional City, which he studied, into top leaders, professionals, and the mass of the citizenry. Whereas the mass of the citizenry manifest silence, and the professionals manifest pessimism, it is the top leadership which manifests fear: Hunter went on to say that "expressions of fear in community life are prevalent among the top leaders" (p. 223). Does Hunter's examination of elite fear discover containment and organizational change to be an outcome of the emotional experience?

Hunter noted that elite fear in Regional City "is apparently rooted in the feeling that any change in the existing relations of power and decision in the community would be disastrous for the leaders who now hold power" (Hunter [1953] 1963, p. 223). He reports that the consequence of elite fear is "a cautious approach to any new issue that might arise" (p. 223). Indeed, Hunter argued that the pervasive fear among the elite of Regional City was responsible for preventing the top leadership from both thinking through the problems they faced and introducing changes which would offset the challenges which confronted them (pp. 228–30). Thus, through an empirical case, Hunter was able to show that elite fear led to caution if not paralysis, and that the organizational consequences of elite fear are the antithesis of innovation and development.

Yet Hunter's conclusions are unconvincing: in fact, when properly understood, his evidence does not contradict the argument advanced in the present chapter. Regional City's elite feared the prospects of social and economic reform. In particular, Hunter reported a fear among the elite that "a more equitable distribution of resources" might become part of the political agenda ([1953] 1963, p. 224). Such a fear was not without foundation, as there was a growing concern about malnutrition and poverty in the region, and the need for relief programs was widely acknowledged (p. 236). Yet, at the same time, Hunter noted that such problems were too large and numerous to be handled by the elite of Regional City, and that there was a consensus that the question of poor relief and social security was a national issue involving federal responsibility (p. 237).

What emerges from the discussion, then, is that while the top leaders of Regional City constituted a local elite, they were simply not in a position to influence national policy on taxation or social security. That is, with regard to the issues which gave rise to their fears, the top leaders of Regional City were not an elite. Their local capacities were insufficient to address the prospects they feared. Hunter's claim, that fear experienced by Regional City's top leaders prevented the organizational changes required to remove the threat they faced, is therefore misplaced. The salient power deficit of Regional City's leaders is in relation to national policy-making and the national power structure, not the local poor. The object of their fear is the prospect of demands coming from the local poor which would reveal their structural power deficit with regard to federal power and policy. Their fear behavior was subjugation: they had neither the capacity nor the resources for containment.

When a genuine case of elite fear is identified it can be shown that containment is its likely behavioral consequence, and that the consequences of elite fear include organizational development and innovation, and social change. A number of epoch-defining socio-political changes are marked by institutional developments effected by elites subject to climates of fear. One such case is that of Britain during the First World War.

## Elite fear and change: some examples

During the period of the First World War and its immediate aftermath both the French and the British governments had the same objectives: preservation of capitalistic structures in the face of impending revolutionary upheaval (Gallie 1983, p. 237). Yet the strategy adopted by each was quite different: the French government "concede[d] as little as possible to the labor movement" it faced, whereas the British government "diffuse[d labor] militancy through accommodation and . . . strengthen[ed] institutional procedures designed to facilitate the peaceful resolution of conflict" (p. 237). The consequence of these differences was that the French working class was simply crushed by the French government, and in many respects the institutional structure of the French state before the war was continuous with its structure in the post-war period. The British government, on the other hand, attempted to contain labor, and in doing so transformed it, but also transformed the institutions of the state.

According to Gallie, the explanation of the difference between France and Britain lies in the British government's "assessment of the potential disruptive power of organized labor in a war situation" (Gallie 1983, p.

247). The French labor movement had no such capacity. The difference, then, is that the British government feared the labor movement it faced, whereas the French government did not. In its endeavors to contain the labor movement it feared, the British elite created new organizations and modified existing ones.

During the course of the First World War the British labor movement grew in numbers, militancy, and organizational capacity. Union membership rose from 23.03 percent of the workforce in 1914 to 25.58 percent in 1916. By 1918, it had risen to 35.68 percent (calculated from Bain and Elsheikh 1976, p. 134). During this period, the militancy of British unionism also grew significantly, measured by numbers involved in strikes. For instance, in 1914, 447,000 workers were involved in strike action; in 1917, 872,000; and in 1918, 1,116,000 (see figures in Cole 1947, p. 484). These developments were all the more remarkable given the war-time legislation against strike action. In addition, socialist and syndicalist ideas and organization developed within the labor movement, and the shop-stewards' movement in particular gave coherence and expression to rank-and-file sentiments and the force of numbers. The success of the Russian Bolsheviks in 1917 exacerbated further the British elite's fear of labor.

Under war-time conditions state intervention in the economy and labor policy was extensive. Labor's grievances were therefore directed against not only employers but also the state. Given British labor's strength and oppositional force, the government not only feared that unionism could disrupt the war-effort, but also threaten post-war reconstruction and the future development of the economy. These fears came to be allayed through the British government's containment of labor by means of a number of organizational and institutional developments.

In the early phase of the war the government incorporated union leadership in the political decision-making process in order to recruit the union movement to the purposes of government, and as a means of exercising intermediary control over a union membership hostile to government initiative (Gallie 1983, pp. 237–8). The government also attempted to enhance the position of unionists in the areas of wages and conditions by integrating unions into a system of industrial relations sponsored and monitored by government. The purpose of such developments was to isolate militant and radical unionism from the labor movement as a whole. Although specific measures were not always successful, they contributed to an emerging pattern of industrial relations which limited the arena of radical action (Cole and Postgate 1946, pp. 547–51; Gallie 1983, p. 240; Middlemas 1979, p. 141).

A number of pieces of social legislation in the immediate post-war period was the price government paid for labor's commitment to the war-effort from 1916 (Cole and Postgate 1946, p. 524; Middlemas 1979, pp. 134–5). In particular, the electoral franchise was extended, the numbers of workers and their families covered by social insurance was increased, and government housing finance was expanded (Gallie 1983, pp. 239–40). Gallie (p. 240) commented that the political effect of these reforms was to indicate to the labor movement and the population at large the virtue of constitutional action over grass-roots and radical mobilization. But for constitutional action to be a choice, government had to provide organizational channels for it which previously had not existed. In order to allay the fear of a powerful and threatening labor movement, the British government engaged in organizational development and change.

The British elite's fear of the labor movement was in the form of a collective emotion, a climate of fear, and it is not required that there be evidence that all members of the elite as individuals had an equal fear of labor. It is sufficient to point to the expressions of fear of ministers, for instance, reported in cabinet minutes, that the revolutionary shop-stewards' movement might lead the sympathy of otherwise patriotic and loyal trade unionists (Middlemas 1979, p. 79). Further expressions of fear of labor's capacities and intentions were contained in contemporary reports from the Intelligence Department, regional conciliation officers of the Ministry of Labour, and of the Industrial Unrest Commissions (pp. 129–30). These and other instruments of elite sensitivity to the currents of the day contributed to a collective climate of fear of labor within the British elite. This elite fear led to the containment of labor. Later, this was implicated in the formation of the organizational innovations and development, which not only transformed labor into a non-threatening force in society, but also lay the foundations for the British welfare state (Barbalet 1991b, pp. 319–22).

It is likely that Hunter's supposition, referred to in the preceding, concerning the high incidence of elite fear is correct. Elites frequently perceive what they take to be shifts in relative power relations. It follows, therefore, that elites will frequently experience social fear. Indeed, changing technical, economic, political, and other circumstances will modify the relative power of all groups in a society. Advantaged groups may lose ground to others who find their position improved through such changes. At crucial periods dominant groups will find that the relative power of subordinate groups increases and threatens existing social and political structures and distributive relations, and therefore the structure of privilege which sustains elite domination. The argument here is that such elite fears of these prospects have been crucial in institutional transformations and historical change.

Two further cases can be briefly added to the one just outlined to indicate the widespread experience of elite fear, and the significance of its consequences. First, the introduction of the suffrage in nineteenth-century Europe was an epoch-defining change marked by organizational developments effected by elites subject to climates of fear. The French Revolution of 1789 gave explosive voice to momentous pressures for change throughout Europe, which generated a high level of elite fear. By the end of the Napoleonic Wars in 1815 the problem of settling the threatening pressures from below was dealt with in most European states by elite-engineered political reforms. These moves constituted a second fear: that the inclusion of ignorant, unruly, and rebellious masses into political society would undermine it.

This tension, between the possibilities of enhancing the power of rule through the political incorporation of the working class on the one hand, and the fears of the political and civic consequences of an extension of the suffrage on the other, constituted the essence of nineteenth-century European politics. The cautious strategies of elite-sponsored working-class political incorporation, realized in the electoral legislation of the period, reflects precisely this fear and the containment strategy it led elites to adopt (Bendix 1964; Moorhouse 1973).

Not all institutional changes are as significant and enduring as these. A more recent and meaner instance of this general pattern of elite fear leading to organizational innovation to offset pressures in the wider political environment is the Iran–Contra affair of 1985–6 in United States politics. In this case the organizational location and practice of key elements of US foreign policy shifted from the State Department to the Office of the Vice-President and the Deputy Director of Political-Military Affairs in the National Security Council, Lieutenant-Colonel Oliver North, in concert with two private citizens, Richard Secord and Albert Hakim. It can be shown that these developments were driven by a pervasive climate of fear in the right-wing of the Republican Party and the Reagan presidency and cabinet.

Three areas of fear can be identified as responsible for the changes in the organization and execution of foreign policy which culminated in the crisis of 1986 (Draper 1991; Emerson 1988; Ledeen 1988; Martin and Walcott 1988). First was the fear of communism and of its perceived new strength through the Sandinista revolution in Nicaragua. Second was the fear of Iranian terrorism in general, and in particular the fear of Iranian-inspired kidnapping of US citizens and officials in Europe and especially in Lebanon. Finally, the Reagan administration feared Congress and

Congressional scrutiny of its activities in Central America. In combination these fears created a climate of fear within the Reagan circle leading to the developments which have become known as the Iran–Contra affair, and which amounted to a criminal reorganization of foreign-policy activity and formation.

## Conclusion

The preceding discussion has attempted to fill a void: it has indicated the significance of fear to an understanding of social and especially organizational change. In the wider literature fear is extensively, almost exclusively, treated as an individual emotion. Immobility, through withdrawal or rebellion, is therefore regarded as the principal consequence of fear. When fear is conceived of in its social form, however, and as having a social object, the possibility of collective action designed to remove the source of fear can be recognized. Such action may take the form of organizational innovation and development.

In both phases, individual and social, fear is central to the apprehension of interest and to an understanding of the direction of action. Indeed, the question of how subjects know that their interests are under threat is readily answered: fear. This disarmingly simple notion, that the emotional experience of fear signals that the subject's interests are likely to be contravened, is central to the account of change proposed in the discussion here.

Most discussion of it confuses the cause and object of fear. And the object of fear is often regarded as physical threat. This latter point partly explains why fear has been ignored in sociological accounts. The argument here is that the cause of fear is in structural insufficiencies of power, which points to the subject's vulnerability. This raises the matter of the object of fear, which is here conceptualized as the prospect of an undesirable event or outcome. Such a perspective allows us to recognize that the specific objects of fear will include the prospect of social dislocations of various sorts.

The social experience of fear has a clear collective aspect, which is treated through the concept of emotional climates. A climate of fear, like emotional climates in general, serves both to maintain social and political identity and to be the pivot of collective behavior or action. The association of fear and interest implies that a climate of fear might lead a social group or collectivity subject to it to appreciate the unity of the fortunes of its members, and also to activate responses to a changing situation which would reshape the context in which their future actions and meanings will be located.

Fear is an emotion which is not confined to the powerless. A relative loss of power by an elite will typically lead to a climate of fear, in which its prospects are evaluated and appropriate courses of corrective action considered and taken. The conventional categories of flight and fight, or subjugation and rebellion, are insufficient to account for the fearful action of elites, and also of non-elite groups who are able to deploy resources in the containment of negative prospects perceived as constituting a threat to their interests and responsible for a feeling of social fear.

The consequences of containment as a response to fear include organizational innovation and development. These divert the threat of the other, enhance the subject's own capacities, and generally realign power relations and render innocuous the prospects which were feared. It has been shown through argument and the evidence of particular cases that an explanation in terms of elite climates of fear constitutes an important addition to sociological accounts of change which until now has been overlooked.

# Epilogue

The conclusion to be drawn from the discussion of emotion, social theory, and social structure conducted in the foregoing chapters is obvious: namely that emotions are basic to social action and to an understanding of social structures and processes. It is unnecessary simply to summarize here what has gone before. But, in closing, it is appropriate to indicate something of the relevance of the perspective developed in this book for some associated themes. Additionally, the implications of these for future research can be stated.

The following remarks, however, are better described as forming an "Epilogue" rather than a "Conclusion." This is because in concluding earlier discussion additional issues are touched upon. Four general matters are treated in what follows. Placing the last first, there is the question of a realignment of intellectual traditions, which comes from an emotions perspective in sociology. As any approach will draw on particular sources, so the orientation of a sociology which regards emotions to be fundamental will find its classic texts in a different part of the library than those belonging to other approaches. Relatedly, and this is the second to last thing that will be dealt with, cognate issues of different perspectives will themselves be different. The particular matter to be dealt with here is that of time or, more properly, temporality. Until quite recently, the general subject of time had drawn very little sociological interest. We shall see that an emotions-based sociology leads to a new recognition of the importance of time, and especially the difference between the past and the future, in social processes.

All sociology, whether based on emotions concepts or not, will have a critical edge. It is the underlying critical thrust of sociology which distinguishes it from sociometry – mere measurement or description. The dimension of critique in the sociology of emotions implicit in the earlier chapters will be briefly indicated in the following. This will be to contrast it with the critical aspects of the concept of emotional labor, developed within a quite different framework than the one employed here. The purpose of this discussion, which is the third to last that will be treated, is to indicate aspects of emotions not fully explored in the preceding arguments, but which are important to them.

The current standing of emotion is a further matter treated in the following. The appeal of the topics just mentioned, indeed, the felt relevance of accounts of social structure and process in terms of emotions, conducted in earlier chapters, will in part depend upon the standing of emotions themselves in our estimation of what is important. This concern, the social conditions or standing of emotions, will be the first to be addressed in what follows.

These different themes, with the exception of that of sociological traditions, are unified by a micro-perspective focussed at the level of "the self." This is in contrast to the macroscopic level of discussion predominant in the preceding chapters. The epilogic shift of focus is not so much to redress a balance as to point to matters which have occupied some recent writings in the sociology of emotions.

## The vernacular standing of emotions today

It is a peculiar thing that the recent rise in sociological interest in emotions corresponds with a decline in emotions themselves. By decline is here meant a narrowing, in the wider society, of what is referred to by the term emotion, and to limitations in or an atrophy of experiences of emotions by members of present-day Western societies. The claim that emotional experiences have somehow shrunk in recent times will no doubt be met with disbelief, in face of the pervasive popular concern with emotions. An apparently contrary view, therefore, is that there has never been given a more focussed attention on the emotions in popular and social scientific discourses. The truth of this latter statement is not denied by the following remarks. Indeed, the purpose of this part of the discussion is to explain the recently risen and current interest in emotions.

The characteristic informality of present-day Western society has been seen by some writers to be at the root of an apparent "emancipation of emotions" (Wouters 1992), which is so frequently identified in popular representations. There is ample evidence of a mushrooming interest in emotion and related themes in popular publications and broadcasts, which are available at a growing rate. The increase in numbers of such things, however, cannot detract from the limited range of topics which they treat. These typically relate to two phases of a single phenomenon, namely particular concerns with the self: such products are directed either to healing the self or to projects of realizing a person's self. Each of these are aspects of self-creation, either by making better an injured self or by expressively forming a self. Indeed, and this is the point, the conventional tendency today is to represent emotion as the foundation and authenticator of experiences of self. It is in this direction rather than in an apparent relaxation of rules underlying informality that the supposed increase in or expression of emotionality is to be found.

It is quite appropriate that a burgeoning of interest in emotions be associated with a growing concern for the self. As William James first clearly stated ([1890a] 1931, pp. 305–6) and as Anthony Giddens (1991) has more recently reminded us, persons know themselves through the emotional apprehension of their needs and aspirations. What is unsatisfactory in this is that today the particular emotions associated with this set of tasks are too often taken to cover the full range of emotions, which they clearly can not. Why they can not was shown in chapters 1 and 2, and in discussion throughout. An apposite note on this process is Alan Davies's (1980, p. 296) observation that the catalog of affects compiled by Dr. Roget and presented in his *Thesaurus*, first published in 1852, simply has no place for what Davies calls the "ego-feelings," which are today the core and content of what are taken to comprise the emotions. Roget lists forty "Common Affections," which fails to include what Davies says are today central: self-esteem, self-hatred, embarrassment, confusion, inspiration, and nostalgia. It is these which fill the present-day handbooks of emotions.

The rise of emotion as a focus of widespread and popular concern at the present time operates through a double process: a shrinking of the phenomenal world to the self, and self-experience as the defining force of what constitutes emotions. Each of these will be dealt with in turn.

### A shrinking world

A shrinking of the phenomenal world to the self requires a larger world which includes markets and states. This is the ground covered by Karl Polanyi ([1944] 1957), who provided a useful sketch of part of the process. Polanyi discussed the subversion of customary society through the development of national markets. A customary society is one in which persons understood themselves as inter-dependent members of larger collectivities. The extension of market prerogatives undermined customary society by constituting persons as self-sufficient selves. In organic and social systems the concept of self-sufficiency can have only a heavily qualified meaning. But Polanyi showed that under conditions of market domination, the basic organizing unit becomes the individual person, whose conceptualization of their own interests and needs is bounded by the conceptualization of the interests and needs of contiguous persons. National markets, therefore, shrink the experience of self, so that selfhood attaches to a person who is the proprietor of their own capacities, rather than a cooperative stake-holder in a joint enterprise.

The political corollary of such a "possessive individualism" (Macpherson 1962) is not merely the individual who stands with the sovereignty of the state by virtue of those political rights and obligations which necessarily attach to singular persons as citizens. In the administration of its obligations to its citizens and subjects, the state provides a unique identification, or a series of such identifications, to each individual person as a subject. These begin with certification of birth, and go on to include the provision of health-care numbers, taxation numbers, and benefits numbers; and also various licenses, to drive, marry, and so on.

These dual processes of market and political individuation converge in constituting the experience of self as essentially isolated from other selves and thus forming a self-contained universe. Such a universe of self is in a galaxy of other self-universes, certainly. But a notion of "the self" in this sense, in the given circumstances, is sufficiently robust or durable adequately to describe a practice of self-possession in which persons can conduct their affairs without primary consideration for or impingement from the needs of other selves. These affairs may include an autopoietic aggrandizement or development of self, again, without regard to other selves.

The general process being described here, the process of individuation, was referred to in the discussion of chapter 6, for instance, in terms of the secular tendency toward an intensification of the social division of labor. In what we might call the classic period of this historical process, under the auspices of self-designated rational – we might say rationalizing – principles, the abstract individuals so created were regarded as constituting "independent centers of consciousness" (Wolff 1968, p. 142), which form the units of a liberal political economy.

The reference to consciousness in this context is both informative and pointed. In the classic phase of individuation, in which "individualism" is the representing doctrine of the process, the emergent self is conceived of as being not only independent but rational, both the proprietor of its own capacities and an able manager of its own interests. For such prospects to be realizable, the unequal capacities between individuals could not be so great that the persons at the lower reaches of the range could not have a sense of being able to exert some influence on processes which effected those at the higher reaches of the range. The sense of rationality, and therefore the effectiveness of consciousness, derives from a sense of possible control available to opinion leaders in market and political relations.

With regard to these matters today, the individuating processes have now clearly reached post-classic proportions. The individual experience of self as an independent being continues, but no longer so clearly as a center of consciousness. The possibility of the self exerting an influence on market and state administrative processes to which it is subject are so remote as to lead to a reconceptualization of the self. An experience of self as a center of consciousness gives way to an experience of self as a center of emotional feeling. This arises in the experiential shift from a sense of control of or meaningful participation in external market and politico-administrative processes to a sense of having no such control or meaningful participation.

The argument here is not that the self as a center of consciousness is without emotion. Rather, the point is that in the experience of self as a center of consciousness, the emotions involved are more likely to be back-grounded in the manner described in chapter 2 when the emotional nature of instrumental rationality was discussed. When opportunities meaningfully to influence economic, political, and other processes are low, then persons are likely to experience themselves as centers of emotion. Again, it is not that such experiences will be without conscious-ness, but that the consciousness involved will be a consciousness of rele-vant foregrounded emotions.

The differences between classic and post-classic processes of individuation can be explained in the following terms. Whereas consciousness provides representations of the external environment of the self, emotions at the level of individual experience are internal repre-sentations of and adjustments to physical and psychic processes of the individual organism. It is true that these both situate the emoting being in its environment or context of relations with others. It was shown in all the earlier chapters that emotions provide information on the significance of their circumstances to social actors. But the experience of self is more likely to be constituted as an emotional rather than as a conscious center when the controlling faculties are effectively directed not to the environ-ment but to inner processes. Whatever increase in informality obtains, it is not the source of a new popular awareness of emotions. Rather, it is the loss of effectiveness in markets and states which leads individuals to become aware of their self-forming emotions as objects of self-regulation.

### Narrowing emotions

This last point is the second aspect of the conjunction of a current popular interest in emotion and a narrowing of emotional experience. In a period of extreme individuation, and under conditions of growing awareness by individual subjects of their own powerlessness, social and political processes are experienced as curtailments of a person's expansive capacities. This is to say that the self is experienced through pressures to limit emotional intensity. Although not treated in the framework developed here, Peter Stearns (1994) has presented much evidence of this process drawn from the historical record of middle-class America during the twentieth century. A number of other studies have also contributed to the overall conclusion that there has been an historical trend to curtail emotional intensity during the present period.

In the economic world of labor markets, over the past century, for instance, there has been a move from simple labor control, sometimes called the drive system, to bureaucratic control (Edwards 1979). In the former, the exhortations of supervisors for the work performance of their subordinates came in the form of expletives and bullying; in the latter, in the form of rules and regulations. Open expressions of anger characterized the former, curtailment of anger and other intense emotions characterize the latter. Indeed, the rise of formal organization over physical discipline in the work-place has been accompanied by the advent of a layer of professional emotions managers (Baritz [1960] 1965). As the service and sales sectors of the economy grew, so grew the requirement that workers be more and not less emotionally restrained, and express only customer-friendly emotions (Hochschild 1983; Mills [1951] 1956).

A development associated with economic changes over this period has been a decline in family size. As families grew smaller, so children, parents, and spouses have been forced to curtail anger and jealousy, and in general to feel their way toward less strident and more low-intensity emotions (Stearns 1989; Stearns and Stearns 1986). Emotions have more recently become a focus in education also, even leading to a redefinition of intelligence. But, in spite of appearances, the attention to emotions here is to enhance self-control, through emotional self-control; and to focus instrumental motivation, not to broaden emotional expressivity or intensity (Goleman 1995).

It can be seen, then, why it is necessary to argue that the contemporary focus on emotions is part of a narrowing of emotional experience. Each of the processes mentioned above expresses a concern identified by Niklas Luhmann ([1984] 1995). Luhmann noted that individuation puts society at risk, "endangered by emotionality," because the "the individual is increasingly subject to the individual's own emotions" (p. 270). But, at the same time, the risk is largely averted through a self-conscious management of these emotions: "individuals are encouraged to talk about themselves and their emotions" (p. 270). The cultural representation of emotion today is largely confined to those emotions constituted by the managed emotions of self-expression. The cultural basis of the significance of emotion, indeed, the elevated presence of emotion, is entailed in the experience of social actors endeavoring to contain the intensity of their emotions in general, and especially in the cultivated development of those emotions associated with what were earlier called ego-feelings.

It is not surprising, then, given this background, that much of the current sociology of emotions is focussed on the problems of emotions management. Only if these prevailing cultural expressions of emotion are taken to be the full meaning of the term is there any justification in saying that the "sociology of emotional management" is equivalent to the "sociology of emotions," as Cas Wouters, for one, has suggested (1992, p. 248). The approach taken in this book, on the other hand, shows why this is too limited a perspective. Emotions which are not covered by the prevailing cultural definition nevertheless continue to be real in their expression and influence, even if persons cannot readily or properly identify their experiences of them.

### Critique of capitalism and the dynamics of emotions

The discussion of the vernacular standing of emotion reiterated what has been demonstrated in the preceding chapters; namely, that social structural developments and not simply cultural processes are necessary to explain the character of emotional experience. Indeed, a reliance on only the cultural aspects of the situation will lead to a partial and distorted account of emotions. In addition to structural accounts of emotions, the approach put forward in this book has explained structural features of social systems through emotions categories.

Much of the discussion in preceding chapters was directed toward a demonstration of the importance of emotions concepts in sociological accounts of social structure. The significance of business or trade cycles to class organization was indicated in chapter 3, for instance. Class is typically understood through the secular vectors of inequalities of earnings, property, or power. The cyclical movements of the economy, on the other hand, have largely been ignored or dismissed as irrelevant to an understanding of class structure. By treating class resentment as necessary to the process of class conflict, however, the role of trade-cycle movements in class formation becomes central, as we have seen. This is because the differential fortunes of real-income groups through the movement of the trade cycle is of primary importance in the formation of that resentment implicated in class mobilization.

This discussion raises another matter, not explicit in the relevant discussion earlier, but about which conclusions can be drawn. Class and class conflict are categories associated not only with the analysis of capitalism but also its critique. Critique is an aspect of much sociology.

Peter Berger's claim that "sociological perspective involves a process of 'seeing through' the facades of social structure" (1966, p. 43) restates Karl Marx's more general proposition that "all science would be superfluous if the outward appearance and the essence of things directly coincided" ([1894] 1971, p. 817). In subverting experientially born accounts, sociological accounts necessarily provide a critique of them. Discussion in this book has not highlighted its critical formations. But it should not be assumed that they are absent.

It is true that emotions accounts, possibly because they have (mistakenly) been thought to function in terms of an invariant "human nature," are widely associated with conservative, not critical, social science. Vilfredo Pareto's sociological system, for instance, emphasizes equilibrium and promotes conservatism. At its foundation are "residues," which are constituted by various sets of emotions (Finer 1976, pp. 38–48; Henderson 1935). But no general implications, concerning emotions and the failure of any critical potency of accounts which are methodologically committed to them, follow from Pareto's emotions-based sociology. Indeed, a directly critical engagement with the social structure of capitalism has come out of an examination of an aspect of emotion management, for instance. It was shown earlier that a certain self-consciousness of emotion management contributes to the pervasive vernacular importance of emotion. Another aspect of this process can be considered here.

Arlie Hochschild (1983) has argued that employment-generated emotion management, what she calls emotional labor, which is associated with many service-sector jobs, is a debilitating distortion of emotional experience, which adds a new layer or dimension to the exploitation of workers in late-capitalist societies. Here a sociology of emotions is at the same time a critique of commercialism. But in her account Hochschild forgets a central aspect of emotion, and this ultimately undermines the particular critique of commercialism she sets out to provide. The purpose of discussion of the concept of emotional labor here is to highlight this further element of emotion. It will first be necessary to restate Hochschild's argument before considering the importance of emotional agency, which Hochschild neglects.

### The managed heart

Hochschild establishes an intended lineage of her account and its focus in the very first sentence of her book, *The Managed Heart: Commercialization of Human Feeling.* She begins with Karl Marx's discussion in *Das Kapital* of child labor and "the human cost of becoming an 'instrument of labor' at all" (Hochschild 1983, p. 3). She immediately goes on to describe a training session for novice airline flight attendants. While acknowledging that the distance between these distinct worlds is extremely wide, Hochschild suggests that "a close examination of the differences between the two can lead us to some unexpected common ground" (p. 5).

Within the common ground which Hochschild wishes to explore are differences which amount to new developments in the exploitative powers of capitalism itself:

> The work done by the boy in the wallpaper factory called for . . . physical labor . . . In the course of doing . . . physical and mental labor [the flight attendant] is also doing . . . *emotional labor*. This labor requires one to induce or suppress feeling in order to sustain the outward countenance that produces the proper state of mind in others . . . Beneath the difference between physical and emotional labor there lies a similarity in the possible cost of doing the work: the worker can become estranged or alienated from an aspect of self . . . that is *used* to do the work. (1983, pp. 6–7, emphasis in original)

Hochschild estimated that approximately one-third of American workers at the time of her writing "have jobs that subject them to substantial demands for emotional labor," and that one-half of all female workers have jobs involving emotional labor (p. 11).

Not only is the incidence of emotional labor high, so are its costs: "it affects the degree to which we listen to feelings and sometimes our very capacity to feel" (Hochschild 1983, p. 21). It is not only the successful operation of emotional labor which has negative consequences for those who engage in it; the very advent of emotional labor has serious deleterious effects on workers: "when the transmutation works, the worker risks losing the signal function of feeling. When it does not work, the risk is losing the signal function of display" (1983, p. 21). Like labor in general, emotional labor is part of the structure of capitalism which robs workers of the products of their (emotional) labor, and these come back as agents of the worker's oppression.

Many of the documented cases of emotional labor offer ready support to Hochschild's argument. One case which has not been treated in the literature but which clearly refers to an early instance of emotional labor in Hochschild's sense is, in the language of the day, that of the "colored" Pullman Car Porters who, from the 1870s to the 1950s, assisted US rail passengers with their baggage, served their food and beverages, and provided for other needs of traveling customers. The Pullman Porters were required to perform smiling services. The presentation of a happy visage was an essential part of the job, as all who were involved in it, as workers, employers, or customers, understood. Another case in which the emotion management of the incumbent is a labor in the sense of difficult and depleting work is that of the police detective when interacting with victims of crime (Stenross and Kleinman 1989). Hospice workers form another category in which the performance of emotional labor is typically experienced as a cost and injury to the worker (James 1989, 1993).

Thus the literature on emotional labor seems to converge on claims of the deleterious consequences such labor has for those who perform it. And yet, because this is predominantly a literature of case studies, there is in each case study no control for other aspects of the work which may be responsible for negative emotional outcomes. In fact, the only empirical study which compares jobs in which emotional labor is a key component and jobs in which emotional labor is ostensibly absent, conducted by Amy Wharton (1993), offers some unexpected findings and conclusions about the affective consequences of service work in general, and the consequences of emotional labor in particular.

Wharton demonstrates that emotional laborers are no more likely than other workers to suffer emotional exhaustion, and are somewhat more likely to be satisfied with their job (1993, p. 218); that emotional laborers are no more likely to experience their emotions as unauthentic (p. 219); and that emotional labor provides rewards not available in comparable jobs which do not have a component of emotional labor (p. 220). Wharton demonstrates that, in failing to control for other jobs and the individual characteristics of particular jobs, previous studies have been unable to disentangle the effects of emotional labor from other factors. Such studies have thus overstated the psychological costs of emotional labor and understated its rewards (pp. 218, 226).

What determines whether work leads to emotional exhaustion or a sense of emotional inauthenticity or alienation, according to Wharton, is the workers' level of job autonomy and job involvement, and their self-monitoring abilities (1993, p. 214). When these are low, then there is a tendency for the jobs involved to produce emotional exhaustion and low job satisfaction, irrespective of whether the job primarily requires emotional labor or not (pp. 220–6). The failure of the emotions–work model satisfactorily to demonstrate an exploitation effect derives from some theoretical problems of understanding both capitalist relations and emotional experience.

### The unmanaged heart

Emotion management refers to "the management of feeling to create a publicly observable facial and bodily display" (Hochschild 1983, p. 7); emotional labor refers to these activities when they are performed in an employment setting for a wage, when they are "sold as labor" (p. 19). Hochschild acknowledges that emotional labor is always performed in conjunction with physical and mental labor. Each of these is known by their effect, in the production of an object, either physical or intellectual. Intellectual objects include a medical diagnosis, stock-purchasing advice, a completed taxation submission. Emotional labor also can only be known by its effects. The emotional labor of a service worker's smile is the production of a sense of satisfaction in the customer. Beyond this point, however, the parallels between physical and mental labor, on the one hand, and emotional labor, on the other, break down. It is necessary to say some things about emotions in general in order to understand why emotional labor is less likely than manual or mental labor, other things being equal, to be depleting of the person performing it.

Hochschild leaves her reader with the impression that emotion can be more or less regarded as a product. The feeling rules, which govern the management of emotion in her account, are authoritatively constructed, and therefore are not under the control of the emoting subject (1983, pp. 75, 85, 250–1). These are the means of emotional production. Emotion management itself is performed by the immediate subject of the emotion. If this is paid for, then emotion management is emotional labor. When she says that the management of feelings contributes to their creation (p. 18), Hochschild means this in the sense that the feeling so created is the output of an application of the feeling rules (pp. 113–14). Hochschildian emotion management is part of discrete and particular processes which conclude with the production of a singular emotion, with emotional objectification. This is irrespective of whether the emotion is produced under paid conditions or not.

Throughout her discussion, Hochschild mentions that emotion "is a sense that tells us about the self-relevance of reality" (p. 85). Apart from the need to distinguish clearly between emotions and senses, it is true to say that persons are provided with information about both what is of value to them and also the potency of such particular things, through the emotional feelings they experience with regard to them. What Hochschild fails to acknowledge, however, is that the experience of the emotional feeling, in directing the subject's disposition to that object, thereby modifies the relationship between the emoting person and the object of their feelings. This emergent situation, therefore, can be described as one of emotional transformation, because this new situation will be appraised by a new emotional feeling. It is therefore primarily in language that emotional objectification occurs; in naming particular experiences as emotions they become things. Emotions themselves are never finished objects but always in process.

Emotion management, then, contrary to Hochschild's assumption, does not produce an object which is a finished emotion. Rather, it generates a stage in a process. Endeavors to manage an emotion lead to emotions which are reactions to the purportedly managed emotion. One emotion leads to another. Hochschild avoids this conclusion through her supposition of a cognitive or cultural management of emotion: others hold, as Spinoza said, that an "emotion can neither be hindered nor removed save by a contrary emotion" (Spinoza [1677] 1970, p. 148). Before explaining why the latter of these accounts is the more likely, we can mention some instances of post-managed emotions.

Industrial workers forced to perform repetitive and dull jobs were shown by the industrial sociologist Donald Roy to engage in diverting activities which relieved the boredom. In "'Banana Time': Job Satisfaction and Informal Interaction," Roy (1959) described how machine production workers devised ritualistic and apparently absurd games to enliven their experience of work-time. He also showed that when the games broke down, time passed more slowly than it had before and that the level of worker exhaustion increased.

The emotional components of "banana time" were not explored by Roy. But it can be said that such games arise as emotional reactions to an absence of positive involvement or emotional engagement with the work at hand. Repetitive activity which serves a direct function does not attract the conscious involvement of those performing it and is therefore not a generator of emotion in those who do it. But when repetitive behavior seems to be without purpose or point to those performing it, as much paid employment does, a strong and negative emotional formation occurs: boredom (Heller 1979, pp. 9–10). In managing their boredom, industrial workers may engage in the playing of ritual games. These carry certain, albeit limited, emotional satisfactions.

The process Roy described is not unlike the "playful flexibility" referred to by Cas Wouters (1989) in the activities reported to him by a KLM air hostess (pp. 116–17). His respondent indicated that in the absence of creating a game – she indicated that it is "enjoyable to find out how one can play together" – the flight would offer only unrelieved boredom. Banana time and playful flexibility suggest that emotional labor is not simply appropriated by the employer in the exploitation of the worker. Emotional labor is an experience which remains within the emotional possession of the employee. The emotions generated by that labor have emotional consequences. These lead the emoting person to apprehend their situation emotionally and to form emotional responses to it. Implicit in this is an element left out of Hochschild's account.

Hochschild's emotion management is the business of making an object which is an emotion. But emotions are both object and agent: persons have feelings about their feelings. A person, in Hochschild's terms, may manage their anger. Such an endeavor can never stand alone, however. In managing anger, a person will unavoidably feel proud that they have done so, or foolish for having bothered, or smug for having tricked another, and so on. Just as the beating heart does not tire of beating by virtue of its performing a beat, so emotion management is unlikely to be a cessation of emotion; it is more likely to be part of a continuing process. Emotions are not necessarily depleted by being experienced or formed, even in an employment situation.

Emotional workers have opportunities for satisfactions which manual and possibly mental workers frequently cannot achieve. Any feelings manual and mental workers have about their jobs, or that arise in performing them, will be regarded by them and others as necessarily external to the work at hand. Emotional workers, though, by virtue of their structural situation in employment, are able explicitly to give emotions their head, are able to develop their emotions. Such workers are subject to the direction of their employers, certainly. But because of the nested quality of emotions, in which one emotion leads to another, and because emotional subjectivization is a processual not an objectificational activity, emotional labor offers emotional experiences not available to manual and mental workers. Such emotional experiences may be enriching of the person subject to them.

The conceptualization of emotional labor outlined in this discussion implies that the category cannot provide a firm foundation for a new critique of capitalism. It is not that emotions cannot be subject to a commercial transaction. Indeed, Marx, for instance, accepts that emotions can be commercialized when he says that "things which in and for themselves are not commodities, things such as conscience, honor, etc., can be offered for sale by their holders, and thus acquire the form of commodities through their price" ([1867] 1976, p. 197). But such things, although taking the price form of commodities are not the result of labor alienation. They retain their pre-commodified quality because they continue to be possessed by those who have the conscience, the honor, or the pleasing smile.

There remains much in an emotions approach, however, which does lead us to "see through the facades of social structure." The critical edge of some of the things which have come from the preceding chapters is their common concern with the changing social context of emotional experiences. In chapter 2, for instance, the separation of emotion and reason was treated as a consequence of systemic processes of instrumental rationality under market conditions. It is not held that capitalism denies emotion; it was noted, in fact, that the cultivation of emotion is possible in capitalist societies. But such cultivation, it was shown, occurs in a diminishing arena in which the familial, sentimental, and non-instrumental aspects of emotion are given license to the exclusion of all other possibilities. It was shown that such constraints on the cultural expression or permissibility of emotion not only limits emotional experiences, but also the scope of rationality. The radical break between them deforms not just emotion but also reason.

A critical aspect of the social context of emotional experience can also be drawn out of the discussion of chapters 5 and 6. In the considerations of shame, for instance, it was shown that changes in social context have introduced a tendency which renders the relationship between shame and conformity problematic through the increasingly likely association of shame and violence. Similarly, in chapter 6, it was shown that changes in social structure, and especially the social division of labor, are responsible for an increase in the likelihood of vengefulness and resentment, irrespective of other factors. Thus the social conditions of emotional experience, which follow developments in capitalist processes, increase the likelihood of violence. These matters have not been emphasized in the text, but conclusions concerning them arise out of the discussions therein.

A further critique of the capitalist system can be drawn from the discussion in chapter 4. It was shown that confidence arises in accommodating relationships, and that governments will always offer incentives to market actors in addition to the outcomes of market exchanges themselves. In other words, in market economies business requires the support of government if investment is to occur. Here exploitation reaches beyond work organizations and forms part of the civic process itself. The costs of state encouragement to business confidence are met out of the taxes and less visible tolls of ordinary workers. A conventional economic radicalism will remain blind to this dimension of capitalist exploitation until led to it by an account which understands the emotional foundations of business confidence.

### Temporality

The critical possibilities of sociology are widely acknowledged. The importance of temporality to social structure, by contrast, is not currently represented as a centrally important concern. And yet the category of temporality encourages an integration of the theories of social action and emotions in such a way as to lead to a reconceptualization of social structure. There is now, it is true, the development of a sociological appreciation of time. Barbara Adam (1990) has summarized the principal dimensions of this theme, and a journal, *Time and Society*, the first issue of which appeared in 1992, is dedicated to the publication of relevant research.

The dominant issues of the sociology of time include the following: the social construction of serial time (Elias 1992; Nowotny 1994); time constraints, including the problems of duration and sequencing (Giddens 1984; Schegloff 1968); and past time as a resource for present action (Game 1991; Giddens 1984, pp. 90–111). Temporality, that is, the difference between the past and the future, including the "time horizon of the future" as a constitutive element of social relations (Luhmann 1978, p. 96), however, remains largely ignored. But an emotions focus in sociology potentially leads in the direction of a full appreciation of the importance of temporality for an understanding of social processes.

It is not only in sociology that time and temporality are not always taken entirely seriously. Physical science tends to reduce time to differential locations in space (Whitrow 1961). Both idealist and analytic philosophy have had little time for time. McTaggart's (1908) disbelief is summarized in a classic article, in which he concluded that "neither time as a whole, nor the A series and B series, really exist." These are respectively the series of positions running from the future to the present to the past, and the series of positions running from earlier to later. Bertrand Russell's (1914) dismissive aside, that "time is an unimportant and superficial characteristic of reality," while not as total as McTaggart's, is nevertheless a forceful depreciation of time. Commenting on Russell's statement, John Passmore (1968, p. 271) remarked that "any philosopher who approaches philosophy through logic is likely to argue in this way: on the face of it, implication is not a temporal relation and 'truth', as logic understands it, is eternal."

Not only logic but calculation has difficulty with temporality. As the future cannot be known, information about it is not available and therefore calculation with regard to it is not possible. If we must remain cognitively ignorant about the future, what of the past and the present? It is now understood that memory is not a system which reliably reconstructs previous experience but is a creative process, psychologically indistinguishable from imagination. Memory, therefore, is not a window on the past. Even the present is problematic, because there are no sensory bases of time perception. How, then, can practical beings be orientated to time and temporality if not through logic, nor calculative reasoning, nor memory, nor sensation? A short answer to this question is: through emotions.

A person's emotions, in evaluating their circumstances in terms of the relevance they hold for that person, provide information on their relations with other persons, with objects, and with events. In doing this, such emotions are necessarily infused with a sense of expectancy. This sense arises in the appraising of circumstances with a view to preparation for action, which emotions provide. As the information about their circumstances given to a person by their emotions is also information about what to do about those circumstances, then an element of expectancy is typically part of most emotions. Expectancy, as an apprehension of a possible future, is also an interpretation of the past: the direction of action is conditioned by its point of departure and the resources bequeathed to it by previous actions. Expectancy, in terms of what it leads an actor to do at any given time, also situates that actor in the present. It is in this sense, then, that emotions are at the root of apprehensions of temporal order. Indeed, this is emotion's unique contribution to action and agency: without it, persons would be lost in time, the past would remain remote, and the future inaccessible.

While more or less neglected in the wider literature on emotion, this aspect of emotions has been accepted by phenomenological philosophers. Martin Heidegger ([1927] 1962) and Maurice Merleau-Ponty ([1962] 1989), for instance, infuse their discussions of temporality with references to particular emotions. Implicit in the phenomenological approach, and its appreciation of temporality, is the importance of the self as a being-in-the-world.

It is not always clear in these and other phenomenological writers (Keen 1975), however, that the notions of self and being-in-the-world can be best understood not as basic categories in their own right but as abstractions from action. This is not necessarily to take issue with these writers, for the formation of self through action appears to be implicit in much of Heidegger's discussion, for instance. Indeed, Merleau-Ponty's statement that "time is not a line, but a network of intentionalities" ([1962] 1989, p. 417), insofar as intention is not a mental but a practical disposition, nicely captures the way in which action is constitutive of time, or more properly, of temporality. This point is important for our purposes, because in the absence of its belonging to a self as actor, anticipation or intention have no dynamic force. The emotional content of anticipation and intention can be taken as given. The connections between emotions and temporality are thus best appreciated through the roles of each in social action.

It is necessary that the notion of action be understood in terms of some continuity between the actor and the actor's "environment." The typical formulation is that action transforms some element of the environment in which it is performed. It is not always noticed, but ever likely, that, in modifying some aspect of their circumstance or relationship with an other, an action will also bring about some change in the actor. Actors *qua* actors, then, can never be assumed to be merely in a state of being, but through their actions are in a state of becoming. It is in the experience of becoming that the question of the difference between the past and the future is core. The matter of becoming is therefore also the question of temporality. The movement of action is always toward a possible future and away from an already experienced past. The direction of action means that the past can be understood in terms of the future, rather than the other way around. Action, which is necessarily an apprehension of a future with the resources of the past, has its animus and telos in emotion. Emotion is the basis of action; it both directs action to the future, and constructs the resources which action draws upon through the emotional apprehension of the past.

There are a number of issues raised by this brief account of action. The first is that emotions and the active apprehension of temporality are directly connected. Indeed, this has been demonstrated with regard to particular emotions in various chapters earlier. In chapter 4, for instance, it was argued that confidence brings one possible future into the present, and in doing so it provides a sense of certainty to what is essentially unknowable, so that assured action may be engaged with regard to it. It is precisely the time perspective integral to confidence which makes it the affective basis of action and agency.

In chapter 7 it was argued that fear, for example, is another emotion best understood as having temporality rather than a discrete other as its object. The object of fear, it was shown, is not adequately conceptualized as a threatening agent or thing who or which should be avoided. Rather the object of fear is an expectation, in the present, of negative outcome. It was shown that one source of the feeling of duration constitutive of what William James ([1890a] 1931, p. 609) called "the specious present" is fear: the anticipation of a threat or danger which is not in the future (as with anxiety), but imminent in the present. Indeed, the anticipation of a present danger in fear extends the saddle back of the specious present, which, in having to be endured, now has duration.

The explicit assimilation of temporality into the account of action, through emotion, enhances the reach of each of these terms. The reality of temporality is in the experience of becoming. The future is created through present action. Present action, by also expanding the past, transforms it. All action changes the context of future action and of past events. It is the actor's emotional apprehension of time which constitutes the basis of action, and gives it direction and form.

Emotion, as movement, is in that sense both external to the subject who experiences it and integral to their being as a consequence of their being moved by the feeling. That emotion has a source outside the self in its relations with others and is internally experienced as a function of active being. It is through the subject's active exchanges with others, through interaction, that emotional experience is both stimulated in the actor and orientating of their conduct. Emotion is directly implicated in the actor's transformation of their environment, and the environment's transformation of the actor. An aspect of this context of action is temporal order, comprising a future the actor realizes and a past which the actor draws upon, and in doing so, expands.

Apprehension of the future is necessarily emotional. The movement of bringing a possible future into the present is through hopeful or fearful, anxious or secure action. The past is appropriated through proud, or depressed, or guilty, or ashamed action. Regret is one emotion in which the failure of the past and the prospects of the future are necessarily integrated (Landman 1993). Something of this connection between time and emotion is captured in Karl Mannheim's ([1936] 1968, p. 188) statement that:

> The innermost structure of the mentality of a group can never be as clearly grasped as when we attempt to understand its conception of time in the light of its hopes, yearnings, and purposes. On the basis of these purposes and expectations, a given mentality orders not merely future events, but also the past.

Mannheim's statement is salutary in the present context, because it reminds us that the subject of an emotion or emotional pattern may be a collective and not necessarily an individual actor.

The bearers of emotions are always individual persons who experience themselves as being or possessing a self. This returns our focus to the beginning of this Epilogue, in which the sense of what is meant by emotion derives from experiences of the self. What has been indicated in the discussion of temporality and emotion, linked through the concept of action, is that the notion of self which is more expansive is that which understands the self to be a resultant of actions and engagement in the world, rather than as an object of subjective intentionality in which a person's project is the conscious making of their own self.

## Intellectual traditions and sociological classics

The relative neglect of temporality in conventional sociology, and its importance to an emotions-based sociology, illustrates a more general point. This is that a distinct research orientation will give attention to particular issues, which another orientation may neglect. Relatedly, different research foci will typically draw upon different intellectual traditions. It is this point which will be briefly pursued here, in conclusion.

It is important to demonstrate, as a number of sociologists writing on emotions have, that the presently constituted set of classical sociologists, especially Marx, Weber, and Durkheim, incorporated emotions categories in much of their basic conceptualizations and theorizing, even though the significance of such activity was not taken up by their intellectual descendants (Denzin 1984, pp. 32–8; Kemper 1978, p. 1). But just as important is to locate additional sources, generally neglected, which offer special encouragement to an emotions approach in sociology.

A new approach requires not only the legitimation which an identification of precursors can provide, but also the intellectual resources which are bequeathed to research by those who had earlier trod the same path (Alexander 1987). The use of Marx, or Weber, or Durkheim, for instance, to found an emotions-based sociology will have its rewards, certainly, but they are likely to be limited in a number of ways. Some of these strictures were discussed in chapters 1 and 2 earlier. The purpose of these remarks is not to deny sociologists of emotions access to these classic sources. It is rather to suggest that an emotions perspective also rethink what are the classics of sociology.

In contrast to the unapologetically cognitivistic underpinnings in the sociology of Max Weber or George Herbert Mead, for example, is the explicitly emotionist approach of, say, Adam Smith or William James. Neither of these last two writers is currently regarded as a leading source of sociological research or theorizing. However, in preparing the present book, these writers proved to be not only inspirational, but their work constitutive of a number of particular discussions, and frequently corrective of conventional distortions of the role and outcome of emotions in social processes and social structures. Additionally, they are each sufficiently well placed in terms of the breadth of their approach and the quality of their output to sustain interest in and provide resources for new research agendas. They are mentioned here as convenient examples of two possible additions to a sociological canon reconstituted through a focus on emotions.

Adam Smith, an eighteenth-century philosopher, is an acknowledged founder of modern economics through his *The Wealth of Nations* ([1776] 1979). This work is also regarded as a contributor to the origins of sociology, by virtue of its analysis of the social structure of class inequality, the division of labor, and stages of historical development. Less frequently mentioned, however, is Smith's *The Theory of Moral Sentiments* ([1759] 1982). This book has been ignored, even ridiculed, precisely because it explains social behavior in terms of emotions.

When prevailing opinion is disfigured by an ideology of instrumental rationality, then such works which focus on emotions in order to explain social processes will be dismissed out of hand. It is ironic that Albion Small, responsible for introducing Georg Simmel to American sociology, made it his business to close the door on Smith's *Moral Sentiments* while praising *Wealth of Nations* (Small [1907] 1972). Yet Smith's work is not only of historic significance, but remains a source of real value today for those who wish to develop sociology through emotions categories. And, because of its theoretical strengths, it offers a real alternative to the prevailing Weberian foundation of sociology on "rational" as opposed to "emotional" principles.

When Smith takes his rightful place as a sociological classic of continuing relevance to present-day practitioners, the importance of his work in addition to *The Wealth of Nations* and *The Theory of Moral Sentiments* will be noticed. In particular, his essay, "The History of Astronomy," published posthumously in a collection of his papers as *Essays on Philosophical Subjects* ([1795] 1980), will be a source and inspiration in the development of an emotions sociology of science. In this essay Smith demonstrates that scientific discovery and the theoretical reorganizations which take the form of what are now called "scientific revolutions" are at root to be explained in terms of emotional process.

Smith's argument, that intellectual discomfort with both unfamiliarity and also complexity set in train emotional processes which culminate in advances of scientific knowledge, goes some way toward providing a solid foundation for a sociology of science which simply goes past the conventional wisdom that science can only proceed in the absence of emotion. Smith's account, which draws a straight line connecting emotion with reason, is in this regard parallel to William James's treatment of the "sentiment of rationality," discussed in chapter 2. James is also a neglected but potentially important source for a sociology grounded in an understanding of the importance of emotions.

The American psychologist and philosopher William James is already known in the emotions literature for his "somatic" theory, which claims that bodily sensations are prior to emotional feeling and not the other way around. The Jamesian theory of emotion summarized in the previous sentence has been almost universally rejected because, as Keith Oatley put it, it treats emotion as no more than "froth" and dismisses the idea that emotion can influence cognition or behavior (1992, p. 133). While James's somatic theory has received enormous attention, largely negative, what it actually attempts, and also its place in his larger treatment of emotion, have been overlooked.

James's somatic theory, contained in chapter 25 of his *Principles of Psychology* ([1890b] 1931), was never intended to be a general theory of emotion but an account of emotional consciousness. Its emphasis on physical processes was to enforce the point that emotion, in being embodied, is necessarily an experience of the self, and not the result of external and "spiritual" forces. This point remains relevant today in face of a view which holds that emotion can be understood with little regard to the physical reality of the emoting self but principally in terms of cultural rules and conventions, so reducing social agents to specters of ideal forces.

Neither was James's account of emotional consciousness designed to deny the significance of emotion in social action, as his critics maintain. This function of emotion is not the concern of chapter 25 of the *Principles*, certainly. However, it is the subject of much else that James wrote, not only in other chapters of the *Principles*, especially chapter 10, "The Consciousness of Self," and chapter 24, "Instinct," but in other papers, including some published in James's first collection of essays, *The Will to Believe and Other Essays in Popular Philosophy*, first published in 1897. These have been neglected by critics of James's account of emotions, but are key sources for a sociology of emotion. Some work in reinterpreting James's contribution to the study of emotion, and indeed his value to sociology, has begun (Barbalet 1996c, 1996d, 1997). The discussion of James in chapter 2 and elsewhere in this book has demonstrated the value of his contribution to a sociological theory of emotions.

The importance of Smith and James in the present context is not that they can be shown to have incorporated emotions categories in some of their basic conceptualizations. Rather, it is that they have demonstrated the fundamentally emotional nature of social life and its products, at all levels. For example, Smith's account of social interaction, the institution of law, and the discoveries of astronomy, in terms of emotional processes, offers a decisive approach which founds an entirely distinct tradition of sociological research and analysis. James's treatment of the self, social relationships, and even logical connectors ("and," "if," "but," etc.) in terms of emotions and feelings, similarly situates inquiry in the social sciences. Neither theorist abandons reason in focussing upon emotions. Rather, each acknowledges that emotions are foundation to reason, and that a rejection of emotion does not enhance rationality but leaves it without sense or direction.

The elemental nature of emotions and their basic location in social processes of every type underlies the need for their inclusion in sociological analysis adequate to the tasks of discovery and explanation. A sociological theory which can support such work will understand that its historical origins are not the same as those which have brought conventional sociology to its present surrender to various fashionable distractions. A future which offers much more promise requires new sociological traditions for new research agendas. And, in realizing the importance of emotions to social processes, the category of emotion itself must be subjected to careful examination and revision. It is as a contribution to this conversation that the present work is offered.

# References

Adam, Barbara. 1990. *Time and Social Theory*. Cambridge: Polity Press.
Adams, James Ring. 1989. *The Big Fix: Inside the S&L Scandal*. New York: Wiley.
Ainslie, George. 1985. "Rationality and the Emotions: a Picoeconomic Approach." *Social Science Information*, 24: 355–74.
Aitken, Hugh George Jeffrey (ed.). 1959. *The State and Economic Growth*. New York: Social Science Research Council.
Albrow, Martin. 1990. *Max Weber's Construction of Social Theory*. London: Macmillan.
Alexander, Jeffrey C. 1987. "The Centrality of the Classics." Pp. 11–57 in *Social Theory Today*, ed. Anthony Giddens and Jonathan Turner. Cambridge: Polity Press.
Allardt, Erik. 1970. "Types of Protest and Alienation." Pp. 45–63 in *Mass Politics: Studies in Political Sociology*, ed. Erik Allardt and Stein Rokkan. New York: Free Press.
Aristotle. [*c*. 330 BC] 1975. *The Art of Rhetoric*. Cambridge, Mass.: Harvard University Press.
Asch, Solomon. 1956. "Studies of Independence and Conformity: 1. A Minority of One against a Unanimous Majority." *Psychological Monographs*, 70: 1–70.
Bacon, Francis. [1605] 1977. *The Advancement of Learning*. London: Dent and Sons.
——— [1625] 1911. "Of Envy." Pp. 52–7 in *The Essays, or Counsels Civil and Moral*. London: William Collins, Sons.
Bain, George S. and Farouk Elsheikh. 1976. *Union Growth and the Business Cycle: an Econometric Analysis*. Oxford: Blackwell.
Barbalet, J. M. 1980. "Principles of Stratification in Max Weber: an Interpretation and Critique." *British Journal of Sociology*, 31(3): 401–18.
——— 1991a. "Class and Rationality: Olson's Critique of Marx." *Science & Society*, 55: 446–68.
——— 1991b. "Power and Group Processes." *Sociological Inquiry*, 61(3): 314–26.
——— 1994. "Ritual Emotion and Body Work: a Note on the Uses of Durkheim." Pp. 111–23 in *Social Perspectives on Emotion*, vol. II, ed. William M. Wentworth and John Ryan. Greenwich, Conn.: JAI Press.
——— 1996a. "Social Emotions: Confidence, Trust and Loyalty." *International Journal of Sociology and Social Policy*, 16(8/9): 75–96.
——— 1996b. "Class Action and Class Theory: Contra Culture, Pro Emotion." *Science & Society*, 60(4): 478–85.
——— 1996c. "James's Theory of Emotions: The Full Picture." Paper to IXth

Conference of the International Society for Research on Emotions, Toronto, Canada.

1996d. "William James: Human Will in a Natural World." Paper to Humanities Research Centre Conference on The Natural Sciences and the Social Sciences, Australian National University, Canberra.

1997. "The Jamesian Theory of Action." *Sociological Review*, 45(1): 102–21.

Baritz, Loren. [1960] 1965. *The Servants of Power: a History of the Use of Social Science in American Industry*. New York: John Wiley.

Bedford, Errol. 1957. "Emotions." *Proceedings of the Aristotelian Society*, n.s. 57: 281–307.

Bendix, Reinhard. 1964. *Nation-Building and Citizenship*. New York: Wiley.

1974. *Work and Authority in Industry*. Second edn. Berkeley: University of California Press.

Bensman, Joseph and Arthur Vidich. 1962. "Business Cycles, Class and Personality." *Psychoanalysis and the Psychoanalytic Review*, 49: 30–52.

Bentley, Arthur F. [1908] 1949. *The Process of Government: a Study of Social Pressures*. Evanston, Ill.: Principia Press.

Berger, Peter L. 1966. *Invitation to Sociology: a Humanistic Perspective*. Harmondsworth: Penguin Books.

Berger, Peter L. and Thomas Luckmann. 1969. *The Social Construction of Reality: a Treatise on the Sociology of Knowledge*. London: Allen Lane.

Béteille, Andre. 1969. *Social Inequality*. Harmondsworth: Penguin.

Beveridge, William H. 1944. *Full Employment in a Free Society*. London: George Allen & Unwin.

Bierstedt, Robert. 1979. "Sociological Thought in the Eighteenth Century." Pp. 3–38 in *A History of Sociological Analysis*, ed. Tom Bottomore and Robert Nisbet. London: Heinemann.

Blackburn, Robert M. and Michael Mann. 1979. *The Working Class in the Labor Market*. London: Macmillan.

Blau, Peter. 1955. *The Dynamics of Bureaucracy*. Chicago: University of Chicago Press.

Bolles, Edmund Blair. 1988. *Remembering and Forgetting: Inquiries into the Nature of Memory*. New York: Walker and Company.

Bourdieu, Pierre. 1990. *The Logic of Practice*. Cambridge: Polity Press.

Bowlby, John. 1969. *Attachment and Loss*, vol. I, *Attachment*. London: Hogarth Press.

1973. *Attachment and Loss*, vol. II, *Separation: Anxiety and Anger*. London: Hogarth Press.

1980. *Attachment and Loss*, vol. III, *Loss: Sadness and Depression*. London: Hogarth Press.

Bradshaw, John. 1988. *Healing the Shame that Binds You*. Pompano Beach, Fla.: Health Communications Inc.

Briggs, Jean L. 1970. *Never in Anger: Portrait of an Eskimo Family*. Cambridge, Mass.: Harvard University Press.

Bruchey, Stuart. 1965. *The Roots of American Economic Growth, 1607–1861: an Essay in Social Causation*. London: Hutchinson University Library.

Bryson, Gladys. 1945. *Man and Society: the Scottish Society of the Eighteenth Century*. Princeton, N.J.: Princeton University Press.

Campbell, Tom. 1981. *Seven Theories of Human Society*. Oxford: Oxford University Press.

Carling, Alan. 1991. *Social Division*. London: Verso.

Cohen, J., L. E. Hazelrigg, and W. Pope. 1975. "De-Parsonising Weber: a Critique of Parsons' Interpretation of Weber's Sociology." *American Sociological Review*, 40(2): 229–41.

Cole, G. D. H. 1947. *A Short History of the British Working-Class Movement, 1789–1947*. London: George Allen & Unwin.

Cole, G. D. H. and Raymond Postgate. 1946. *The Common People, 1746–1946*. London: Methuen.

Coleman, James S. 1990. *Foundations of Social Theory*. Cambridge, Mass.: The Belknap Press of Harvard University Press.

Collins, Randall. 1975. *Conflict Sociology: Towards an Explanatory Science*. New York: Academic Press.

— 1981. "On the Microfoundations of Macrosociology." *American Journal of Sociology*, 86 (5): 984–1014.

— 1990. "Stratification, Emotional Energy, and the Transient Emotions." Pp. 27–57 in *Research Agendas in the Sociology of Emotions*, ed. Theodore D. Kemper. Albany, N.Y.: SUNY Press.

— 1994. *Four Sociological Traditions*. New York: Oxford University Press.

Cooley, Charles Horton. [1922] 1964. *Human Nature and the Social Order*. New York: Schocken Books.

Cox, Oliver C. [1948] 1970. *Caste, Class and Race: a Study in Social Dynamics*. New York: Monthly Review Press.

Crouch, Colin. 1978. "The Intensification of Industrial Conflict in the United Kingdom." Pp. 191–256 in *The Resurgence of Class Conflict in Western Europe Since 1968*, vol. I, *National Studies*, ed. Colin Crouch and Alessandro Pizzorno. London: Macmillan.

Dahrendorf, Ralf. 1959. *Class and Class Conflict in Industrial Society*. London: Routledge & Kegan Paul.

Damasio, Antonio R. 1994. *Descartes' Error: Emotion, Reason, and the Human Brain*. New York: Putnam.

Darwin, Charles. [1872] 1965. *The Expression of the Emotions in Man and Animals*. Chicago: University of Chicago Press.

Davies, Alan F. 1980. *Skills, Outlooks and Passions: a Psychoanalytic Contribution to the Study of Politics*. Cambridge: Cambridge University Press.

Dawe, Alan. 1970. "The Two Sociologies." *British Journal of Sociology*, 21(2): 207–18.

Denzin, Norman K. 1984. *On Understanding Emotion*. San Francisco: Jossey-Bass Publishers.

de Rivera, Joseph. 1977. *A Structural Theory of the Emotions*. Psychological Issues Monograph 40. New York: International Universities Press.

— 1992. "Emotional Climate: Social Structure and Emotional Dynamics." Pp. 199–218 in *International Review of Studies on Emotion*, vol. II, ed. K. T. Strongman. New York: John Wiley.

de Rivera, Joseph and Carmen Grinkis. 1986. "Emotions as Social Relationships." *Motivation and Emotion*, 10: 351–69.

Descartes, René. [1649] 1931. "The Passions of the Soul." Pp. 329–427 in

*Philosophical Works of Descartes*, trans. Elizabeth S. Haldane and G. R. T. Ross, vol. I. Cambridge: Cambridge University Press.

de Sousa, Ronald. 1990. *The Rationality of Emotion*. Cambridge, Mass.: MIT Press.

de Tocqueville, Alexis. [1835] 1945. *Democracy in America*. New York: Alfred A. Knopf.

Draper, Theodore. 1991. *A Very Thin Line: the Iran–Contra Affairs*. New York: Hill and Wang.

Edwards, Richard. 1979. *Contested Terrain: the Transformation of the Workplace in the Twentieth Century*. New York: Basic Books.

Elias, Norbert. [1939] 1978. *The History of Manners*. Oxford: Basil Blackwell.

1992. *Time: an Essay*. Oxford: Blackwell.

Elster, Jon. 1985. *Making Sense of Marx*. Cambridge: Cambridge University Press.

Emde, Rober N. 1984. "Levels of Meaning in Infant Emotions: a Biosocial View." Pp. 77–107 in *Approaches to Emotion*, ed. Klaus R. Scherer and Paul Ekman. Hillsdale, N.J.: Lawrence Erlbaum Associates.

Emerson, Steven. 1988. *Secret Warriors: Inside the Covert Military Operations of the Reagan Era*. New York: G. P. Putnam's Sons.

Engels, Frederick. [1893] 1965. "Letter to Franz Mehring, July 14." Pp. 458–62 in Karl Marx and Frederick Engels, *Selected Correspondence*. Moscow: Progress Publishers.

Fantasia, Rick. 1988. *Cultures of Solidarity: Consciousness, Action and Contemporary American Workers*. Berkeley: University of California Press.

Farr, Robert M. and Serge Moscovici (eds.). 1984. *Social Representations*. Cambridge: Cambridge University Press.

Ferguson, Adam. [1767] 1966. *An Essay on the History of Civil Society*. Edinburgh: Edinburgh University Press.

Finer, S. E. 1976. *Vilfredo Pareto: Sociological Writings*. Oxford: Basil Blackwell.

Fishbein, Martin and Icek Ajzen. 1972. "Attitudes and Opinions." *Annual Review of Psychology*, 23: 487–544.

Fisher, Gene A. and Kyum Koo Chon. 1989. "Durkheim and the Social Construction of Emotions." *Social Psychology Quarterly*, 52(1): 1–9.

Flam, Helena. 1993. "Fear, Loyalty and Greedy Organizations." Pp. 58–75 in *Emotion in Organizations*, ed. Stephen Fineman. London: Sage.

Fossum, Merle A. and Marilyn J. Mason. 1986. *Facing Shame: Families in Recovery*. New York: Norton.

Foucault, Michel. [1975] 1977. *Discipline and Punish: the Birth of the Prison*. Harmondsworth: Penguin.

[1976] 1978. *The History of Sexuality, vol. I, An Introduction*. Harmondsworth: Penguin.

[1984a] 1985. *The History of Sexuality, vol. II, The Use of Pleasure*. New York: Viking.

[1984b] 1987. *The History of Sexuality, vol. III, The Care of the Self*. New York: Viking.

Frank, Robert H. 1988. *Passions within Reason: the Strategic Role of the Emotions*. New York: Norton.

Fricker, Miranda. 1991. "Reason and Emotion." *Radical Philosophy*, 57: 14–19.

Gallie, Duncan. 1983. *Social Inequality and Class Radicalism in France and Britain*. Cambridge: Cambridge University Press.

Gambetta, Diego. 1990. "Can We Trust Trust?" Pp. 213–37 in *Trust: Making and Breaking Cooperative Relations*, ed. Diego Gambetta. Oxford: Blackwell.

Game, Ann. 1991. *Undoing the Social: Towards a Deconstructive Sociology*. Milton Keynes: Open University Press.

Garfinkel, Harold. 1967. *Studies in Ethnomethodology*. Englewood Cliffs, N.J.: Prentice-Hall.

Gazzaniga, Michael. 1985. *The Social Brain*. New York: Basic Books.

Geiger, Theodor. 1969. *On Social Order and Mass Society*. Chicago: University of Chicago Press.

Gerschenkron, Alexander. 1965. *Economic Backwardness in Historical Perspective*. New York: Frederick A. Praeger.

Giddens, Anthony. 1971. *Capitalism and Modern Social Theory*. Cambridge: Cambridge University Press.

1984. *The Constitution of Society: Outline of a Theory of Structuration*. Cambridge: Polity Press.

1991. *Modernity and Self-Identity: Self and Society in the Late Modern Age*. Cambridge: Polity Press.

Ginsberg, Morris. 1965. *On Justice in Society*. Harmondsworth: Penguin.

Goffman, Erving. 1952. "On Cooling the Mark Out: Some Aspects of Adaptation to Failure." *Psychiatry*, 15: 451–63.

1956. "Embarrassment and Social Organization." *American Journal of Sociology*, 62 (3): 264–74.

1967. *Interaction Ritual: Essays on Face-to-Face Behavior*. Garden City, N.Y.: Anchor Books.

Goldthorpe, John H., David Lockwood, Frank Bechhoffer, and Jennifer Platt. 1968a. *The Affluent Worker: Industrial Attitudes and Behavior*. Cambridge: Cambridge University Press.

1968b. *The Affluent Worker: Political Attitudes and Behavior*. Cambridge: Cambridge University Press.

1969. *The Affluent Worker in the Class Structure*. Cambridge: Cambridge University Press.

Goleman, Daniel. 1995. *Emotional Intelligence*. New York: Bantam Books.

Goodrich, Carter L. 1921. *The Frontier of Control: a Study in British Workshop Politics*. New York: Harcourt, Brace & Company.

Gordon, Steven L. 1981. "The Sociology of Sentiments and Emotions." Pp. 261–78 in *Social Psychology: Sociological Perspectives*, ed. Morris Rosenberg and Ralph H. Turner. New York: Basic Books.

Gouldner, Alvin W. 1954. *Patterns of Industrial Bureaucracy*. New York: Free Press.

1955. "Metaphysical Pathos and the Theory of Bureaucracy." *American Political Science Review*, 49 (2): 496–507.

1970. *The Coming Crisis of Western Sociology*. London: Heinemann.

Green, Penny. 1990. *The Enemy Without: Policing and Class Consciousness in the Miners Strike*. Milton Keynes: Open University Press.

Harré, Rom. 1990. "Embarrassment: a Conceptual Analysis." Pp. 181–204 in *Shyness and Embarrassment: Perspectives from Social Psychology*, ed. Roy Crozier. Cambridge: Cambridge University Press.

Hart, Keith. 1990. "Kinship, Contract, and Trust: the Economic Organization of Migrants in an African City Slum." Pp. 176–93 in *Trust: Making and Breaking Cooperative Relations*, ed. Diego Gambetta. Oxford: Blackwell.

Hebb, D. O. 1946. "On the Nature of Fear." *Psychological Review*, 53(5): 259–76.

Hechter, Michael. 1983. *The Microfoundations of Macrosociology*. Philadelphia, Pa.: Temple University Press.

Heidegger, Martin. [1927] 1962. *Being and Time*. New York: Harper & Row.

Heise, David. 1977. "Social Action as the Control of Affect." *Behavioral Science*, 22: 163–77.

1979. *Understanding Events: Affect and the Construction of Social Action*. Cambridge: Cambridge University Press.

Heller, Agnes. 1979. *A Theory of Feelings*. Assen, The Netherlands: Van Gorcum.

Henderson, Lawrence J. 1935. *Pareto's General Sociology: a Physiologist's Interpretation*. Cambridge, Mass.: Harvard University Press.

Hildreth, Richard. 1856. *The History of the United States of America*, vol. IV. New York: Harper & Brothers

Hindess, Barry. 1988. *Choice, Rationality and Social Theory*. London: Unwin-Hyman.

Hirschman, Albert O. 1970. *Exit, Voice and Loyalty: Responses to Decline in Firms, Organizations, and States*. Cambridge, Mass.: Harvard University Press.

Hobbes, Thomas. [1651] 1962. *Leviathan*. London: Dent.

Hobhouse, Leonard T. 1911. *Liberalism*. London: Williams and Norgate.

Hochschild, Arlie Russell. 1975. "The Sociology of Feelings and Emotion: Selected Possibilities." Pp. 280–307 in *Another Voice: Feminist Perspectives on Social Life and Social Science*, ed. Marcia Millman and Rosabeth Moss Kanter. Garden City, N.Y.: Anchor Books.

1979. "Emotion Work, Feeling Rules, and Social Structure." *American Journal of Sociology*, 85 (3): 551–75.

1983. *The Managed Heart: Commercialization of Human Feeling*. Berkeley: University of California Press.

1990. "Ideology and Emotion Management: a Perspective and Path for Future Research." Pp. 117–42 in *Research Agendas in the Sociology of Emotions*, ed. Theodore D. Kemper. Albany, N.Y.: SUNY Press.

Homans, George C. 1951. *The Human Group*. London: Routledge & Kegan Paul.

Hume, David. [1740] 1911. *A Treatise of Human Nature*, vol. II. London: J. M. Dent and Sons.

[1751] 1962. *Enquiries Concerning the Principles of Morals*. Oxford: Oxford University Press.

Hunter, Floyd. [1953] 1963. *Community Power Structure: a Study of Decision Makers*. Garden City, N.Y.: Anchor Books.

Ichheiser, Gustav. 1949. *Misunderstandings in Human Relations: a Study in False Social Perceptions*. Supplement to *American Journal of Sociology*, 55(2): 1–70.

James, Nicky. 1989. "Emotional Labour: Skill and Work in the Social Regulation of Feelings." *Sociological Review*, 37(1): 15–42.

1993. "Divisions of Emotional Labour: Disclosure and Cancer." Pp. 94–117 in *Emotion in Organizations*, ed. Stephen Fineman. London: Sage.

James, William. [1890a] 1931. *The Principles of Psychology*, vol. I. New York: Henry Holt.

[1890b] 1931. *The Principles of Psychology*, vol. II. New York: Henry Holt.

[1897a] 1956. "The Sentiment of Rationality." Pp. 63–110 in *The Will to Believe and Other Essays in Popular Philosophy*. New York: Dover Publications.

[1897b] 1956. "Reflex Action and Theism." Pp. 111–44 in *The Will to Believe and Other Essays in Popular Philosophy*. New York: Dover Publications.

[1897c] 1956. "The Will to Believe". Pp. 1–31 in *The Will to Believe and Other Essays in Popular Philosophy*. New York: Dover Publications.

[1897d] 1956. "Is Life Worth Living?" Pp. 32–62 in *The Will to Believe and Other Essays in Popular Philosophy*. New York: Dover Publications.

[1909] 1932. *A Pluralistic Universe*. New York: Longmans, Green.

Kalecki, Michael. [1943] 1972. "Political Aspects of Full Employment." Pp. 420–30 in *A Critique of Economic Theory*, ed. E. K. Hunt and Jesse G. Schwartz. Harmondsworth: Penguin.

Karen, Robert. 1992. "Shame." *The Atlantic Monthly*, 269(2): 40–70.

Katona, George. 1979. "Toward a Macropsychology." *American Psychologist*, 34(2): 118–26.

Katznelson, Ira. 1981. *City Trenches: Urban Politics and the Patterning of Class in the United States*. New York: Pantheon Books.

Keen, Ernest. 1975. *A Primer in Phenomenological Psychology*. New York: Holt, Rinehart & Winston.

Kemper, Theodore D. 1978. *A Social Interactional Theory of Emotions*. New York: John Wiley.

1987. "How Many Emotions are There? Wedding the Social and the Autonomic Components." *American Journal of Sociology*, 93(2): 263–89.

1991. "An Introduction to the Sociology of Emotions." Pp. 301–49 in *International Review of Studies on Emotion*, vol. I, ed. K. T. Stongman. New York: John Wiley.

Kemper, Theodore D. and Randall Collins. 1990. "Dimensions of Microinteraction." *American Journal of Sociology*, 96: 32–68.

Kenny, Anthony. 1964. *Action, Emotion and Will*. London: Routledge & Kegan Paul.

Keynes, John Maynard. [1936] 1981. *The General Theory of Employment, Interest and Money*. London: Macmillan.

Landman, Janet. 1993. *Regret: the Persistence of the Possible*. New York: Oxford University Press.

Lane, Robert E. 1991. *The Market Experience*. Cambridge: Cambridge University Press.

Lauderdale, Pat, Steve McLaughlin, and Annamarie Oliverio. 1990. "Levels of Analysis, Theoretical Orientations and Degrees of Abstraction." *American Sociologist*, 21: 29–40.

Lazarus, Robert. 1984. "Thoughts on the Relations between Emotion and Cognition." Pp. 247–58 in *Approaches to Emotion*, ed. Klaus R. Scherer and Paul Ekman. Hillsdale, N.J.: Lawrence Erlbaum.

Le Bon, Gustave. 1895. *Psychologie des foules [The Crowd]*. Paris: F. Alcan.

Ledeen, Michael A. 1988. *Perilous Statecraft: an Insider's Account of the Iran Contra Affair*. New York: Charles Scribner's Sons.

Leeper, R. W. 1948. "A Motivational Theory of Emotion to Replace Emotion as Disorganized Response." *Psychological Review*, 55: 5–21.

Lehmann, William C. 1930. *Adam Ferguson and the Beginnings of Modern Sociology.* New York: Columbia University Press.

Leventhal, Howard. 1984. "A Perceptual Motor Theory of Emotion." Pp. 272–91 in *Approaches to Emotion,* ed. Klaus R. Scherer and Paul Ekman. Hillsdale, N.J.: Lawrence Erlbaum.

Leventhal, Howard and Andrew J. Tomarken. 1986. "Emotion: Today's Problems." *Annual Review of Psychology,* 37: 565–610.

Levy, Robert I. 1973. *Tahitians: Mind and Experience in the Society Island.* Chicago: Chicago University Press.

Lewin, Kurt. [1942] 1973. "Time Perspective and Morale." Pp. 103–24 in *Resolving Social Conflict: Selected Papers in Group Dynamics.* London: Souvenir Press.

Lewis, Helen Block. [1971] 1974. *Shame and Guilt in Neurosis.* New York: International Universities Press.

Lewis, Michael and Carolyn Saarni (eds.). 1985. *The Socialization of Emotions.* New York: Plenum.

Lindblom, Charles. 1977. *Politics and Markets: the World's Political Economic Systems.* New York: Harper & Row.

Lockwood, David. 1982. "Fatalism: Durkheim's Hidden Theory of Order." Pp. 101–18 in *Social Class and the Division of Labor: Essays in Honour of Ilya Neustadt,* ed. Anthony Giddens and Gavin Mackenzie. Cambridge: Cambridge University Press.

Lockwood, William W. 1954. *The Economic Development of Japan: Growth and Structural Change, 1868–1938.* Princeton, N.J.: Princeton University Press.

Lomax, Louis E. 1963. *The Negro Revolt.* New York: Signet Books.

Luhmann, Niklas. 1978. "Temporalization and Complexity." Pp. 95–111 in *Sociocybernetics,* ed. R. F. Geyer and J. van der Zouwen. Leiden: Martinus Nijhoff.

1979. *Trust and Power.* New York: Wiley.

[1984] 1995. *Social Systems.* Stanford, Calif.: Stanford University Press.

Lukes, Steven. 1977. *Essays in Social Theory.* London: Macmillan.

Lutz, Catherine and Geoffrey M. White. 1986. "The Anthropology of Emotions." *Annual Review of Anthropology,* 15: 405–36.

Lynd, Helen Merrill. 1958. *On Shame and the Search for Identity.* New York: Harcourt, Brace & Company.

Macfie, A. L. and D. D. Raphael. 1976. "Introduction." Pp. 1–52 in *Adam Smith: the Theory of Moral Sentiments.* Oxford: Oxford University Press.

Mackenzie, Gavin. 1974. "The 'Affluent Worker' Study: an Evaluation and Critique." Pp. 237–56 in *The Social Analysis of Class Structure,* ed. Frank Parkin. London: Tavistock.

MacKinnon, Neil J. 1994. *Symbolic Interactionism as Affect Control.* Albany, N.Y.: SUNY Press.

Macpherson, C. B. 1962. *The Political Theory of Possessive Individualism.* Oxford: Clarendon Press.

McCarthy, E. Doyle. 1989. "Emotions are Social Things: an Essay in the Sociology of Emotions." Pp. 51–72 in *The Sociology of Emotions: Original Essays and Research Papers,* ed. David Franks and E. Doyle McCarthy. Greenwich, Conn.: JAI Press.

1994. "The Social Construction of Emotions: New Directions from Culture Theory." Pp. 267–79 in *Social Perspectives on Emotion*, vol. II, ed. William M. Wentworth and John Ryan. Greenwich, Conn.: JAI Press.

McClelland, J. S. 1989. *The Crowd and the Mob*. London: Unwin.

McDougall, William. [1908] 1948. *An Introduction to Social Psychology*. 29th edn. London: Methuen and Company.

1933. *The Energies of Men*. New York: Scribner.

McGill, V. J. 1954. *Emotions and Reason*. Springfield, Ill.: Charles C. Thomas.

McTaggart, J. Ellis. 1908. "The Unreality of Time." *Mind*, 17.

Maine, Henry Sumner. [1884] 1905. *Ancient Law: Its Connection with the Early History of Society and its Relation to Modern Ideas*. 10th edn. London: John Murray.

Mannheim, Karl. [1936] 1968. *Ideology and Utopia*. London: Routledge & Kegan Paul.

Marshall, Thomas H. [1938] 1973. "The Nature of Class Conflict." Pp. 164–173 in *Class, Citizenship and Social Development*. Westport, Conn.: Greenwood Press.

Marshall, Thomas H. [1956] 1973. "Changes in Social Stratification in the Twentieth Century." Pp. 123–43 in *Class, Citizenship and Social Development*. Westport, Conn.: Greenwood Press.

Martin, David C. and John Walcott. 1988. *Best Laid Plans: the Inside Story of America's War Against Terrorism*. New York: Harper & Row.

Martindale, Don. 1961. *The Nature and Types of Sociological Theory*. London: Routledge & Kegan Paul.

Marx, Karl. [1844] 1967. *Economic and Philosophic Manuscripts*. Moscow: Progress Publishers.

[1867] 1976. *Capital: a Critique of Political Economy*, vol. I. Harmondsworth: Penguin Books.

[1894] 1971. *Capital: a Critique of Political Economy*, vol. III. Moscow: Progress Publishers.

Marx, Karl and Frederick Engels. [1848] 1970. "Manifesto of the Communist Party." Pp. 31–63 in *Marx and Engels Selected Works in One Volume*. Moscow: Progress Publishers.

Meek, Ronald L. 1976. *Social Science and the Ignoble Savage*. Cambridge: Cambridge University Press.

Merleau-Ponty, Maurice. [1962] 1989. *Phenomenology of Perception*. London: Routledge.

Merton, Robert K. [1940] 1968. "Bureaucratic Structure and Personality." Pp. 249–60 in *Social Theory and Social Structure*. New York: Free Press.

1968. *Social Theory and Social Structure*. New York: Free Press.

Middlemas, Keith. 1979. *Politics in an Industrial Society: the Experience of the British System Since 1911*. London: André Deutsch.

Mill, John Stuart. [1863] 1960. "Utilitarianism." Pp. 1–60 in *Utilitarianism, Liberty, Representative Government*. London: J. M. Dent & Sons.

Mills, C. Wright. [1940] 1967. "Situated Actions and Vocabularies of Motive." Pp. 439–52 in *Power, Politics and People: the Collected Essays of C. Wright Mills*. New York: Oxford University Press.

[1951] 1956. *White Collar: the American Middle Classes*. New York: Oxford University Press.

Mommsen, Wolfgang J. 1989. *The Political and Social Theory of Max Weber.* Cambridge: Polity Press.

Moore, Barrington. 1967. *Social Origins of Dictatorship and Democracy.* Boston: Beacon Press.

1978. *Injustice: the Social Bases of Obedience and Revolt.* London: Macmillan.

Moorhouse, H. F. 1973. "The Political Incorporation of the British Working Class: an Interpretation." *Sociology,* 7(3): 341–59.

Moscovici, Serge. 1987. "Social Collectivities." Pp. 42–59 in *Essays in Honor of Elias Canetti,* trans. Michael Hulse. London: André Deutsch.

Neu, Jerome. 1977. *Emotion, Thought and Therapy: Hume and Spinoza, Theories of Emotion and Therapy.* London: Routledge & Kegan Paul.

Nietzsche, Friedrich. [1887] 1992. "On the Genealogy of Morals." Pp. 451–599 in *Basic Writings of Nietzsche,* trans. and ed. Walter Kaufman. New York: Random House.

Nowotny, Helga. 1994. *Time: the Modern and Postmodern Experience.* Cambridge: Cambridge University Press.

Oatley, Keith. 1992. *Best Laid Schemes: the Psychology of Emotions.* Cambridge: Cambridge University Press.

Ollman, Bertell. 1993. *Dialectical Investigations.* New York: Routledge.

Ortony, Andrew, Gerald L. Clore, and Allan Collins. [1988] 1990. *The Cognitive Structure of Emotions.* Cambridge: Cambridge University Press.

Paine, Thomas. [1791] 1992. *Rights of Man,* ed. with an Introduction and notes by Gregory Claeys. Indianapolis: Hacket Publishing Company.

Parsons, Talcott. [1937] 1968. *The Structure of Social Action.* New York: Free Press.

1951. *The Social System.* New York: Free Press.

[1953] 1991. "The Marshall Lectures: the Integration of Economic and Sociological Theory." *Sociological Inquiry,* 61(1): 10–59.

1956. "Suggestions for a Sociological Approach to the Theory of Organizations." *Administrative Science Quarterly,* 1: 63–85; 2: 225–39.

[1963] 1969. "On the Concept of Political Power." Pp. 352–404 in *Politics and Social Structure.* New York: Free Press.

[1970] 1977. "On Building Social System Theory: a Personal History." Pp. 22–76 in *Social Systems and the Evolution of Action Theory.* New York: Free Press.

Parsons, Talcott and Edward A. Shils. 1951. *Toward a General Theory of Action.* Cambridge, Mass.: Harvard University Press.

Parsons, Talcott, Robert F. Bales, and Edward A. Shils. 1953. *Working Papers in the Theory of Action.* New York: Free Press.

Passmore, John. 1968. *A Hundred Years of Philosophy.* Harmondsworth: Penguin.

Peristiany, Jean G. (ed.). 1965. *Honour and Shame: the Values of Mediterranean Society.* London: Weidenfeld & Nicolson.

Pizzo, Stephen, Mary Fricker, and Paul Muolo. 1989. *Inside Job: the Looting of America's Savings and Loans.* New York: McGraw-Hill.

Polanyi, Karl. [1944] 1957. *The Great Transformation: the Political and Economic Origins of Our Time.* Boston: Beacon Press.

Potok, Chaim. 1970. *The Promise.* London: William Heinemann.

Przeworski, Adam. 1985. *Capitalism and Social Democracy.* Cambridge: Cambridge University Press.

Reddy, William M. 1987. *Money and Liberty in Modern Europe: a Critique of Historical Understanding*. Cambridge: Cambridge University Press.

Ridker, Ronald G. 1967. *Economic Costs of Air Pollution: Studies in Measurement*. New York: Frederick A. Praeger.

Robinson, Joan. 1964. *Economic Philosophy*. Harmondsworth: Penguin.

Roemer, John. 1982. *A General Theory of Exploitation and Class*. Cambridge, Mass.: Harvard University Press.

Rousseau, Jean-Jacques. [1754] 1973. "A Discourse on the Origin of Inequality." Pp. 27–113 in *The Social Contract and Discourses*, ed. G. D. H. Cole. London: Dent.

[1762] 1973. "The Social Contract." Pp. 164–278 in *The Social Contract and Discourses*, ed. G. D. H. Cole. London: Dent.

Roy, Donald F. 1959. "'Banana Time': Job Satisfaction and Informal Interaction." *Human Organizations*, 18(4): 156–68

1980. "Repression and Incorporation: Fear Stuff, Sweet Stuff and Evil Stuff: Management's Defence against Unionization in the South." Pp. 395–415 in *Capital and Labor*, ed. Theo Nichols. Glasgow: Fontana.

Rueschemeyer, Dietrich and Peter B. Evans. 1985. "The State and Economic Transformation: Toward an Analysis of the Conditions Underlying Effective Intervention." Pp. 44–77 in *Bringing the State Back In*, ed. Peter B. Evans, Dietrich Rueschemeyer, and Theda Skocpol. Cambridge: Cambridge University Press.

Runciman, W. G. 1972. *Relative Deprivation and Social Justice: a Study of Attitudes to Social Inequality in Twentieth Century England*. Harmondsworth: Penguin.

Russell, Bertrand. 1914. *Our Knowledge of the External World*. London: Allen & Unwin.

Russell, James A. 1991. "Culture and the Categorization of Emotions." *Psychological Bulletin*, 110(3): 426–50.

Ryle, Gilbert. 1949. *The Concept of Mind*. London: Hutchinson.

Scheff, Thomas J. 1983. "Towards Integration in the Social Psychology of Emotions." *Annual Review of Sociology*, 9: 333–54.

1984. "The Taboo on Coarse Emotions." Pp. 146–69 in *Review of Personality and Social Psychology*, ed. Phillip Shaver. Beverly Hills, Calif.: Sage.

1988. "Shame and Conformity: the Deference–Emotion System." *American Sociological Review*, 53: 395–406.

1990. *Microsociology: Discourse, Emotion and Social Structure*. Chicago: University of Chicago Press.

1994. *Bloody Revenge: Emotions, Nationalism, and War*. Boulder, Colo.: Westview Press.

Scheff, Thomas J. and Suzanne M. Retzinger. 1991. *Emotions and Violence: Shame and Rage in Destructive Conflict*. Lexington, Mass.: D. C. Heath.

Schegloff, Emmanuel. 1968. "Sequencing in Conversational Openings." *American Anthropologist*, 70: 1075–95.

Scheler, Max. [1912] 1961. *Ressentiment*. New York: Free Press.

[1913] 1954. *The Nature of Sympathy*, trans. Peter Heath. London: Routledge & Kegan Paul.

Scherer, Klaus R. 1984. "On the Nature and Function of Emotion: a Component Process Approach." Pp. 293–317 in *Approaches to Emotion*, ed. Klaus R. Scherer and Paul Ekman. Hillsdale, N.J.: Lawrence Erlbaum.

Scherer, Klaus R., Harold G. Wallbott, and Angela B. Summerfield. 1986. *Experiencing Emotion: a Cross-cultural Study.* Cambridge: Cambridge University Press.

Schneider, Herbert W. 1948. "Editor's Introduction." Pp. xv–xxvii in *Adam Smith's Moral and Political Philosophy.* New York: Hafner Publishing.

Scott, James C. 1985. *Weapons of the Weak: Everyday Forms of Peasant Resistance.* New Haven, Conn.: Yale University Press.

Selznick, Philip. 1948. "Foundations of the Theory of Organization." *American Sociological Review,* 13(1): 25–35.

Sen, Amartya. 1982. *Poverty and Famine: an Essay on Entitlement and Deprivation.* Oxford: Oxford University Press.

Sennett, Richard. 1974. *The Fall of Public Man.* New York: Alfred A. Knopf.

Sennett, Richard and Jonathan Cobb. [1972] 1983. *The Hidden Injuries of Class.* New York: Vintage.

Shonfield, Alan. 1965. *Modern Capitalism: the Changing Balance of Public and Private Power.* Oxford: Oxford University Press.

Shott, Susan. 1979. "Emotions and Social Life: a Symbolic Interactionist Analysis." *American Journal of Sociology,* 84(6): 1317–34.

Simmel, Georg. [1903] 1971. "The Metropolis and Mental Life." Pp. 324–39 in *Georg Simmel: On Individuality and Social Forms,* ed. Donald N. Levine. Chicago: University of Chicago Press.

——— [1906] 1964. "Types of Social Relationships." Pp. 317–29 in *The Sociology of Georg Simmel,* ed. Kurt H. Wolf. New York: Free Press.

Small, Albion W. [1907] 1972. *Adam Smith and Modern Sociology: a Study in the Methodology of the Social Sciences.* Clifton, N.J.: Augustus M. Kelley.

Smelser, Neil J. 1959. *Social Change in the Industrial Revolution.* London: Routledge & Kegan Paul.

Smelt, Simon. 1980. "Money's Place in Society." *British Journal of Sociology,* 31(2): 204–23.

Smith, Adam. [1759] 1982. *The Theory of Moral Sentiments.* Oxford: Oxford University Press.

——— [1776] 1979. *An Inquiry in the Nature and Causes of the Wealth of Nations.* Oxford: Oxford University Press.

——— [1795] 1980. "The History of Astronomy." Pp. 31–105 in *Essays on Philosophical Subjects.* Oxford: Oxford University Press.

Smith, Vincent Kerry. 1976. *The Economic Consequences of Air Pollution.* Cambridge, Mass.: Ballinger Publishing.

Solomon, Robert C. 1976. *The Passions.* Garden City, N.Y.: Anchor Press and Doubleday.

——— 1991. *A Passion for Justice: Emotions and the Origins of the Social Contract.* New York: Addison-Wesley.

Spinoza, Baruch. [1677] 1970. *Ethics.* London: Dent.

Stearns, Peter N. 1989. *Jealousy: the Evolution of an Emotion in American History.* New York: New York University Press.

——— 1994. *American Cool: Constructing a Twentieth-century Emotional Style.* New York: New York University Press.

Stearns, Peter N. and Carol Z. Stearns. 1986. *Anger: the Struggle for Emotional Control in American History.* Chicago: Chicago University Press.

Stenross, Barbara and Sherryl Kleinman. 1989. "The Highs and Lows of

Emotional Labor: Detectives' Encounters with Criminals and Victims."
*Journal of Contemporary Ethnography*, 17: 435–52.

Suttie, Ian. 1935. *The Origins of Love and Hate*. London: Kegan Paul.

Swingewood, Alan. 1991. *A Short History of Sociological Thought*. 2nd edn.
London: Macmillan.

Tarde, Gabriel. 1890. *Les lois de l'imitation* [*The Laws of Imitation*]. Paris: F. Alcan.

Tawney, Richard Henry. [1926] 1948. *Religion and the Rise of Capitalism*. West
Drayton: Penguin.

Thoits, Peggy A. 1989. "The Sociology of Emotions." *Annual Review of Sociology*,
15: 317–42.

Tomkins, Silvan S. 1963. *Affect, Imagery, Consciousness, vol. II, The Negative Affects*.
New York: Springer Publishing.

Tomkins, Silvan S. and Carroll E. Izard. 1966. *Affect, Cognition, and Personality:
Empirical Studies*. London: Tavistock.

Tönnies, Ferdinand. [1887] 1963. *Community and Society. (Gemeinschaft und
Gesselschaft)*. New York: Harper & Row.

Toulmin, Stephen. 1990. *Cosmopolis: the Hidden Agenda of Modernity*. New York:
Free Press.

Turner, Bryan S. 1993. "Outline of a Theory of Human Rights." *Sociology*, 27(3):
489–512.

Turner, Jonathan. 1987. "Analytical Theorizing." Pp. 156–94 in *Social Theory
Today*, ed. Anthony Giddens and Jonathan Turner. Cambridge: Polity Press.

Turner, Stephen P. and Regis A. Factor. 1984. *Max Weber and the Dispute over
Reason and Value*. London: Routledge & Kegan Paul.

Vaughan, Ted R. and Gideon Sjoberg. 1986. "Human Rights Theory and the
Classical Sociological Tradition." Pp. 127–41 in *Sociological Theory in
Transition*, ed. Mark L. Wardell and Stephen P. Turner. London: Allen &
Unwin.

Walter, Eugene Victor. 1969. *Terror and Resistance: a Study of Political Violence*.
New York: Oxford University Press.

Webb, Sidney and Beatrice. 1920. *Industrial Democracy*. London: Longmans,
Green.

Weber, Max. [1904] 1949. "'Objectivity' in Social Science." Pp. 50–112 in *The
Methodology of the Social Sciences*, ed. Edward A. Shils and Henry A. Finch.
New York: Free Press.

[1905a] 1991. *The Protestant Ethic and the Spirit of Capitalism*. London:
HarperCollins.

[1905b] 1975. "Knies and the Problem of Irrationality." Pp. 93–207 in *Roscher
and Knies: the Logical Problems of Historical Economics*, ed. Guy Oakes. New
York: Free Press.

[1915a] 1970. "The Social Psychology of World Religions." Pp. 267–301 in
*From Max Weber: Essays in Sociology*, ed. H. H. Gerth and C. Wright Mills.
London: Routledge & Kegan Paul.

[1915b] 1970. "Religious Rejections of the World and their Directions." Pp.
323–59 in *From Max Weber: Essays in Sociology*, ed. H. H. Gerth and C.
Wright Mills. London: Routledge & Kegan Paul.

[1917] 1967. *Ancient Judaism*. New York: Free Press.

[1919] 1970. "Science as a Vocation." Pp. 129–56 in *From Max Weber: Essays in*

*Sociology*, ed. H. H. Gerth and C. Wright Mills. London: Routledge & Kegan Paul.

[1920] 1991. "Author's Introduction." Pp. 13–31 in *The Protestant Ethic and the Spirit of Capitalism*. London: HarperCollins.

[1921a] 1978. *Economy and Society: an Outline of Interpretive Sociology*. Berkeley: University of California Press.

[1921b] 1970. "Politics as a Vocation." Pp. 77–128 in *From Max Weber: Essays in Sociology*, ed. H. H. Gerth and C. Wright Mills. London: Routledge & Kegan Paul.

Weissbrodt, David. 1988. "Human Rights: an Historical Perspective." Pp. 1–20 in *Human Rights*, ed. Peter Davies. London: Routledge.

Westergaard, John and Henrietta Resler. 1976. *Class in a Capitalist Society*. Harmondsworth: Penguin.

Wharton, Amy S. 1993. "The Affective Consequences of Service Work: Managing Emotions on the Job." *Work and Occupations*, 20(2): 205–32.

Whitrow, G. J. 1961. *The Natural Philosophy of Time*. New York: Harper.

Wiley, Norbert F. 1983. "The Congruence of Weber and Keynes." Pp. 30–57 in *Sociological Theory, 1983*, ed. Randall Collins. San Francisco: Jossey-Bass Publishers.

Williams, Juan. 1987. *Eyes on the Prize: America's Civil Rights Years, 1954–1965*. New York: Viking Penguin.

Wirth, Louis. [1938] 1957. "Urbanism as a Way of Life." Pp. 46–63 in *Cities and Society: the Revised Reader in Urban Sociology*, ed. Paul K. Hatt and Albert J. Reiss. New York: Free Press.

Wolff, Robert Paul. 1968. *The Poverty of Liberalism*. Boston: Beacon Press.

Wood, Ellen. 1989. "Rational Choice Marxism: Is the Game Worth the Candle?" *New Left Review*, 177: 41–88.

Wouters, Cas. 1989. "The Sociology of Emotions and Flight Attendants: Hochschild's *Managed Heart*." *Theory, Culture and Society*, 6: 95–123.

1992. "Of Status Competition and Emotion Management: the Study of Emotions as a New Field." *Theory, Culture and Society*, 9: 229–52.

Zweig, Ferdynand. 1961. *The Worker in an Affluent Society: Family Life and Industry*. London: Heinemann.

# Index